CASENOTE® Legal Briefs®

CONTRACTS

Keyed to Courses Using

Knapp, Crystal, Prince, Hart, and Silverstein's Problems in Contract Law: Cases and Materials Tenth Edition

Authored by: Publisher's Editorial Staff

ASPEN PUBLISHING

This publication is designed to provide accurate and authoritative information in regard to the subject matter covered. It is sold with the understanding that the publisher is not engaged in rendering legal, accounting, or other professional services. If legal advice or other expert assistance is required, the services of a competent professional person should be sought.

— From a Declaration of Principles adopted jointly by a Committee of the American Bar Association and a Committee of Publishers and Associates

To contact Customer Service, e-mail customer.service@aspenpublishing.com, call 1-800-950-5259, or mail correspondence to:

Aspen Publishing
Attn: Order Department
1 Wall Street
Burlington, MA 01803

Printed in the United States of America.

1 2 3 4 5 6 7 8 9 0

ISBN 979-8-8861-4351-5

SUSTAINABLE FORESTRY INITIATIVE Certified Sourcing
www.forests.org
SFI-00756

About Aspen Publishing

Aspen Publishing is a leading provider of educational content and digital learning solutions to law schools in the U.S. and around the world. Aspen provides best-in-class solutions for legal education through authoritative textbooks, written by renowned authors, and breakthrough products such as Connected eBooks, Connected Quizzing, and PracticePerfect.

The Aspen Casebook Series (famously known among law faculty and students as the "red and black" casebooks) encompasses hundreds of highly regarded textbooks in more than eighty disciplines, from large enrollment courses such as Torts and Contracts to emerging electives such as Sustainability and the Law of Policing. Study aids such as the *Examples & Explanations* and the *Emanuel Law Outlines* series, both highly popular collections, help law students master complex subject matter.

Major products, programs, and initiatives include:

- **Connected eBooks** are enhanced digital textbooks and study aids that come with a suite of online content and learning tools designed to maximize student success. Designed in collaboration with hundreds of faculty and students, the Connected eBook is a significant leap forward in the legal education learning tools available to students.
- **Connected Quizzing** is an easy-to-use formative assessment tool that tests law students' understanding and provides timely feedback to improve learning outcomes. Delivered through CasebookConnect.com, the learning platform already used by students to access their Aspen casebooks, Connected Quizzing is simple to implement and integrates seamlessly with law school course curricula.
- **PracticePerfect** is a visually engaging, interactive study aid to explain commonly encountered legal doctrines through easy-to-understand animated videos, illustrative examples, and numerous practice questions. Developed by a team of experts, PracticePerfect is the ideal study companion for today's law students.
- The **Aspen Learning Library** enables law schools to provide their students with access to the most popular study aids on the market across all of their courses. Available through an annual subscription, the online library consists of study aids in e-book, audio, and video formats with full text search, note-taking, and highlighting capabilities.
- Aspen's **Digital Bookshelf** is an institutional-level online education bookshelf, consolidating everything students and professors need to ensure success. This program ensures that every student has access to affordable course materials from day one.
- **Leading Edge** is a community centered on thinking differently about legal education and putting those thoughts into actionable strategies. At the core of the program is the Leading Edge Conference, an annual gathering of legal education thought leaders looking to pool ideas and identify promising directions of exploration.

Format for the Casenote® Legal Brief

Nature of Case: This section identifies the form of action (e.g., breach of contract, negligence, battery), the type of proceeding (e.g., demurrer, appeal from trial court's jury instructions) or the relief sought (e.g., damages, injunction, criminal sanctions).

Palsgraf v. Long Island R.R. Co.

Injured bystander (P) v. Railroad company (D)

N.Y. Ct. App., 248 N.Y. 339, 162 N.E. 99 (1928).

NATURE OF CASE: Appeal from judgment affirming verdict for plaintiff seeking damages for personal injury.

FACT SUMMARY: Helen Palsgraf (P) was injured on R.R.'s (D) train platform when R.R.'s (D) guard helped a passenger aboard a moving train, causing his package to fall on the tracks. The package contained fireworks which exploded, creating a shock that tipped a scale onto Palsgraf (P).

RULE OF LAW

The risk reasonably to be perceived defines the duty to be obeyed.

FACTS: Helen Palsgraf (P) purchased a ticket to Rockaway Beach from R.R. (D) and was waiting on the train platform. As she waited, two men ran to catch a train that was pulling out from the platform. The first man jumped aboard, but the second man, who appeared as if he might fall, was helped aboard by the guard on the train who had kept the door open so they could jump aboard. A guard on the platform also helped by pushing him onto the train. The man was carrying a package wrapped in newspaper. In the process, the man dropped his package, which fell on the tracks. The package contained fireworks and exploded. The shock of the explosion was apparently of great enough strength to tip over some scales at the other end of the platform, which fell on Palsgraf (P) and injured her. A jury awarded her damages, and R.R. (D) appealed.

ISSUE: Does the risk reasonably to be perceived define the duty to be obeyed?

HOLDING AND DECISION: (Cardozo, C.J.) Yes. The risk reasonably to be perceived defines the duty to be obeyed. If there is no foreseeable hazard to the injured party as the result of a seemingly innocent act, the act does not become a tort because it happened to be a wrong as to another. If the wrong was not willful, the plaintiff must show that the act as to her had such great and apparent possibilities of danger as to entitle her to protection. Negligence in the abstract is not enough upon which to base liability. Negligence is a relative concept, evolving out of the common law doctrine of trespass on the case. To establish liability, the defendant must owe a legal duty of reasonable care to the injured party. A cause of action in tort will lie where harm, though unintended, could have been averted or avoided by observance of such a duty. The scope of the duty is limited by the range of danger that a reasonable person could foresee. In this case, there was nothing to suggest from the appearance of the parcel or otherwise that the parcel contained fireworks. The guard could not reasonably have had any warning of a threat to Palsgraf (P), and R.R. (D) therefore cannot be held liable. Judgment is reversed in favor of R.R. (D).

DISSENT: (Andrews, J.) The concept that there is no negligence unless R.R. (D) owes a legal duty to take care as to Palsgraf (P) herself is too narrow. Everyone owes to the world at large the duty of refraining from those acts that may unreasonably threaten the safety of others. If the guard's action was negligent as to those nearby, it was also negligent as to those outside what might be termed the "danger zone." For Palsgraf (P) to recover, R.R.'s (D) negligence must have been the proximate cause of her injury, a question of fact for the jury.

ANALYSIS

The majority defined the limit of the defendant's liability in terms of the danger that a reasonable person in defendant's situation would have perceived. The dissent argued that the limitation should not be placed on liability, but rather on damages. Judge Andrews suggested that only injuries that would not have happened but for R.R.'s (D) negligence should be compensable. Both the majority and dissent recognized the policy-driven need to limit liability for negligent acts, seeking, in the words of Judge Andrews, to define a framework "that will be practical and in keeping with the general understanding of mankind." The Restatement (Second) of Torts has accepted Judge Cardozo's view.

Quicknotes

FORESEEABILITY A reasonable expectation that change is the probable result of certain acts or omissions.

NEGLIGENCE Conduct falling below the standard of care that a reasonable person would demonstrate under similar conditions.

PROXIMATE CAUSE The natural sequence of events without which an injury would not have been sustained.

Fact Summary: This is included to refresh your memory and can be used as a quick reminder of the facts.

Rule of Law: Summarizes the general principle of law that the case illustrates. It may be used for instant recall of the court's holding and for classroom discussion or home review.

Facts: This section contains all relevant facts of the case, including the contentions of the parties and the lower court holdings. It is written in a logical order to give you a clear understanding of the case. The plaintiff and defendant are identified by their proper names throughout and are always labeled with a (P) or (D).

Issue: The issue is a concise question that brings out the essence of the opinion as it relates to the section of the casebook in which the case appears. Both substantive and procedural issues are included if relevant to the decision.

Party ID: Quick identification of the relationship between the parties.

Concurrence/Dissent: All concurrences and dissents are briefed whenever they are included by the casebook author.

Analysis: This last paragraph gives you a broad understanding of where the case "fits in" with other cases in the section of the book and with the entire course. It is a hornbook-style discussion indicating whether the case is a majority or minority opinion and comparing the principal case with other cases in the casebook. It may also provide analysis from restatements, uniform codes, and law review articles.

Holding and Decision: This section offers a clear and in-depth discussion of the rule of the case and the court's rationale. It is written in easy-to-understand language and answers the issue presented by applying the law to the facts of the case. When relevant, it includes a thorough discussion of the exceptions to the case as listed by the court, any major cites to the other cases on point, and the names of the judges who wrote the decisions.

Quicknotes: Conveniently defines legal terms found in the case.

Note to Students

Aspen Publishing is proud to offer *Casenote® Legal Briefs*—continuing thirty years of publishing America's best-selling legal briefs.

Casenote® Legal Briefs are designed to help you save time when briefing assigned cases. Organized under convenient headings, they show you how to abstract the basic facts and holdings from the text of the actual opinions handed down by the courts. Used as part of a rigorous study regimen, they can help you spend more time analyzing and critiquing points of law than on copying bits and pieces of judicial opinions into your notebook or outline.

Casenote® Legal Briefs should never be used as a substitute for assigned casebook readings. They work best when read as a follow-up to reviewing the underlying opinions themselves. Students who try to avoid reading and digesting the judicial opinions in their casebooks or online sources will end up shortchanging themselves in the long run. The ability to absorb, critique, and restate the dynamic and complex elements of case law decisions is crucial to your success in law school and beyond. It cannot be developed vicariously.

In addition to *Casenote® Legal Briefs*, Aspen Publishing offers the following study aids:

- *Casenote® Legal Briefs*
- *Emanuel® Law Outlines*
- Emanuel® *Law in a Flash* Flash Cards
- Emanuel® *CrunchTime®* Series

Each of these series is designed to provide you with easy-to-understand explanations of complex points of law. Each volume offers guidance on the principles of legal analysis and, consulted regularly, will hone your ability to spot relevant issues. We have titles that will help you prepare for class, prepare for your exams, and enhance your general comprehension of the law along the way.

To find out more about our law school tools for success, visit us at *www.AspenPublishing.com* or e-mail us at *customer.service@aspenpublishing.com*. We'll be happy to assist you.

How to Brief a Case

A. Decide on a Format and Stick to It

Structure is essential to a good brief. It enables you to arrange systematically the related parts that are scattered throughout most cases, thus making manageable and understandable what might otherwise seem to be an endless and unfathomable sea of information. There are, of course, an unlimited number of formats that can be utilized. However, it is best to find one that suits your needs and stick to it. Consistency breeds both efficiency and the security that when called upon you will know where to look in your brief for the information you are asked to give.

Any format, as long as it presents the essential elements of a case in an organized fashion, can be used. Experience, however, has led *Casenote® Legal Briefs* to develop and utilize the following format because of its logical flow and universal applicability.

NATURE OF CASE: This is a brief statement of the legal character and procedural status of the case (e.g., "Appeal of a burglary conviction").

There are many different alternatives open to a litigant dissatisfied with a court ruling. The key to determining which one has been used is to discover *who is asking this court for what.*

This first entry in the brief should be kept as *short as possible.* Use the court's terminology if you understand it. But since jurisdictions vary as to the titles of pleadings, the best entry is the one that addresses who wants what in this proceeding, not the one that sounds most like the court's language.

RULE OF LAW: A statement of the general principle of law that the case illustrates (e.g., "An acceptance that varies any term of the offer is considered a rejection and counteroffer").

Determining the rule of law of a case is a procedure similar to determining the issue of the case. Avoid being fooled by red herrings; there may be a few rules of law mentioned in the case excerpt, but usually only one is *the* rule with which the casebook editor is concerned. The techniques used to locate the issue, described below, may also be utilized to find the rule of law. Generally, your best guide is simply the chapter heading. It is a clue to the point the casebook editor seeks to make and should be kept in mind when reading every case in the respective section.

FACTS: A synopsis of only the essential facts of the case, i.e., those bearing upon or leading up to the issue.

The facts entry should be a short statement of the events and transactions that led one party to initiate legal proceedings against another in the first place. While some cases conveniently state the salient facts at the beginning of the decision, in other instances they will have to be culled from hiding places throughout the text, even from concurring and dissenting opinions. Some of the "facts" will often be in dispute and should be so noted. Conflicting evidence may be briefly pointed up. "Hard" facts must be included. Both must be *relevant* in order to be listed in the facts entry. It is impossible to tell what is relevant until the entire case is read, as the ultimate determination of the rights and liabilities of the parties may turn on something buried deep in the opinion.

Generally, the facts entry should not be longer than three to five *short* sentences.

It is often helpful to identify the role played by a party in a given context. For example, in a construction contract case the identification of a party as the "contractor" or "builder" alleviates the need to tell that that party was the one who was supposed to have built the house.

It is always helpful, and a good general practice, to identify the "plaintiff" and the "defendant." This may seem elementary and uncomplicated, but, especially in view of the creative editing practiced by some casebook editors, it is sometimes a difficult or even impossible task. Bear in mind that the *party presently* seeking something from this court may not be the plaintiff, and that sometimes only the cross-claim of a defendant is treated in the excerpt. Confusing or misaligning the parties can ruin your analysis and understanding of the case.

ISSUE: A statement of the general legal question answered by or illustrated in the case. For clarity, the issue is best put in the form of a question capable of a "yes" or "no" answer. In reality, the issue is simply the Rule of Law put in the form of a question (e.g., "May an offer be accepted by performance?").

The major problem presented in discerning what is *the* issue in the case is that an opinion usually purports to raise and answer several questions. However, except for rare cases, only one such question is really the issue in the case. Collateral issues not necessary to the resolution of the matter in controversy are handled by the court by language known as *"obiter dictum"* or merely *"dictum."* While dicta may be included later in the brief, they have no place under the issue heading.

To find the issue, ask *who wants what* and then go on to ask *why did that party succeed or fail in getting it.* Once this is determined, the "why" should be turned into a question.

The complexity of the issues in the cases will vary, but in all cases a single-sentence question should sum up the issue. *In a few cases,* there will be two, or even more rarely, three issues of equal importance to the resolution of the case. Each should be expressed in a single-sentence question.

Since many issues are resolved by a court in coming to a final disposition of a case, the casebook editor will reproduce the portion of the opinion containing the issue or issues most relevant to the area of law under scrutiny. A noted law professor gave this advice: "Close the book; look at the title on the cover." Chances are, if it is Property, you need not concern yourself with whether, for example, the federal government's treatment of the plaintiff's land really raises a federal question sufficient to support jurisdiction on this ground in federal court.

The same rule applies to chapter headings designating sub-areas within the subjects. They tip you off as to what the text is designed to teach. The cases are arranged in a casebook to show a progression or development of the law, so that the preceding cases may also help.

It is also most important to remember to *read the notes and questions* at the end of a case to determine what the editors wanted you to have gleaned from it.

HOLDING AND DECISION: This section should succinctly explain the rationale of the court in arriving at its decision. In capsulizing the "reasoning" of the court, it should always include an application of the general rule or rules of law to the specific facts of the case. Hidden justifications come to light in this entry: the reasons for the state of the law, the public policies, the biases and prejudices, those considerations that influence the justices' thinking and, ultimately, the outcome of the case. At the end, there should be a short indication of thedisposition or procedural resolution of the case (e.g., "Decision of the trial court for Mr. Smith (P) reversed").

The foregoing format is designed to help you "digest" the reams of case material with which you will be faced in your law school career. Once mastered by practice, it will place at your fingertips the information the authors of your casebooks have sought to impart to you in case-by-case illustration and analysis.

B. Be as Economical as Possible in Briefing Cases

Once armed with a format that encourages succinctness, it is as important to be economical with regard to the time spent on the actual reading of the case as it is to be economical in the writing of the brief itself. This does not mean "skimming" a case. Rather, it means reading the case with an "eye" trained to recognize into which "section" of your brief a particular passage or line fits and having a system for quickly and precisely marking the case so that the passages fitting any one particular part of the brief can be easily identified and brought together in a concise and accurate manner when the brief is actually written.

It is of no use to simply repeat everything in the opinion of the court; record only enough information to trigger your recollection of what the court said. Nevertheless, an accurate statement of the "law of the case," i.e., the legal principle applied to the facts, is absolutely essential to class preparation and to learning the law under the case method.

To that end, it is important to develop a "shorthand" that you can use to make marginal notations. These notations will tell you at a glance in which section of the brief you will be placing that particular passage or portion of the opinion.

Some students prefer to underline all the salient portions of the opinion (with a pencil or colored underliner marker), making marginal notations as they go along. Others prefer the color-coded method of underlining, utilizing different colors of markers to underline the salient portions of the case, each separate color being used to represent a different section of the brief. For example, blue underlining could be used for passages relating to the rule of law, yellow for those relating to the issue, and green for those relating to the holding and decision, etc. While it has its advocates, thecolor-coded method can be confusing and time-consuming (all that time spent on changing colored markers). Furthermore, it can interfere with the continuity and concentration many students deem essential to the reading of a case for maximum comprehension. In the end, however, it is a matter of personal preference and style. Just remember, whatever method you use, underlining must be used sparingly or its value is lost.

If you take the marginal notation route, an efficient and easy method is to go along underlining the key portions of the case and placing in the margin alongside them the following "markers" to indicate where a particular passage or line "belongs" in the brief you will write:

N	(NATURE OF CASE)
RL	(RULE OF LAW)
I	(ISSUE)
HL	(HOLDING AND DECISION, relates to the RULE OF LAW behind the decision)
HR	(HOLDING AND DECISION, gives the RATIONALE or reasoning behind the decision)
HA	(HOLDING AND DECISION, applies the general principle(s) of law to the facts of the case to arrive at the decision)

Remember that a particular passage may well contain information necessary to more than one part of your brief, in which case you simply note that in the margin. If you are using the color-coded underlining method instead of marginal notation, simply make asterisks or checks in the margin next to the passage in question in the colors that indicate the additional sections of the brief where it might be utilized.

The economy of utilizing "shorthand" in marking cases for briefing can be maintained in the actual brief writing process itself by utilizing "law student shorthand" within the brief. There are many commonly used words and phrases for which abbreviations can be substituted in your briefs (and in your class notes also). You can develop abbreviations that are personal to you and which will save you a lot of time. A reference list of briefing abbreviations can be found on page x of this book.

C. Use Both the Briefing Process and the Brief as a Learning Tool

Now that you have a format and the tools for briefing cases efficiently, the most important thing is to make the time spent in briefing profitable to you and to make the most advantageous use of the briefs you create. Of course, the briefs are invaluable for classroom reference when you are called upon to explain or analyze a particular case. However, they are also useful in reviewing for exams. A quick glance at the fact summary should bring the case to mind, and a rereading of the rule of law should enable you to go over the underlying legal concept in your mind, how it was applied in that particular case, and how it might apply in other factual settings.

As to the value to be derived from engaging in the briefing process itself, there is an immediate benefit that arises from being forced to sift through the essential facts and reasoning from the court's opinion and to succinctly express them in your own words in your brief. The process ensures that you understand the case and the point that it illustrates, and that means you will be ready to absorb further analysis and information brought forth in class. It also ensures you will have something to say when called upon in class. The briefing process helps develop a mental agility for getting to the *gist* of a case and for identifying, expounding on, and applying the legal concepts and issues found there. The briefing process is the mental process on which you must rely in taking law school examinations; it is also the mental process upon which lawyers rely in serving their clients and in making a living.

Abbreviations for Briefs

acceptance	acp
affirmed	aff
answer	ans
assumption of risk	a/r
attorney	atty
beyond a reasonable doubt	b/r/d
bona fide purchaser	BFP
breach of contract	br/k
cause of action	c/a
common law	c/l
Constitution	Con
constitutional	con
contract	K
contributory negligence	c/n
cross	x
cross-complaint	x/c
cross-examination	x/ex
cruel and unusual punishment	c/u/p
defendant	D
dismissed	dis
double jeopardy	d/j
due process	d/p
equal protection	e/p
equity	eq
evidence	ev
exclude	exc
exclusionary rule	exc/r
felony	f/n
freedom of speech	f/s
good faith	g/f
habeas corpus	h/c
hearsay	hr
husband	H
injunction	inj
in loco parentis	ILP
inter vivos	I/v
joint tenancy	j/t
judgment	judgt
jurisdiction	jur
last clear chance	LCC
long-arm statute	LAS
majority view	maj
meeting of minds	MOM
minority view	min
Miranda rule	Mir/r
Miranda warnings	Mir/w
negligence	neg
notice	ntc
nuisance	nus
obligation	ob
obscene	obs
offer	O
offeree	OE
offeror	OR
ordinance	ord
pain and suffering	p/s
parol evidence	p/e
plaintiff	P
prima facie	p/f
probable cause	p/c
proximate cause	px/c
real property	r/p
reasonable doubt	r/d
reasonable man	r/m
rebuttable presumption	rb/p
remanded	rem
res ipsa loquitur	RIL
respondeat superior	r/s
Restatement	RS
reversed	rev
Rule Against Perpetuities	RAP
search and seizure	s/s
search warrant	s/w
self-defense	s/d
specific performance	s/p
statute	S
statute of frauds	S/F
statute of limitations	S/L
summary judgment	s/j
tenancy at will	t/w
tenancy in common	t/c
tenant	t
third party	TP
third party beneficiary	TPB
transferred intent	TI
unconscionable	uncon
unconstitutional	unconst
undue influence	u/e
Uniform Commercial Code	UCC
unilateral	uni
vendee	VE
vendor	VR
versus	v
void for vagueness	VFV
weight of authority	w/a
weight of the evidence	w/e
wife	W
with	w/
within	w/i
without	w/o
without prejudice	w/o/p
wrongful death	wr/d

Table of Cases

Note: There are no principal cases in Chapter 1 of the casebook.

CHAPTER 2

The Basis of Contractual Obligation: Mutual Assent and Consideration

Quick Reference Rules of Law

Ray v. William G. Eurice & Bros., Inc.

Engineer (P) v. Builder (D)

Md. Ct. App., 201 Md. 115, 93 A.2d 272 (1952)

NATURE OF CASE: Appeal from denial of damages for breach of contract.

FACT SUMMARY: The trial court found a mistake precluded a meeting of the minds between the parties, and thus no contract existed to be breached.

RULE OF LAW

A party is bound to a signed document that he or she has read with the capacity to understand, and in the absence of fraud, duress, or mutual mistake.

FACTS: Ray (P), an engineer, presented architect's plans to Eurice (D) to solicit a bid for the construction of a house. Eurice (D), an experienced builder, rendered an estimate based upon revisions to the plans. Revised plans were attached to a contract that was read and signed by Eurice (D). Subsequently, Eurice (D) refused to perform, and Ray (P) sued for breach. Eurice (D) contended he never saw the specifications referred to by the contract and believed the contract referred to his own standard specifications. Thus, a mistake precluded a meeting of the minds preventing the formation of a contract. The trial court found for Eurice (D), and Ray (P) appealed.

ISSUE: Is a party bound to a signed document that he or she has read with the capacity to understand, and in the absence of fraud, duress, or mutual mistake?

HOLDING AND DECISION: (Hammond, J.) Yes. A party is bound to a signed document that he or she has read with the capacity to understand, and in the absence of fraud, duress, or mutual mistake. The contractor was very experienced and had no logical basis for assuming the specifications were his rather than those referred to in the contract. His mistake was unilateral rather than mutual. Thus, the contract was enforceable and was breached. The proper measure of damages is the cost in excess of the contract price that would be incurred by Ray (P) in having the house built. That amount is ascertainable with sufficient definiteness here and equals $5,993.40. Reversed.

ANALYSIS

Only a mutual mistake will prevent a meeting of the minds and thereby defeat the existence of an enforceable contract. A party's outward manifestations of an intent to contract are sufficient to bind him or her to the agreement. A party who is damaged by his or her lack of diligence in reviewing the contract has no remedy.

Quicknotes

DURESS Unlawful threats or other coercive behavior by one person that causes another to commit acts he or she would not otherwise do.

FRAUD A false representation of facts with the intent that another will rely on the misrepresentation to his or her detriment.

MUTUAL MISTAKE A mistake by both parties to a contract, who are in agreement as to what the contract terms should be, but the agreement as written fails to reflect that common intent; such contracts are voidable or subject to reformation.

UNILATERAL MISTAKE A mistake or misunderstanding as to the terms of a contract made by one party; it is generally not a basis for relief by rescission or reformation.

Lonergan v. Scolnick

Interested potential buyer (P) v. Seller (D)

Cal. Dist. Ct. App., 129 Cal. App. 2d 179, 276 P.2d 8 (1954)

NATURE OF CASE: Appeal from judgment for defendant in action for specific performance/damages.

FACT SUMMARY: After Lonergan (P) made several inquiries concerning some advertised land, the land was sold to another.

RULE OF LAW

There is no meeting of the minds and, therefore, no enforceable contract, where communications between the parties do not evidence a definite offer and acceptance.

FACTS: Lonergan (P) read about some property being offered for sale. Lonergan (P) wrote Scolnick (D), the seller, requesting additional information. Lonergan (P) later wrote requesting a legal description and whether a certain escrow company would be satisfactory to Scolnick (D). Scolnick (D) informed Lonergan (P) that if he wanted the property, he would have to act fast, as Scolnick (D) expected to sell the property to a third party in a week. Lonergan (P) sent a letter one week later stating that he wanted the property. Scolnick (D) had already sold it several days before. Lonergan (P) brought suit for specific performance and/or damages alleging that a valid contract had been formed. Scolnick (D) alleged that the parties had merely negotiated, no offer and acceptance had occurred, and there had been no meeting of the minds as to forming a valid contract. The trial court rendered judgment for Scolnick (D). The state appellate court granted review.

ISSUE: Is there a meeting of the minds and, therefore, an enforceable contract, where communications between the parties do not evidence a definite offer and acceptance?

HOLDING AND DECISION: (Barnard, P.J.) No. There is no meeting of the minds and, therefore, no enforceable contract, where communications between the parties do not evidence a definite offer and acceptance. Until there is a definite offer and acceptance, the parties are merely in a negotiation stage, which creates no binding relationship between them. The meeting of the minds is normally evidenced by an offer and acceptance. The ad herein was merely the solicitation of offers for the property. None of the letters, on either side, constituted an offer and acceptance. Scolnick's (D) final letter made clear that he would accept the first valid offer tendered. Lonergan (P) could not arbitrarily change negotiations into a contract unless Scolnick (D) had made a firm offer, a fact not established by the evidence. From Scolnick's (D) statement in his letter, alone, Lonergan (P) knew or should have known that he was not being given time in which to accept an offer that was being made, but that some further assent on the part of Scolnick (D) was required. Under the language used, Lonergan (P) was not being given a right to act within a reasonable time after receiving the letter. Because there was no offer, there could not be an acceptance and, therefore, there was no meeting of the minds of the parties. Consequently, no enforceable contract was formed. Affirmed.

ANALYSIS

In *Fairmount Glass Works v. Crunden-Martin Woodenware*, 106 Ky. 659, 51 S.W. 196 (1899), the plaintiff inquired as to the defendant's lowest price on ten loads of Mason jars. The reply was "$4.50 and $5.00 for immediate acceptance." The defendant refused to fill plaintiff's order. The court held that defendant's reply "was not a quotation of prices, but a definite order to sell." In *Harvey v. Facey*, A.C. 552 (1893), plaintiff telegraphed defendant, "Will you sell us Bumper Hall Pen? Telegraph lowest price." The defendant replied, "Lowest price for Bumper Hall Pen 900 Pounds." Plaintiff responded, "We agree to buy Bumper Hall Pen for 900 Pounds." The court held that there was no contract.

Quicknotes

ACCEPTANCE Assent to the specified terms of an offer, resulting in the formation of a binding agreement.

FIRM OFFER Under the Uniform Commercial Code, a signed, written offer to enter into a contract for the sale of goods that is irrevocable for a specified period of time, or if no time is stated, then for a reasonable time period not exceeding three months.

OFFER A proposed promise to undertake performance of an action, or to refrain from acting, that is to become binding upon acceptance by the offeree.

SPECIFIC PERFORMANCE An equitable remedy whereby the court requires the parties to perform their obligations pursuant to a contract.

Normile v. Miller

Purchaser (P) v. Seller (D)

N.C. Sup. Ct., 313 N.C. 98, 326 S.E.2d 11 (1985)

NATURE OF CASE: Appeal from denial of summary judgment motion for specific performance.

FACT SUMMARY: Normile (P) sought specific performance for the sale of Miller's (D) property after he accepted Miller's (D) counteroffer (which did not specify a time of acceptance) within the time period set for acceptance in his original offer, but after Miller (D) sold the property to Segal (P), thus revoking her counteroffer.

RULE OF LAW

A prospective purchaser does not have the power to accept a counteroffer after receiving notice of its revocation by accepting the counteroffer within the time period specified in the prospective purchaser's original offer.

FACTS: Miller (D) placed real estate for sale. Normile (P) completed a form purchase offer, and through brokers, presented it to Miller (D). The form had a set expiration period and called for other particulars of the sale. Miller (P) made changes in the terms—i.e., a counteroffer—and returned the form to Normile (P), who erroneously believed he was free to wait and think about the proposed counteroffer terms until the time set forth in the original offer that he had submitted to Miller (D). The counteroffer did not specify a time of acceptance. Prior to the expiration period on the original offer, Miller (D) accepted Segal's (P) offer to purchase the property, thus revoking her counteroffer. This revocation was communicated to Normile (P) by his broker, but Normile (P) attempted to accept the counteroffer, after being informed of its revocation, within the period for acceptance specified in the original offer. After this attempt was rejected, Normile (P) sued for specific performance and moved for summary judgment. However, the trial court granted Segal (P) summary judgment, and Normile (P) appealed the denial of his summary judgment motion. The state's highest court granted review.

ISSUE: Does a prospective purchaser have the power to accept a counteroffer after receiving notice of its revocation by accepting the counteroffer within the time period specified in the prospective purchaser's original offer?

HOLDING AND DECISION: (Frye, J.) No. A prospective purchaser does not have the power to accept a counteroffer after receiving notice of its revocation by accepting the counteroffer within the time period specified in the prospective purchaser's original offer. The original offer and its terms were rejected when Miller (D) made her qualified or conditional acceptance, which became a counteroffer. Although Normile (P) controlled the time for acceptance of his original offer, he could not control the time for acceptance of the counteroffer, since the counteroffer was a completely new offer and did not incorporate the original offer's time-of-acceptance term. If the terms of an offer are changed or qualified, there is no meeting of the minds, and, therefore, no contract. Here, Miller (D) did not accept the original offer, and her counteroffer did not include either a time limitation or a valid option supported by consideration, whereby it would remain open. Thus, when Miller (D) sold the property to Segal (P), she revoked her counteroffer to Normile (P), and Normile (P) was put on notice of this revocation by his broker. Normile's (P) failure to accept the counteroffer prior to its revocation precluded him from creating an enforceable contract based on the counteroffer. Affirmed as modified.

ANALYSIS

Offers must be accepted entirely or the conditional acceptance constitutes a counteroffer. The offer grants the offeree the power to enter into an enforceable contract through acceptance. Acceptance of an offer, when supported by valuable consideration, creates an enforceable contract.

Quicknotes

ACCEPTANCE Assent to the specified terms of an offer resulting in the formation of a binding agreement.

COUNTEROFFER An offer made by the offeree that has the effect of rejecting the offer deemed unsatisfactory and of proposing a different offer.

OFFER A proposed promise to undertake performance of an action, or to refrain from acting, that is to become binding upon acceptance by the offeree.

OFFEREE A person or party to whom an offer to enter into a contractual agreement is made.

REVOCATION The cancellation or withdrawal of some authority conferred, or destruction or making void an instrument drafted.

SPECIFIC PERFORMANCE An equitable remedy whereby the court requires the parties to perform their obligations pursuant to a contract.

Cook v. Coldwell Banker/Frank Laiben Realty Co.

Former salesperson (P) v. Employer (D)

Mo. Ct. App., 967 S.W.2d 654 (1998)

NATURE OF CASE: Appeal from a jury verdict and judgment for plaintiff for damages for breach of a bonus agreement contract.

FACT SUMMARY: Cook (P), a former employee of Coldwell Banker/Frank Laiben Realty Co. (D), alleged that she had accepted Coldwell's (D) offer of a bonus by substantial performance.

RULE OF LAW

In the context of an offer for a unilateral contract, the offer may not be revoked when the offeree has accepted the offer by substantial performance.

FACTS: Cook (P) worked for Coldwell Banker/Frank Laiben Realty Co. (collectively, Coldwell) (D) as a licensed real estate broker. In March 1991, Coldwell (D) announced a bonus program in order to retain its agents. The bonuses awarded for commissions earned by the brokers were to be paid at the end of each year. In September, Coldwell (D) indicated that the bonuses would be paid in March of the following year instead. Cook (P) had earned a $500 bonus, which was paid to her in September, and was also entitled to another bonus, staying with Coldwell (D) until the end of the year in reliance on its promise of that bonus. In January 1992 Cook (P) accepted a position with another firm and was told she would not be receiving her bonus from Coldwell (D). Cook (P) sent a demand letter to Coldwell (D), who refused to pay. Cook (P) then filed an action for breach of a bonus contract and sought damages, which a jury awarded her. Coldwell Banker (D) appealed.

ISSUE: In the context of an offer for a unilateral contract, may the offer be revoked when the offeree has accepted the offer by substantial performance?

HOLDING AND DECISION: (Crane, P.J.) No. In the context of an offer for a unilateral contract, the offer may not be revoked when the offeree has accepted the offer by substantial performance. An offer to make a unilateral contract is accepted when the requested performance is rendered. A promise to pay a bonus in return for an at-will employee's continued employment is an offer for a unilateral contract that becomes enforceable when accepted by the employee's performance. Part performance or tender may furnish consideration for the implied subsidiary promise that the offeror will not revoke his or her offer if part of the requested performance is given. In this case, there was evidence that, before the offer was modified in September 1991, Cook (P) had remained with Coldwell Banker/Frank Laiben Realty Co. (D) and had earned enough in commissions to be eligible for the offered bonus. This evidence was sufficient to make a submissible case for breach of a unilateral contract. Affirmed.

ANALYSIS

The holding of this case reflects a modern expansion of the concept of a unilateral contract. In a unilateral contract, an offeree's performance is considered both the acceptance of, and the consideration for, the offeror's promise to pay. The Restatement (Second) of Contracts abandoned the distinction between unilateral and bilateral contracts.

Quicknotes

PART PERFORMANCE Partial performance of a contract, promise, or obligation.

SUBSTANTIAL PERFORMANCE Performance of all the essential obligations pursuant to an agreement.

UNILATERAL CONTRACT An agreement pursuant to which a party agrees to act without an express exchange for performance on the part of the other party.

Sateriale v. R.J. Reynolds Tobacco Co.

Consumer (P) v. Tobacco company (D)

697 F.3d 777 (9th Cir. 2012)

NATURE OF CASE: Appeal from dismissal for failure to state a claim, inter alia, of breach of contract.

FACT SUMMARY: Consumers (P) contended they sufficiently made out a claim for R.J. Reynolds Tobacco Co.'s (RJR) (D) breach of contract by alleging RJR (D) initiated a customer loyalty program through which customers who purchased RJR (D) products could obtain merchandise, and RJR (D) refused to provide merchandise to consumers in accordance with the terms of the program months before RJR (D) officially terminated the program.

RULE OF LAW

(1) To state a claim for breach of contract, a plaintiff does allege the existence of an offer for a unilateral contract by alleging a manufacturer has advertised a consumer loyalty program that is designed to induce consumers to purchase the manufacturer's product by offering a reward for such purchases.

(2) To state a claim for breach of contract, a plaintiff must assert that the purported contract is sufficiently definite by alleging a discernable breach of the alleged contract, and that the breach is susceptible of some remedy.

(3) Lack of mutuality is not fatal to a claim of breach of a unilateral contract.

(4) Where a plaintiff alleges a defendant reserved the right to terminate its obligations under a unilateral contract at any time without notice, but does not allege the defendant reserved an unrestricted right to so terminate its obligations, and the plaintiff alleges the defendant waived its right to terminate by announcing a definite termination date and conditions of termination, dismissal of the plaintiff's breach of contract claim is not warranted.

FACTS: R.J. Reynolds Tobacco Co. (RJR) (D) initiated a customer loyalty program in 1991, whereby purchasers of RJR's (D) Camel cigarettes could accumulate, and redeem for merchandise, Camel Cash certificates (also known as C-Notes) included in Camel cigarette packages. As part of the program, RJR (D) provided consumers (P) with catalogs of merchandise for which consumers (P) could redeem their Camel Cash certificates. The number of certificates needed varied depending on the value of the merchandise, so consumers (P) could obtain merchandise for as little as 100 certificates, and they could get more valuable merchandise for thousands of certificates. This encouraged consumers (P) to purchase more cigarettes and to save certificates for more expensive merchandise. RJR (D) allegedly reserved the right to terminate the program without notice at any time. However, RJR (D) notified consumers (P) in October 2006, it would be terminating the program effective as of March 2007, and RJR (D) also informed consumers (P) they would be able to redeem their C-Notes for merchandise through March 2007. Several consumers (P) brought a class action in federal district court alleging that beginning in October 2006, RJR (D) stopped making catalogs available to consumers (P), and also refused to honor redemption submissions, so consumers (P) were stuck with hundreds or thousands of C-Notes they had saved. The consumers (P) asserted claims, inter alia, for breach of contract and promissory estoppel. RJR (D) defended on four grounds: the absence of an offer, indefiniteness, lack of mutuality of obligation (premised on RJR's right to terminate its contractual obligations), and untimeliness. The district court dismissed the action for failure to state a claim under Fed. R. Civ. P. 12(b)(6), and the court of appeals granted review.

ISSUE:

(1) To state a claim for breach of contract, does a plaintiff allege the existence of an offer for a unilateral contract by alleging a manufacturer has advertised a consumer loyalty program that is designed to induce consumers to purchase the manufacturer's product by offering a reward for such purchases?

(2) To state a claim for breach of contract, must a plaintiff assert that the purported contract is sufficiently definite by alleging a discernable breach of the alleged contract, and that the breach is susceptible of some remedy?

(3) Is lack of mutuality fatal to a claim of breach of a unilateral contract?

(4) Where a plaintiff alleges a defendant reserved the right to terminate its obligations under a unilateral contract at any time without notice, but does not allege the defendant reserved an unrestricted right to so terminate its obligations, and the plaintiff alleges the defendant waived its right to terminate by announcing a definite termination date and conditions of termination, is dismissal of the plaintiff's breach of contract claim warranted?

Continued on next page.

HOLDING AND DECISION: (Fisher, J.)

(1) Yes. To state a claim for breach of contract, a plaintiff does allege the existence of an offer for a unilateral contract by alleging a manufacturer has advertised a consumer loyalty program that is designed to induce consumers to purchase the manufacturer's product by offering a reward for such purchases. An offer is the manifestation of willingness to enter a bargain, so made as to justify another person in understanding his or her assent to that bargain is invited and he or she will conclude it. Whether an offer has been made depends on all the circumstances, and the key is whether the person to whom a communication was directed had reason to believe it was intended as an offer. As a preliminary matter, if there was an offer made by R.J. Reynolds Tobacco Co. (RJR) (D), it could not have been an offer for a bilateral contract. The consumers (P) have identified an alleged promise by RJR (D) (to allow customers to redeem C-Notes for rewards), but they have not pointed to any promise they made to RJR (D), nor do they argue RJR (D) sought a return promise in exchange for its own promise to allow consumers to exchange C-Notes for merchandise. Nonetheless, the consumers (P) have alleged an offer for a unilateral contract, which involves the exchange of a promise for a performance. RJR's (D) argument, that its C-Notes, whether read in isolation or in combination with the catalogs, were not offers, but invitations to make an offer, is rejected. RJR (D) relies on the common law's general rule that advertisements are not ordinarily intended or understood as offers to sell. It is not clear state law applies the common-law rule, but even assuming it does, that rule contains an exception for offers of a reward, including offers of a reward for the redemption of coupons. This exception has been applied to consumer loyalty rewards programs, and there is no reason not to apply that exception here. In any event, the concerns of the general rule—that there will be over-acceptance of a limited quantity of a product—do not arise here because RJR's (D) purpose was not to sell a limited inventory, but to induce as many consumers (P) as possible to purchase its product. RJR (D) alone decided how many C-Notes to distribute, so it exercised absolute control over the number of acceptances. Accordingly, there are no reasons for presuming RJR's (D) communications did not constitute an offer merely because they were addressed to the general public in the form of advertisements. Construing the complaint in the light most favorable to the consumers (P) and drawing all reasonable inferences from the complaint in their favor, the court finds the consumers (P) have adequately alleged the existence of an offer. This conclusion rests on the totality of the circumstances, including the repeated use of the word "offer" in the C-Notes; the absence of any language disclaiming the intent to be bound; the inclusion of specific restrictions in the C-Notes; the formal enrollment process, through which consumers submitted registration forms and RJR (D) issued enrollment numbers; and the substantial reliance expected from consumers. Under the common law, advertisements have been held to constitute offers where they invite the performance of a specific act without further communication and leave nothing for negotiation, and these requirements are satisfied here. RJR's (D) alleged offer invited the performance of specific acts (saving C-Notes and redeeming them for rewards in accordance with the catalog) without further communication and leaving nothing for negotiation. Although RJR (D) correctly observes performance of certain aspects of the program were entirely within its discretion, the consumers (P) do not allege these aspects were essential terms. Instead, they allege a contract the essence of which was their general right to redeem their certificates, during the life of the program, for whatever rewards merchandise RJR (D) made available, with RJR's discretion limited only by the implied duty of good faith performance. The presence of discretion thus does not preclude the existence of an offer. Judgment for consumers (P) as to this issue.

(2) Yes. To state a claim for breach of contract, a plaintiff must assert that the purported contract is sufficiently definite by alleging a discernable breach of the alleged contract, and that the breach is susceptible of some remedy. The terms of a contract are reasonably definite if they provide a basis for determining the existence of a breach and for giving an appropriate remedy. Here, the consumers (P) have stated a discernable breach of the alleged contract. They allege RJR (D) was required to make reasonable quantities of rewards merchandise (which RJR (D) chose at its discretion) available during the life of the Camel Cash program—a duty RJR (D) allegedly breached by failing to make any merchandise available after October 1, 2006. Whether the consumers (P) have stated an available remedy for this alleged breach is a closer call. Because it is unknown what rewards the consumers (P) may have obtained from RJR (D), since the nature of those rewards was solely within RJR's (D) discretion, it is difficult to know how to remedy a breach of RJR's (D) performance. Nevertheless, it is likewise not clear damages could not be rationally assessed, since RJR's internal documents assigned C-Notes values, such as 15 cents per \$1 note, that might afford a basis for assessing damages. Given that the allegations suggest the parties intended to contract, it would be premature at this

Continued on next page.

early stage of the pleadings to conclude no remedy will be available. RJR's (D) conduct demonstrates it believed it was contractually bound by its program, and the consumers (P) substantially relied on RJR's (D) promises. Accordingly, dismissal for indefiniteness is unwarranted. Judgment for consumers (P) as to this issue.

(3) No. Lack of mutuality is not fatal to a claim of breach of a unilateral contract. Because the consumers (P) have alleged an offer to enter into a unilateral rather than a bilateral contract, RJR's (D) reliance on mutuality of obligation necessarily fails: that doctrine does not apply to unilateral contracts and has no relevance in the unilateral contract context. [Judgment for consumers (P) as to this issue.]

(4) No. Where a plaintiff alleges a defendant reserved the right to terminate its obligations under a unilateral contract at any time without notice, but does not allege the defendant reserved an unrestricted right to so terminate its obligations, and the plaintiff alleges the defendant waived its right to terminate by announcing a definite termination date and conditions of termination, dismissal of the plaintiff's breach of contract claim is not warranted. If RJR (D) had in fact reserved an unrestricted right to terminate the Camel Cash program at any time without notice, this would have been fatal to the consumers' (P) claim, since if an offeror expressly reserves not only the right to revoke the offer at will and without notice, but also the unrestricted right not to perform, then the offer is not legally effective as an offer at all, and it is better viewed as an invitation to submit an offer. Moreover, such an expression constitutes an unenforceable illusory promise, at least so long as the purported contract remains wholly executory. The consumers (P) did not, however, allege RJR (D) reserved an unrestricted right to terminate its duty to perform, but only that some, but not all, of RJR's (D) catalogs stated RJR (D) could terminate the Camel Cash program without notice. Moreover, the consumers (P) alleged RJR (D) waived any right to terminate without notice when, on or about October 1, 2006, it announced by mailing a notice to program members, that the program would terminate as of March 31, 2007. Accordingly, on this record, dismissal is unwarranted. Judgment for consumers (P) as to this issue. The court also ruled the consumers' (P) promissory estoppel claim should go forward; but it ruled two statutory consumer protection claims should not. Affirmed in part, reversed in part, and remanded.

ANALYSIS

It is possible for a consumer rewards program to involve a bilateral contract. Frequent flyer programs, for example, may be governed by membership agreements that impose contractual duties on both sides of the bargain, exposing airlines and travelers alike to potential contractual liability. See, e.g., *Ginsberg v. Northwest, Inc.*, 653 F.3d 1033, 1035, 1040 (9th Cir. 2011); *Am. Airlines, Inc. v. Am. Coupon Exch., Inc.*, 721 F. Supp. 61, 63 (S.D.N.Y.1989). Here, however, the consumers (P) had not alleged an offer or contract involving reciprocal duties, and therefore they had not alleged a bilateral contract.

Quicknotes

BILATERAL CONTRACT An agreement pursuant to which each party promises to undertake an obligation, or to forbear from acting.

BREACH OF CONTRACT Unlawful failure by a party to perform its obligations pursuant to contract.

FORBEARANCE The act of refraining from doing something that one has the legal right to do.

INDEFINITENESS Indeterminable; not definite or permanent; a contract is void for indefiniteness when its terms are so uncertain as to render it incapable of being enforced.

MUTUALITY OF OBLIGATION Requires that both parties to a contract be bound or else neither is bound.

OFFER A proposed promise to undertake performance of an action, or to refrain from acting, that is to become binding upon acceptance by the offeree.

OFFEREE A person or party to whom an offer to enter into a contractual agreement is made.

PERFORMANCE The fulfillment of a contractual duty.

PROMISEE The party to whom a promise is made.

PROMISOR The party who promises to render an obligation to another in the future.

PROMISSORY ESTOPPEL A promise that is enforceable if the promisor should reasonably expect that it will induce action or forbearance on the part of the promisee, does in fact cause such action or forbearance, and is the only means of avoiding injustice.

UNILATERAL CONTRACT An agreement pursuant to which a party agrees to act without an express exchange for performance on the part of the other party.

Walker v. Keith

Lessor (D) v. Lessee (P)

Ky. Ct. App., 382 S.W.2d 198 (1964)

NATURE OF CASE: Appeal from declaratory judgment for plaintiff lessee in action for breach of an option to renew a lease clause.

FACT SUMMARY: Walker (D), the lessor, contended that the option provision in his lease with Keith (P), the lessee, did not fix rent with sufficient certainty to constitute an enforceable contract between the parties.

RULE OF LAW

Where essential terms such as price are not contained in an option contract, and no standards are included whereby such terms may be judicially determined, no contract exists.

FACTS: Walker (D), the lessor, entered a ten-year lease with Keith (P), the lessee. The contract gave Keith (P) an option to renew the lease for ten additional years. The parties were to agree on a fair rental at that time to be fixed based on the "comparative basis of rental values at the date of renewal with rental values at this time reflected by the comparative business conditions of the two periods." Keith (P) attempted to renew his lease, but Walker (D) refused. Keith (P) brought suit for damages or specific performance. The trial court fixed the reasonable rental value at $125 per month. Walker (D) appealed, alleging that there was no way to fix the price and, therefore, no contract existed. The intermediate court of appeals granted review.

ISSUE: Where essential terms such as price are not contained in an option contract, and no standards are included whereby such terms may be judicially determined, does a contract exist?

HOLDING AND DECISION: (Clay, Commr.) No. Where essential terms such as price are not contained in an option contract, and no standards are included whereby such terms may be judicially determined, no contract exists. The price term is essential in a lease contract. The option clause fails to fix it or to provide any standard whereby the court could fix it. Equity cannot rewrite a contract supplying essential terms that the parties failed to provide. Reasonable rent to one party may be unreasonable to the other. The parties herein have merely agreed to agree. Their failure to agree renders the option/offer incapable of being accepted. No contract was ever formed. Reversed.

ANALYSIS

A number of courts have tried to supply missing terms, even essential ones by making "reasonable" judgments as to value, rental, etc. *Hull v. Weatherford*, 32 Ariz. 370 (1927). Courts feel that "reasonable" rental can be determined by comparison with the rental of similar property, for a similar period of time and for a similar use. *Edwards v. Tobin*, 132 Or. 38 (1930). In *Walker*, the court focuses on whether a contract exists. Only if one is found to exist may the court supply terms.

Quicknotes

LEASE An agreement or contract that creates a relationship between a landlord and tenant (real property) or lessor and lessee (real or personal property).

LESSEE One who leases property from a landlord, receiving the right to immediate possession of the property but not legal title.

LESSOR One who leases property to another, relinquishing the right to immediate possession of the property but retaining legal title.

MATERIAL TERM OF CONTRACT A fact without the existence of which a contract would not have been entered.

SPECIFIC PERFORMANCE An equitable remedy whereby the court requires the parties to perform their obligations pursuant to a contract.

Quake Construction, Inc. v. American Airlines, Inc.

Construction subcontractor (P) v. Owner (D)

Ill. Sup. Ct., 141 Ill. 2d 281, 565 N.E.2d 990 (1990)

NATURE OF CASE: Appeal from reversal of dismissal of suit for damages resulting from alleged breach of contract.

FACT SUMMARY: When American Airlines, Inc. (D) canceled its agreement with the general contractor for construction of an expansion of its airport facilities, Quake Construction, Inc. (P), a subcontractor, alleged that the letter of intent it had received from the general contractor constituted an enforceable, binding contract.

RULE OF LAW

Although letters of intent may be enforceable, such letters are not necessarily enforceable unless the parties intend them to be contractually binding.

FACTS: American Airlines, Inc. (D) hired a general contractor to prepare and accept bids and award contracts for construction of the expansion of American Airlines' (D) facilities at O'Hare International Airport. Quake Construction, Inc. (Quake) (P) was invited by the general contractor to bid on the employee facilities and automotive maintenance shop projects. Quake (P) was orally informed that it had been awarded the contract for the project. To induce Quake (P) and its subcontractors to provide their license numbers, the general contractor sent Quake (P) a letter of intent stating that the formal contract agreement was being prepared and would be available for signature shortly. The letter also contained a cancellation clause. American Airlines (D) later terminated Quake's (P) involvement with the project, and Quake (P) sued for the damages it had allegedly suffered in procuring the contract, preparing to perform under the contract, and its loss of anticipated profit from the contract. The circuit court held that the letter was not an enforceable contract and dismissed the complaint. The appellate court found the letter ambiguous regarding the parties' intent to be bound by it and remanded. American Airlines (D) appealed.

ISSUE: Although letters of intent may be enforceable, are such letters necessarily enforceable if the parties do not intend them to be contractually binding?

HOLDING AND DECISION: (Calvo, J.) No. Although letters of intent may be enforceable, such letters are not necessarily enforceable unless the parties intend them to be contractually binding. It is settled law in Illinois regarding letters of intent that the intent of the parties is controlling. A circuit court must initially determine, as a question of law, whether the language of a purported contract is ambiguous as to the parties' intent. If the terms of an alleged contract are ambiguous or capable of more than one interpretation, parol evidence is admissible to ascertain the parties' intent. The cancellation clause here exhibited the parties' intent to be bound by the letter because no need would exist to provide for the cancellation of the letter unless the letter had some binding effect. The cancellation clause could also, however, be interpreted to mean that the parties did not intend to be bound until they entered into a formal agreement. Therefore, the appellate court correctly concluded that the letter was ambiguous regarding the parties' intent to be bound by it. Affirmed.

CONCURRENCE: (Stamos, J.) Because dismissal is unwarranted unless clearly no set of facts can be proved under the pleadings that will entitle a plaintiff to recover, the circuit court should not have dismissed. The letter of intent is just ambiguous enough for Quake Construction Inc.'s (P) complaint to survive a motion to dismiss. Drafters of letters of intent would be well advised to avoid ambiguity on the point of whether the issuers are bound if they want to avoid further litigation and undesired contractual obligations.

ANALYSIS

An "agreement to agree" is a type of incomplete bargaining. In such a case, only one or two terms may be left for future agreement, and the parties have reached agreement on most other matters. Under the Uniform Commercial Code § 2-204(3), a contract for sale does not fail for indefiniteness if the parties have intended to make a contract and there is a reasonably certain basis for giving an appropriate remedy.

Quicknotes

AMBIGUITY Language that is capable of more than one interpretation.

CONSTRUCTION CONTRACT A contract containing provisions that specify the terms pursuant to which a building is to be constructed.

CONTRACT An agreement pursuant to which a party agrees to act, or to forbear from acting, in exchange for performance on the part of the other party.

FORBEAR Refrain from doing something that one has the legal right to do.

PAROL EVIDENCE RULE Doctrine precluding parties to an agreement from introducing evidence of prior or contemporaneous agreements in order to repudiate or alter the terms of a written contract.

Hamer v. Sidway

Assignor of nephew (P) v. Executor (D)

N.Y. Ct. App., 124 N.Y. 538, 27 N.E. 256 (1891)

NATURE OF CASE: Appeal from denial of damages in an action for breach of contract.

FACT SUMMARY: Sidway's (D) decedent promised to pay $5,000 to Hamer's (P) assignor if he would forbear from the use of liquor, tobacco, swearing, or playing cards or billiards for money until his 21st birthday.

RULE OF LAW

In general a waiver of any legal right at the request of another party is a sufficient consideration for a promise.

FACTS: Story, of whose estate Sidway (D) was executor, agreed with his nephew, William, that he, Story, would pay him $5,000 if he refrained from drinking liquor, using tobacco, swearing, or playing cards or billiards for money until his 21st birthday. Upon turning 21, William wrote Story saying that he had fulfilled his part of this deal and was entitled to the money. Story replied that William had in fact earned the money, but because Story feared that William might squander it, Story told William that he would keep the money set aside for him at interest. William agreed to this arrangement. Story died 12 years later without having paid the $5,000. William assigned his right in the money to his wife who, in turn, assigned her right to Hamer (P), who brought this action for breach of contract when Sidway (D) refused to pay on the ground that William gave no consideration nor did he suffer a detriment, but rather that his health and habits were benefited. Hamer (P) appealed judgment for Sidway (D).

ISSUE: In general is a waiver of any legal right at the request of another party a sufficient consideration for a promise?

HOLDING AND DECISION: (Parker, J.) Yes. In general a waiver of any legal right at the request of another party is a sufficient consideration for a promise. The Exchequer Chamber, in 1875, defined consideration as follows: "A valuable consideration in the sense of the law may consist either in some right, interest, profit or benefit accruing to the one party, or some forbearance, detriment, loss or responsibility given, suffered or undertaken by the other." To follow Sidway's (D) contention would be to leave open to controversy whether a consideration was erased by the degree to which a detriment is given by a promisee also benefited him. Second, the letter to William stating that the money would be set aside, coupled with his assent to that arrangement, changed the relationship of Story and William from debtor-creditor to trustee-beneficiary. If before a declaration of trust a party was a mere debtor, a subsequent agreement recognizing the fund as already in his hands and stipulating for its investment on the creditor's account will have the effect to create a trust. While the word "trust" was never used, the language of the letter assured William that the money would be set apart and kept without interference until he was capable of managing it himself. Reversed.

ANALYSIS

The trust question was raised above because a pure contract action would have been barred by the running of the statute of limitations while an action on a trust would not have been so barred. "Consideration means not so much that one party is profiting as that the other abandons some legal right in the present or limits his legal freedom of action in the future as an inducement for the promise of the first." Pollock, *Contracts*, 166. Abstinence from liquor or giving up the use of liquor has independently been held to be sufficient consideration for a promise.

Quicknotes

CONSIDERATION Value given by one party in exchange for performance, or a promise to perform, by another party.

FORBEARANCE The act of refraining from doing something that one has the legal right to do.

PERFORMANCE The fulfillment of a contractual duty.

PROMISE The expression of an intention to act, or to forbear from acting, granting a right to the promisee to expect and enforce its performance.

PROMISEE The party to whom a promise is made.

TRUST The holding of property by one party for the benefit of another.

Pennsy Supply, Inc. v. American Ash Recycling Corp. of Pennsylvania

Subcontractor (P) v. Materials supplier (D)

Pa. Super. Ct., 895 A.2d 595 (2006)

NATURE OF CASE: Appeal from grant of demurrer dismissing an action for breach of contract, breach of implied and express warranties of merchantability, breach of warranty of fitness for a particular purpose, and promissory estoppel.

FACT SUMMARY: Pennsy Supply, Inc. (Pennsy) (P) contended that its disposal of a hazardous material it had obtained for free from American Ash Recycling Corp. of Pennsylvania (American Ash) (D) constituted consideration necessary to support various breach of contract, warranty, and merchantability claims.

RULE OF LAW

Relief of a manufacturer's legal obligation to dispose of a material classified as hazardous waste, such that the manufacturer avoids the costs of disposal, constitutes sufficient consideration to ground contract and warranty claims brought by the disposer.

FACTS: Pennsy Supply, Inc. (Pennsy) (P), a paving subcontractor, obtained paving material, known as Treated Ash Aggregate (TAA) or AggRite, for free from American Ash Recycling Corp. of Pennsylvania (American Ash) (D). Pennsy (P) used the material for driveways and a parking lot in a school district construction project. When the paving started to crack extensively, Pennsy (P) remedied at no cost to the district. The scope and cost of the remedial work included the removal and appropriate disposal of the AggRite, which the state classified as a hazardous waste material. Pennsy (P) requested American Ash (D) to arrange for the removal and disposal of the AggRite, but American Ash (D) refused. Pennsy (P) provided notice to American Ash (D) of its intention to recover costs, and then filed suit for breach of contract, breach of implied warranty of merchantability, breach of express warranty of merchantability, breach of warranty of fitness for a particular purpose, and promissory estoppel. American Ash (D) demurred, and the trial court sustained its demurrers on the basis of its finding that any alleged agreement between the parties was unenforceable for lack of consideration. The trial court found that there was no evidence that disposal costs were part of any bargaining process or that American Ash (D) offered the AggRite with an intent to avoid disposal costs. The state's intermediate court of appeals granted review.

ISSUE: Does relief of a manufacturer's legal obligation to dispose of a material classified as hazardous waste, such that the manufacturer avoids the costs of disposal, constitute sufficient consideration to ground contract and warranty claims brought by the disposer?

HOLDING AND DECISION: (Melvin, J.) Yes. Relief of a manufacturer's legal obligation to dispose of a material classified as hazardous waste, such that the manufacturer avoids the costs of disposal, constitutes sufficient consideration to ground contract and warranty claims brought by the disposer. Consideration—a benefit to the promisor or a detriment to the promisee—is an essential element of an enforceable contract and must be bargained for as an exchange for a promise. It is not enough, however, that the promisee has suffered a legal detriment at the request of the promisor. The detriment incurred must be the "quid pro quo," or the "price" of the promise, and the inducement for which it was made. If the promisor merely intends to make a gift to the promisee upon the performance of a condition, the promise is gratuitous, and the satisfaction of the condition is not consideration for a contract. Here, the facts alleged do not show only that American Ash Recycling Corp. of Pennsylvania (American Ash) (D) made a conditional gift of the AggRite to Pennsy Supply, Inc. (P). Pennsy (P) alleged that American Ash (D) gave away the AggRite in an effort to have others dispose of it so that American Ash (D) could avoid incurring disposal costs. Thus, here, American Ash's (D) promise to supply AggRite free of charge induced Pennsy (P) to assume the detriment of collecting and taking title to the material, and it was this detriment that induced American Ash (D) to make the promise to provide free AggRite for the project. Moreover, the lack of an actual bargaining process between the parties is unnecessary to establish consideration; the facts, if proven, need merely show that the promise induced the detriment and the detriment induced the promise. Therefore, Pennsy (P) alleged facts that, if proven true, would indicate sufficient consideration to support breach of contract, breach of warranty, and promissory estoppel claims. Reversed and remanded.

ANALYSIS

As this case demonstrates, the distinction between conduct that constitutes consideration and conduct that is a condition to a gift is not a clear one because the very same conduct may be consideration or a condition to a gift depending on how the parties treat the conduct. As indicated in 17A Am. Jur. 2d § 104 (2004 & 2005 Supp.),

Continued on next page.

"[a]n aid, though not a conclusive test, in determining which construction of the promise is more reasonable is an inquiry into whether the occurrence of the condition would benefit the promisor. If so, it is a fair inference that the occurrence was requested as consideration. On the other hand, if the occurrence of the condition is no benefit to the promisor but is merely to enable the promisee to receive a gift, the occurrence of the event on which the promise is conditional, though brought about by the promisee in reliance on the promise, is not properly construed as consideration."

Quicknotes

BREACH OF CONTRACT Unlawful failure by a party to perform its obligations pursuant to contract.

BREACH OF EXPRESS WARRANTY The breach of an express promise made by one party to a contract on which the other party may rely, relieving that party from the obligation of determining whether the fact is true and indemnifying the other party from liability if that fact is shown to be false.

BREACH OF WARRANTY The breach of a promise made by one party to a contract on which the other party may rely, relieving that party from the obligation of determining whether the fact is true and indemnifying the other party from liability if that fact is shown to be false.

CONSIDERATION Value given by one party in exchange for performance, or a promise to perform, by another party.

DEMURRER The assertion that the opposing party's pleadings are insufficient and that the demurring party should not be made to answer.

EXPRESS PROMISE The expression of an intention to act, or to forbear from acting, granting a right to the promisee to expect and enforce its performance.

FORBEARANCE The act of refraining from doing something that one has the legal right to do.

IMPLIED WARRANTY An implied promise made by one party to a contract that the other party may rely on a fact, relieving that party from the obligation of determining whether the fact is true and indemnifying the other party from liability if that fact is shown to be false.

PERFORMANCE The fulfillment of a contractual duty.

PROMISE The expression of an intention to act, or to forbear from acting, granting a right to the promisee to expect and enforce its performance.

PROMISEE The party to whom a promise is made.

PROMISOR The party who promises to render an obligation to another in the future.

PROMISSORY ESTOPPEL A promise that is enforceable if the promisor should reasonably expect that it will induce action or forbearance on the part of the promisee, does in fact cause such action or forbearance, and is the only means of avoiding injustice.

QUID PRO QUO Something for something; in contract law, the consideration, something of value, passed between the parties to render the contract binding.

WARRANTY OF FITNESS An implied promise made by a merchant in a contract for the sale of goods that such goods are suitable for the purpose for which they are purchased.

WARRANTY OF MERCHANTABILITY An implied promise made by a merchant in a contract for the sale of goods that such goods are suitable for the purpose for which they are purchased.

Dougherty v. Salt

Minor and guardian (P) v. Executor (D)

N.Y. Ct. App., 227 N.Y. 200, 125 N.E. 94 (1919)

NATURE OF CASE: Appeal from reinstatement of verdict for plaintiff in breach of contract action.

FACT SUMMARY: The trial court dismissed Dougherty's (P) action to recover on a note finding no consideration supported the note.

RULE OF LAW

A note that is not supported by consideration is unenforceable.

FACTS: Dougherty (P), a minor, was visited by his aunt, who indicated she wished to take care of him. The note was a preprinted form and carried no indication of consideration. Dougherty's (P) guardian was the sole witness who testified the aunt wanted to take care of the child, and thus was motivated to execute the note payable at her death. After her death, suit was brought to enforce the note, which was dismissed, although the jury found the note was supported by consideration. The appellate court reversed, finding sufficient consideration and holding the trial court erred in overruling the jury. Salt (D), the executor, appealed.

ISSUE: Is a note that is not supported by consideration enforceable?

HOLDING AND DECISION: (Cardozo, J.) No. A note that is not supported by consideration is unenforceable. The only evidence available indicated the note was given out of the generosity of the maker. The payee was not a creditor and was not owed support by the maker. Thus, the note was not supported by consideration and was unenforceable. Reversed.

ANALYSIS

The note in this case was labeled an executory gift, one that is to be performed or executed in the future. The triggering event here was the death of the aunt. No consideration was found despite the fact the preprinted form stated value had been received. Thus, the court looked to the substance rather than the appearance of the note.

Quicknotes

CONSIDERATION Value given by one party in exchange for performance, or a promise to perform, by another party.

GIFT A transfer of property to another person that is voluntary and that lacks consideration.

Plowman v. Indian Refining Co.

Employer (P) v. Oil company (D)

20 F. Supp. 1 (E.D. Ill. 1937)

NATURE OF CASE: Action for breach of contract.

FACT SUMMARY: Plowman (P) and others sought to enforce a benefit agreement between them and their former employer, Indian Refining Co. (D).

RULE OF LAW

Past services are not sufficient consideration to support the enforceability of a contract to provide continuing payments to former employees.

FACTS: Plowman (P) and others were employed by Indian Refining Co. (Indian) (D) for several years. They were told, orally and in writing, that because of their past service to the company they would be retired at half-pay. The length of such payments was not established at trial. The payments were conditioned upon the recipients' picking up their checks at the factory. The payments were made for approximately one year and then summarily discontinued. The employees sued, contending there was an enforceable contract created. Indian (D) defended on the basis of a lack of consideration, rendering any agreement unenforceable.

ISSUE: Are past services sufficient consideration to support the enforceability of a contract to provide continuing payments to former employees?

HOLDING AND DECISION: (Lindley, J.) No. Past services are not sufficient consideration to support the enforceability of a contract to provide continuing payments to former employees. The only consideration for the promise to pay was the company's (D) purported concern for its employees who had to be laid off. This concern was a reward for past services and thus the promise was unsupported by consideration. The requirement that the checks be picked up was merely a condition. Thus, no enforceable agreement existed.

ANALYSIS

Consideration consists of a voluntary detriment or forbearance by the party in return for a promise. If the detriment already has been performed, it could not be in exchange for the promise, and thus could not be considered consideration. Thus, "past consideration" cannot support an enforceable contract.

Quicknotes

CONDITION Requirement; potential future occurrence upon which the existence of a legal obligation is dependent.

FORBEARANCE The act of refraining from doing something that one has the legal right to do.

PAST CONSIDERATION Consideration made before a contract is created and is usually not legally sufficient consideration to support a contract.

PROMISE The expression of an intention to act, or to forbear from acting, granting a right to the promisee to expect and enforce its performance.

Harris v. Time, Inc.

Junk mail recipient (P) v. Subscription magazine publisher (D)

Cal. Ct. App., 191 Cal. App. 3d 449, 237 Cal. Rprt. 584 (1987)

NATURE OF CASE: Appeal from dismissal on summary judgment of class action for, inter alia, breach of contract.

FACT SUMMARY: After receiving junk mail from Time, Inc. (D) that promised to "GIVE YOU THIS VERSATILE NEW CALCULATOR WATCH FREE Just for Opening this Envelope Before Feb. 15, 1985," and after notifying Time (D) that he had satisfied the conditions of what he asserted was an offer, and demanding such watch from Time (D), Joshua Gnaizda (P), along with others similarly situated, sued Time (D) for, inter alia, breach of contract. Time (D) contended that its mailer did not constitute an offer, or, alternatively, that there was no consideration of value, and that, in any event, the action should be dismissed because it concerned a de minimis matter.

RULE OF LAW

(1) An advertisement can constitute an offer, and form the basis of a unilateral contract, if it calls for performance of a specific act without further communication and leaves nothing for further negotiation.

(2) Any bargained-for act or forbearance can constitute adequate consideration for a unilateral contract, regardless of equivalence of value.

(3) Where a promisor of a unilateral contract has no means of learning of the acceptance of its offer by performance, the promisee must give the promisor notice of performance within a reasonable time period for the contract to be enforceable.

(4) Where a plaintiff states a cause of action, that cause of action nevertheless may be dismissed where it concerns a trifling, de minimis, matter.

FACTS: Joshua Gnaizda (Joshua) (P), the three-year-old son of a public interest attorney, received what he (or his mother) thought was a tantalizing offer in the mail from Time, Inc. (D). The front of the envelope contained two see-through windows partially revealing the envelope's contents. One window showed Joshua's (P) name and address. The other revealed the following statement: "JOSHUA A GNAIZDA, I'LL GIVE YOU THIS VERSATILE NEW CALCULATOR WATCH FREE Just for Opening this Envelope Before Feb. 15, 1985." Beneath the offer was a picture of the calculator watch itself. Joshua's (P) mother opened the envelope and apparently realized she had been deceived by a ploy to get her to open a piece of junk mail. The see-through window had not revealed the full text of Time's (D) offer. Printed below the picture of the calculator watch, and not viewable through the see-through window, were the following additional words: "AND MAILING THIS CERTIFICATE TODAY!" The certificate itself clearly required that Joshua (P) purchase a subscription to Fortune magazine to receive the free calculator watch. Joshua's (P) father, after notifying Time (D) that Joshua (P) had satisfied the conditions set forth in the mailer, and demanding a calculator watch, which Time (D) refused to provide, brought a class action for $15 million in punitive damages on behalf of Joshua (P) and others who had received the mailing, asserting a cause of action for breach of contract, and other causes of action based on fraud, promissory estoppel, and unfair advertising. The trial court dismissed the entire action on summary judgment. Joshua (P) appealed as to the dismissal of the claims for breach of contract and unfair advertising. The state's intermediate appellate court granted review.

ISSUE:

(1) Can an advertisement constitute an offer, and form the basis of a unilateral contract, if it calls for performance of a specific act without further communication and leaves nothing for further negotiation?

(2) Can any bargained-for act or forbearance constitute adequate consideration for a unilateral contract, regardless of equivalence of value?

(3) Where a promisor of a unilateral contract has no means of learning of the acceptance of its offer by performance, must the promisee give the promisor notice of performance within a reasonable time period for the contract to be enforceable?

(4) Where a plaintiff states a cause of action, may that cause of action nevertheless be dismissed where it concerns a trifling, de minimis, matter?

HOLDING AND DECISION: (King, J.)

(1) Yes. An advertisement can constitute an offer, and form the basis of a unilateral contract, if it calls for performance of a specific act without further communication and leaves nothing for further negotiation. Thus, the text of Time, Inc.'s (D) unopened mailer was, technically, an offer to enter into a unilateral contract: the promisor made a promise to do something (give the recipient a calculator watch) in exchange for the performance of an act by the promisee (opening the envelope).

(2) Yes. Any bargained-for act or forbearance can constitute adequate consideration for a unilateral contract,

Continued on next page.

regardless of equivalence of value. If a performance is bargained for, there is no further requirement of benefit to the promisor or detriment to the promisee, and courts will not require equivalence in values exchanged or otherwise question the adequacy of consideration. Moreover, although the opening of the envelope may have had trivial value to Joshua Gnaizda (Joshua) (P), it had great value to Time (D). For an advertiser such as Time (D), it is of great value to get the recipient of a direct advertising mailer to open the mailer—which is why Time (D) resorted to the ruse it did. Accordingly, Time (D) made an offer that was accepted by Joshua (P) and supported by consideration.

(3) Yes. Where a promisor of a unilateral contract has no means of learning of the acceptance of its offer by performance, the promisee must give the promisor notice of performance within a reasonable time period for the contract to be enforceable. Here, because Time (D) had no means of learning whether a recipient of its mailer had in fact opened the mailer's envelope, and because the complaint alleged that Joshua (P) had given Time (D) notice of his acceptance prior to commencing the action, the complaint—at least as to Joshua (P)—stated a cause of action for breach of contract. If such notice had not been given to Time (D), it could have treated its offer as lapsed.

(4) Yes. Where a plaintiff states a cause of action, that cause of action nevertheless may be dismissed where it concerns a trifling, de minimis, matter. Notwithstanding that technically a unilateral contract had been formed between Joshua (P) and Time (D), and that Time (D) breached that contract, the action here is "de minims" in the extreme, and a court will apply the legal maxim "de minimis non curat lex," or "the law disregards trifles" to dismiss such an action. At the heart of the complaint is that the plaintiffs were tricked into opening a junk mail envelope, not that they were misled into buying anything or doing anything more significant than opening an envelope. Thus, the suit itself, for $15 million, is an abuse of the judicial system and is an extreme overreaction. A remedy for misleading junk mail must rest with Congress, which not the courts, which cannot solve every complaint or right every technical wrong, particularly one that causes no actual damage beyond the loss of the few seconds it takes to open an envelope and examine its contents. Affirmed.

ANALYSIS

As to Joshua Gnaizda's (Joshua) (P) co-plaintiffs (P), there had been no allegation in the complaint that they provided Time, Inc. (D) with timely notice of their acceptance. Accordingly, the court indicated it would dismiss the breach of contract action as to them. In response, the co-plaintiffs argued that because the complete contents of Time's (D) mailer indicated the recipient would not receive a calculator watch without subscribing to Fortune magazine, there was an anticipatory breach of the unilateral contract, so that the recipient should not have been obligated to give notice of performance. The court rejected this argument because courts in the state (California) had taken the approach that the doctrine of anticipatory breach – by which an anticipatory repudiation will support an action for breach of contract without further performance by the plaintiff – is not applicable to unilateral contracts. The rationale for such an approach is that the aggrieved party has already fully performed and would not be harmed by awaiting counterperformance at the time promised.

Quicknotes

ACCEPTANCE Assent to the specified terms of an offer resulting in the formation of a binding agreement.

ANTICIPATORY BREACH Breach of a contract subsequent to formation but prior to the time performance is due.

ANTICIPATORY REPUDIATION Breach of a contract subsequent to formation but prior to the time performance is due.

BREACH OF CONTRACT Unlawful failure by a party to perform its obligations pursuant to contract.

CAUSE OF ACTION A fact or set of facts the occurrence of which entitles a party to seek judicial relief.

CLASS ACTION A suit commenced by a representative on behalf of an ascertainable group that is too large to appear in court, shares a commonality of interests, and will benefit from a successful result.

CONSIDERATION Value given by one party in exchange for performance, or a promise to perform, by another party.

DE MINIMIS Insignificant; trivial; not of sufficient significance to require legal action.

FORBEARANCE The act of refraining from doing something that one has the legal right to do.

FRAUD A false representation of facts with the intent that another will rely on the misrepresentation to his or her detriment.

PERFORMANCE The fulfillment of a contractual duty.

PROMISE The expression of an intention to act, or to forbear from acting, granting a right to the promisee to expect and enforce its performance.

PROMISEE The party to whom a promise is made.

Continued on next page.

PROMISOR The party who promises to render an obligation to another in the future.

PROMISSORY ESTOPPEL A promise that is enforceable if the promisor should reasonably expect that it will induce action or forbearance on the part of the promisee, does in fact cause such action or forbearance, and is the only means of avoiding injustice.

PUNITIVE DAMAGES Damages exceeding the actual injury suffered for the purposes of punishment of the defendant, deterrence of the wrongful behavior, or comfort to the plaintiff. Also called "exemplary damages."

UNILATERAL CONTRACT An agreement pursuant to which a party agrees to act without an express exchange for performance on the part of the other party.

Marshall Durbin Food Corp. v. Baker

Former employer (D) v. Former employee (P)

Miss. Ct. App., 909 So. 2d 1267 (2005)

NATURE OF CASE: Appeal from judgment awarding former employee payments in action to enforce a severance contract.

FACT SUMMARY: Marshall Durbin Food Corp. (D) contended that a contract that purported to pay Baker (P), a former employee, his salary for five years upon the happening of certain triggering events, was invalid for want of consideration.

RULE OF LAW

An agreement is supported by sufficient consideration to create an enforceable contract where one party has made an illusory promise, the second party has made a promise of a unilateral contract that is contingent on the first party's performance, and the first party has performed to fulfillment of the contingency.

FACTS: Baker (P) had been an employee of Marshall Durbin Food Corp. (the Company) (D), which was controlled by Mr. Durbin. During a period when the Company (D) was experiencing hardship and chaos, Baker (P) obtained from Mr. Durbin an agreement that upon certain triggering events, Baker (P) would be entitled to five years of his then-current salary. One of those triggering events was Mr. Durbin's incapacity. The agreement specified how the payments would be calculated, specified an "effective date," and recited that it was not intended to create a contract of employment, which remained at-will. The agreement also recited that it was entered for consideration of $10 and other valuable consideration, the receipt of which was acknowledged. The Company's (D) board ratified this agreement. Around a year and a half later, Mr. Durbin was diagnosed with malignant cancer, and Baker (P) took over as the Company's (D) president. About a month later, Mr. Durbin was judicially declared incapacitated, whereupon Baker (P) informed the Company (D) that the agreement had been triggered and that he would no longer be working as an employee but would continue to do work for the Company (D) as a contractor. The following month Mr. Durbin died; and a new board was elected. Baker (P) sued for specific performance of the agreement, he and was informed by the Company (D) that the new board, believing the agreement was invalid, had repudiated it. In answer to Baker's (P) suit, the Company (D) asserted the agreement was invalid for lack of consideration. The trial court, determining that the agreement had been entered into to retain top management, including Baker (P), at a time the Company (D) was experiencing difficulties, and that Baker (P), in reliance on the agreement, had not sought employment elsewhere, held for Baker (P). The state's intermediate appellate court granted review.

ISSUE: Is an agreement supported by sufficient consideration to create an enforceable contract where one party has made an illusory promise, the second party has made a promise of a unilateral contract that is contingent on the first party's performance, and the first party has performed to fulfillment of the contingency?

HOLDING AND DECISION: (Barnes, J.) Yes. An agreement is supported by sufficient consideration to create an enforceable contract where one party has made an illusory promise, the second party has made a promise of a unilateral contract that is contingent on the first party's performance, and the first party has performed to fulfillment of the contingency. As a threshold matter, the agreement's recital of consideration creates a rebuttable presumption that consideration actually existed. Here, Marshall Durbin Food Corp. (the Company) (D) has failed to present sufficient evidence to rebut the presumption by a clear preponderance of the evidence. That unrebutted presumption is sufficient to affirm the trial court's decision as to the existence of consideration. Nonetheless, the parties' arguments about the issue will be addressed. First, the Company (D) argues that both Baker's (P) promise and the Company's (D) promise were illusory, since their relationship remained at-will. This argument, while valid as to Baker (P), must be rejected as to the Company (D). Baker's (P) promise was illusory because he had the right to look for other employment at any time, so he did not give up anything when he promised to stay with the Company (D). In turn, the Company's (D) promise was that if Baker (P) continued his employment until the happening of a triggering event, the Company (D) would compensate him as set forth in the contract. The Company's (D) promise, although contingent was not illusory. Accordingly, Baker (P) could, and did, supply consideration for the Company's (D) promise by "an act other than a promise"—Baker's (P) act of continuing to work for the Company (D) and the Company's (D) corresponding receipt of benefit from his services. Here, the contingency (Baker (P) being employed during the triggering event of Mr. Durbin's incapacity) has been fulfilled. Thus, Baker's (P) consideration was not supplied by a promise but by his actual performance during the fulfillment of the contingency. Additionally, the Company (D) argues that Baker's (P) forbearance from

Continued on next page.

seeking other employment was not a legal detriment and cannot constitute consideration because Baker (P) had the legal right to look for other employment, since his employment was at will. This issue need not be addressed because the trial court found—and the evidence supports its finding—Baker (P) experienced detriment in forbearing from seeking or accepting other employment and the Company (D) benefitted from retaining his services. It is established law that a benefit to the promisor or detriment to the promisee is sufficient consideration for a contract. This may consist either in some interest, right, profit or benefit accruing to the one party, or some forbearance, detriment, loss or responsibility given, suffered or undertaken by the other. For all these reasons, the trial court correctly determined there to be consideration for the contract. Affirmed as to this issue and reversed as to the agreement's effective date.

ANALYSIS

This case illustrates the principle that the presence of an illusory promise does not destroy the possibility of a contract. Instead, it may create a unilateral contract and the promisor who made the illusory promise – here, Baker (P) – can accept the contract by performance. Other courts, however, hold that an illusory promise by one party renders the return promise unenforceable, unless some other consideration is present.

Quicknotes

AT-WILL EMPLOYMENT The rule that an employment relationship is subject to termination at any time, or for any cause, by an employee or an employer in the absence of a specific agreement otherwise.

FORBEARANCE The act of refraining from doing something that one has the legal right to do.

ILLUSORY PROMISE A promise that is not legally enforceable because performance of the obligation by the promisor is completely within the promisor's discretion.

PERFORMANCE The fulfillment of a contractual duty.

PROMISE The expression of an intention to act, or to forbear from acting, granting a right to the promisee to expect and enforce its performance.

PROMISEE The party to whom a promise is made.

PROMISOR The party who promises to render an obligation to another in the future.

REBUTTABLE PRESUMPTION Rule of law inferred from the existence of a particular set of facts that is conclusive in the absence of contrary evidence.

SEVERANCE Dividing or separating; setting aside one or more claims in a lawsuit to be tried separately.

SPECIFIC PERFORMANCE An equitable remedy whereby the court requires the parties to perform their obligations pursuant to a contract.

UNILATERAL CONTRACT An agreement pursuant to which a party agrees to act without an express exchange for performance on the part of the other party.

Jannusch v. Naffziger

Business seller (P) v. Business buyer (D)

Ill. App. Ct., 379 Ill. App. 3d 381, 883 N.E.2d 711 (2008)

NATURE OF CASE: Appeal from judgment for defendants in action for breach of contract.

FACT SUMMARY: The Jannusches (P) owned Festival Foods, a concessions business. The Jannusches (P) contended that they had an enforceable oral contract with the Naffzigers (D) to buy Festival Foods because essential terms were identified, i.e., price and the goods to be conveyed, and that the Naffzigers (D) breached that contract.

RULE OF LAW

Under the Uniform Commercial Code, a contract that is primarily for the sale of goods is enforceable where, although many terms are missing, essential terms, including price and the identification of the goods to be sold, have been agreed upon.

FACTS: The Jannusches (P) owned and operated Festival Foods, a concessions business that owned a truck and servicing trailer and equipment such as refrigerators and freezers, roasters, chairs and tables, fountain service, and signs and lighting equipment. The Naffzigers (D) expressed interest in purchasing the business, and, after meeting several times, the parties orally agreed on a $150,000 purchase price, in exchange for which the Naffzigers (D) would receive the truck and trailer, all necessary equipment, and the opportunity to work at event locations secured by the Jannusches (P). The Naffzigers (D) paid $10,000 immediately and took possession of Festival Foods the next day. They operated the business for the remainder of the season, i.e., for over four months. Throughout this period, the Naffzigers (D) received the income from the business, purchased inventory, replaced equipment, paid taxes on the business, and paid employees. At the end of the season, unhappy with the income the business was generating, the Naffzigers (D) returned Festival Foods to the storage facility where it previously had been stored. The Jannusches (P) sued for breach of contract. The Naffzigers (D) testified they had agreed only to run the business while they pursued buying it. They also testified they had rejected putting their agreement into writing because they had not received the bank loan. However, the following week, the Naffzigers (D) consulted with an attorney regarding the legal aspects of buying and owning a business and asked the attorney to prepare a contract for the purchase. Ultimately, the bank approved the loan. The Jannusches (P) testified that the Naffzigers (D) hired them as consultants during some of the events and paid for their lodging. There was other, conflicting, testimony as to the chain of events. Ultimately, the trial court held that even though a contract had been formed, the evidence was insufficient to establish by a preponderance of the evidence that there was a meeting of the minds as to what that agreement was. Accordingly, the court rendered judgment for the Naffzigers (D). The state's intermediate appellate court granted review.

ISSUE: Under the Uniform Commercial Code, is a contract that is primarily for the sale of goods enforceable where, although many terms are missing, essential terms, including price and the identification of the goods to be sold, have been agreed upon?

HOLDING AND DECISION: (Cook, J.) Yes. Under the Uniform Commercial Code (U.C.C.), a contract that is primarily for the sale of goods is enforceable where, although many terms are missing, essential terms, including price and the identification of the goods to be sold, have been agreed upon. First, the trial court correctly determined that the contract at issue is governed by the U.C.C. Where a contract is for both goods and services, the "predominant purpose" test is applied to determine if the contract falls within U.C.C. Article 2 governing the sale of goods. This test is generally a question of fact. Here, significant tangible assets were involved, so that the evidence presented was sufficient to support the conclusion that the proposed agreement was predominantly one for the sale of goods. Second, under the U.C.C., a contract for the sale of goods worth over $500 must be in writing unless certain exceptions apply. Here, two exceptions apply: (1) the party against whom enforcement is sought admits in its pleading, testimony, or otherwise in court that a contract for sale was made (the Naffzigers (D) so admitted) and (2) an oral contract for the sale of goods that has been partially performed is enforceable. Thus, the key question is whether a binding contract was formed. The Naffzigers (D) argue that nothing was said in the contract about many terms that are customarily in—and essential to—contracts for the sale of a business, including terms relating to allocating a price for good will, a covenant not to compete, allocating a price for the equipment, how to release liens, what would happen if there was no loan approval, and other issues. This argument is unpersuasive. Although the Naffzigers (D) are correct that a contract that is missing essential terms is unenforceable, the essential terms of the contract at issue were agreed upon. The purchase price was $150,000, and the items to be transferred were specified. No essential terms remained

Continued on next page.

to be agreed upon; the only action remaining was the performance of the contract. The Naffzigers (D) took possession of the items to be transferred and used them as their own, and they paid $10,000 of the purchase price. Merely because they were disappointed with the income the business generated while they operated it does not negate the existence of a contract. Although the parties had different subjective ideas as to what occurred in their course of dealing, their objective conduct indicated an agreement to the essential terms. Parties discussing the sale of goods do not transfer those goods and allow them to be retained for a substantial period before reaching agreement. The Naffzigers (D) replaced equipment, reported income, paid taxes, and paid the Jannusches (P) as consultants, all of which is inconsistent with the idea that the Naffzigers (D) were only "pursuing buying the business." Moreover, the fact the parties did not enter a written contract is not dispositive; the fact that a formal written document is anticipated does not preclude enforcement of a specific preliminary promise. At issue was not an agreement to enter into an agreement; there was more. Although the agreement could have been fleshed out with additional terms, the essential terms were agreed upon. Therefore, the Naffziger's (D) return of the goods at the end of the season was not a rejection of the Jannusches (P) offer to sell, but a breach of contract. Reversed and remanded.

ANALYSIS

The Uniform Commercial Code (U.C.C.), as opposed to common law, does not ask whether there was mutual assent to a contract. Instead, as in this case, the U.C.C. focuses the inquiry on the parties' intent to be bound, notwithstanding that some (nonessential) terms have not been addressed.

Quicknotes

BREACH OF CONTRACT Unlawful failure by a party to perform its obligations pursuant to contract.

ORAL CONTRACT A contract that is not reduced to written form.

PERFORMANCE The fulfillment of a contractual duty.

E.C. Styberg Engineering Co. v. Eaton Corp.

Components manufacturer (P) v. Parts producer (D)

492 F.3d 912 (7th Cir. 2007)

NATURE OF CASE: Appeal from judgment for defendant in action for breach of contract.

FACT SUMMARY: E.C. Styberg Engineering Co. (Styberg) (P), a components manufacturer, contended that Eaton Corp. (D), an automobile parts producer, and Styberg (P) had a contract for Eaton (D) to purchase 13,000 transmission components from Styberg (P).

RULE OF LAW

Under the Uniform Commercial Code, a contract for the sale of goods is not formed where the parties' communications evidence ongoing negotiations, but no agreement, as to key terms, such as price, quantity, and monthly production volume.

FACTS: E.C. Styberg Engineering Co. (Styberg) (P) manufactured components. Eaton Corp. (D), an automobile parts producer, purchased various components from Styberg (P). For a two-year period, Styberg (P) manufactured an automobile transmission component known as the I-brake, which Eaton (D) used in certain transmissions it produced. At first, Styberg (P) began selling prototype I-brake units to Eaton (D), and Eaton (D) began purchasing limited quantities of I-brakes so it could test the product in the marketplace. Subsequently, Eaton (D) decided to pursue full production of I-brakes, and the parties began negotiating an agreement under which Styberg (P) would produce large quantities of I-brakes for Eaton (D). Getting a minimum unit commitment from Eaton (D) was important to Styberg (P) because it had to expend significant capital to mass-produce the custom-designed parts. The parties went back and forth with various proposals, in e-mails, phone calls, letters, and meetings. On July 8, 1999, Styberg (P) sent Eaton (D) a proposal for a 60,000-unit order. According to the proposal, the first 13,000 units sold would have an average price of $544.88, with the initial price of the units being $595, but progressively decreasing as Styberg (P) tweaked and perfected its manufacturing process. The proposal also requested $343,000 in "tooling money" to assist Styberg (P) in acquiring materials for its customized production and set forth a production schedule. On July 29, 1999, Eaton (D) communicated to Styberg (P) that it would purchase 13,000 units at $544.88 each and provide $293,000 for tooling. On August 9, 1999, Styberg (P) thanked Eaton (D) for its July 29 commitment, but also communicated to Eaton (D)—as it had previously—that it needed a minimum commitment of between 25,000 and 30,000 units to cover its capital expenditures. On September 1, 1999, employees from both parties participated in a conference call. Styberg (P) again indicated to Eaton (D) that a 13,000-unit commitment was not enough to cover its costs, and that it needed a minimum 30,000 commitment. Eaton's (D) notes from the call said, "Styberg will come back w/capacity + quotes for 13K flat out." On September 9, 1999, Styberg (P) sent Eaton (D) a production schedule that included a detailed breakdown of Styberg's (P) anticipated monthly production capacity for 13,000 units as well as a quote for an initial unit price of $595 plus $31 per unit until a certain part became available. Allegedly, on September 27, 1999, Eaton (D) confirmed that this was acceptable, but there was also evidence that such a communication never occurred. Eaton (D) did not issue a specific purchase order for 13,000 I-brakes, nor did Styberg (P) send a purchase order acknowledgment for 13,000 I-brakes. In April 2000, Eaton (D) notified Styberg (P) that it expected delivery of 240 units. Styberg (P) shipped the units under an existing purchase order, and Eaton (D) paid for the units. On May 8, 2000, Eaton (D) requested another 240 units for shipment, which were to be delivered the following month. Three days later, however, Eaton (D) cancelled the request. After May 11, 2000, Eaton (D) neither ordered nor paid for any I-brakes. In May 2003, Styberg (P) sued Eaton (D) in district court for breach of contract, seeking approximately $3.4 million in damages. The district court, concluding that no contract had been formed for the purchase by Eaton (D) of 13,000 I-brakes, rendered judgment for Eaton (D). In reaching its conclusion, the court characterized the e-mail, telephone, and letter exchanges as evidence of continuing negotiations in which the parties could not agree on key terms like quantity, price, and monthly production volume. The court of appeals granted review.

ISSUE: Under the Uniform Commercial Code, is a contract for the sale of goods formed where the parties' communications evidence ongoing negotiations, but no agreement, as to key terms, such as price, quantity, and monthly production volume?

HOLDING AND DECISION: (Flaum, J.) No. Under the Uniform Commercial Code (U.C.C.), a contract for the sale of goods is not formed where the parties' communications evidence ongoing negotiations, but no agreement, as to key terms, such as price, quantity, and monthly production volume. Styberg's (P) appeal challenges the district court's factual findings and the legal conclusions that flow therefrom. However, the evidence

Continued on next page.

and relevant case law shows that the district court's conclusions were not clearly erroneous. Under U.C.C. § 2-204, a contract for the sale of goods may be made in any manner sufficient to show agreement, including conduct by both parties that recognizes the existence of such a contract. This is a liberal view of what is required to create a contract for the sale of goods. Notwithstanding this liberal approach, for a contract for the sale of goods to be formed, its essential terms must be agreed upon. E.C. Styberg Engineering Co. (Styberg) (P) contends that there was agreement as to such essential terms. It argues that the parties agreed that Eaton Corp. (Eaton) (D) would purchase 13,000 I-brakes from Styberg (P) at an average unit price of $544.88. Styberg (P) identifies three possible sources for the alleged contract: (1) Eaton's July 29, 1999, letter; (2) Styberg's (P) September 9, 1999, schedule; and (3) Eaton's (D) request for I-brakes in 2000. Styberg (P) argues that the July 29 letter was either an acceptance of Styberg's (P) July 8 offer to supply Eaton (D) with 13,000 I-brakes or an offer to purchase I-brakes that Styberg (P) accepted on August 9, 1999, by saying "thank you." Then, according to Styberg (P), although the parties had a contract with the price and quantity terms firmly in place, they continued to negotiate about larger orders and other open terms. Eaton (D), on the other hand, characterized the July 29 letter as part of a series of ongoing negotiations, during which Eaton (D) and Styberg (P) could not agree on the essential terms, with Styberg (P) wanting a minimum commitment of 20,000 I-brakes to justify its capital investment and Eaton (D) not wanting to be bound by such a large commitment. Case law provides that a price quotation is considered an invitation for an offer, rather than an offer to form a binding contract. Thus, Styberg's (P) July 8 letter was an invitation for an offer; if it was not, then Eaton's (D) July 29 letter could not have constituted an acceptance of that offer. However, even assuming the July 29 letter was an offer in response to the price quotation, the district court did not clearly err in finding that Styberg (P) rejected the offer and continued to push for a higher minimum-unit commitment. After all, the parties had a conference call on September 1, during which Styberg (P) again indicated that a 13,000-unit commitment was not enough. The district court also did not clearly err in finding that Eaton (D) did not communicate on September 27 an acceptance of Styberg's (P) September 9 proposed schedule, as conflicting evidence and the district court's judgment of witnesses' veracity supported such a finding. Finally, the district court did not clearly err in rejecting Styberg's (P) argument that the parties' conduct manifested the existence of a contract. Two 240-unit orders at the price specified in Styberg's (P) quotes were insufficient to prove an agreement for the sale of 13,000 units. Courts finding contracts based on parties' conduct have typically done so either where there was repeated and ongoing conduct manifesting an agreement or where the parties had an established course of dealing to which they adhered. Here, Eaton's (D) two requests for 240 I-brakes, one of which was cancelled, did not come close to the repeated, ongoing dealing necessary to establish a course of dealing required to prove the existence of a contract. Affirmed.

ANALYSIS

This case illustrates the potentially fact-heavy nature of cases involving ongoing negotiations where the formation of a contract is at issue. As in this case, the outcome in such cases typically is not clear-cut. Here, the district court accepted Eaton Corp.'s (Eaton) (D) interpretation of ambiguous evidence, and the court of appeals affirmed because the district court's choice between two reasonable interpretations of that evidence was not clearly erroneous. In all fairness to E.C. Styberg Engineering Co. (Styberg) (P), it seems Styberg (P) had some strong arguments why it was led to believe that Eaton (D) had agreed to the minimum 13,000-unit purchase.

Quicknotes

BREACH OF CONTRACT Unlawful failure by a party to perform its obligations pursuant to contract.

DAMAGES Monetary compensation that may be awarded by the court to a party who has sustained injury or loss to his or her person, property, or rights due to another party's unlawful act, omission, or negligence.

Princess Cruises, Inc. v. General Electric Co.

Shipowner (P) v. Ship repairer (D)

143 F.3d 828 (4th Cir. 1998)

NATURE OF CASE: Appeal by General Electric (D) from federal district court's refusal to grant its motion for summary judgment to vacate the jury's award in favor of Princess Cruises (P) for incidental and consequential damages for breach of contract.

FACT SUMMARY: In October 1994, Princess Cruises, Inc. (Princess) (P) issued a Purchase Order and scheduled its SS Sky Princess for routine inspection services and repairs to be done in December by General Electric Co. (GE) (D), the original manufacturer of the ship's main turbines, for a proposed contract price of $260,000. Upon inspection of the ship, GE (D) found additional work needed to be done, and, as a result, Princess (P) canceled a ten-day Christmas cruise. Princess (P) paid the full amount of the contract. At trial, Princess (P) alleged the repairs had not been properly done and it had been forced to cancel a ten-day Easter cruise. In April 1996, Princess (P) filed a complaint against GE (D) alleging breach of contract, breach of express and implied maritime warranty, and negligence.

RULE OF LAW

When the predominant purpose of a maritime or land-based contract is the rendering of services rather than the furnishing of goods, the Uniform Commercial Code is inapplicable, and courts must draw on common-law doctrines when interpreting the contract.

FACTS: Princess Cruises, Inc. (Princess) (P) and General Electric Company (GE) (D) entered into a maritime contract for inspection and repair services relating to Princess's (P) cruise ship, the SS Sky Princess. A jury found GE (D) liable for breach of contract and awarded Princess (P) $4,577,743.00 in damages. On appeal, GE (D) contended that the district court erred in denying its renewed motion for judgment as a matter of law, which had requested that the court vacate the jury's award of incidental and consequential damages. Specifically, GE (D) argued that the district court erroneously applied Uniform Commercial Code (U.C.C.) principles rather than common-law principles to a contract primarily for services. Although Princess's (P) fine-print terms and conditions mentioned the sale of goods, Princess's (P) actual purchase description requested a GE (D) "service engineer" to perform service functions: the opening of valves for survey and the inspection of the ship's port main turbine. GE's (D) Final Price Quotation (Quotation) also contemplated service functions, stating in large print on every page that it was a "Quotation for Services." The Quotation's first page noted that GE (D) was offering a quotation for "engineering services." GE's (D) Quotation further specified that the particular type of service offered was "Installation/Repair/Maintenance." The Quotation then listed the scope of the contemplated work (opening, checking, cleaning, inspecting, disassembling), in short, service functions. Although GE's (D) materials list showed that GE (D) planned to manufacture a small number of parts for Princess (P), Princess (P) appeared to have had most of the needed materials already onboard.

ISSUE: When the predominant purpose of a maritime or land-based contract is the rendering of services rather than the furnishing of goods, must courts draw on common-law doctrines when interpreting the contract rather than looking to the Uniform Commercial Code?

HOLDING AND DECISION: (Goodwin, J.) Yes. When the predominant purpose of a maritime or land-based contract is the rendering of services rather than the furnishing of goods, the Uniform Commercial Code (U.C.C.) is inapplicable, and courts must draw on common-law doctrines when interpreting the contract. Here, in analyzing a mixed maritime contract for goods and services, the court must first determine whether the predominant purpose of the transaction is the sale of goods, and, once this initial analysis has been performed, the court then may properly decide whether the common law, the U.C.C., or other statutory law governs the transaction. In the instant case, the contract for inspection and repair of the ship was predominantly for services, not goods, and the contract thus was governed by common-law doctrines rather than the U.C.C. The purchase description and the final price quotation contemplated a provision of services, and, although the repairer was known to manufacture goods, its correspondence and quotations came from its service engineering department. It is plain the GE-Princess transaction principally concerned the rendering of services, specifically, the routine inspection and repair of the SS Sky Princess, with incidental, albeit expensive, parts supplied by GE (D). The language of both the Purchase Order and the Final Price Quotation (Quotation) indicated that although GE (D) planned to supply certain parts, the parts were incidental to the contract's predominant purpose, which was inspection, repair, and maintenance services. As a matter of law, the jury should only have awarded damages consistent with the terms and conditions of GE's Quotation under common-law doctrines of contract law and should

Continued on next page.

not have awarded incidental or consequential damages. Reversed and remanded.

ANALYSIS

As noted in the *Princess Cruises* decision, before applying the Uniform Commercial Code, courts generally examine the transaction to determine whether the sale of goods predominates. In this regard, the test for inclusion or exclusion is not whether the transaction is for both sales and services, but granting that it is, whether the predominant factor of the transaction—its thrust, its purpose—reasonably stated, is the rendition of service, with goods incidentally involved (e.g., contract with artist for painting) or is a transaction of sale, with labor incidentally involved (e.g., installation of a water heater in a bathroom). As an aid in the making of this determination, the Fourth Circuit has deemed the following factors significant in determining the nature of the contract: (1) the language of the contract, (2) the nature of the business of the supplier, and (3) the intrinsic worth of the materials.

Quicknotes

BREACH OF CONTRACT Unlawful failure by a party to perform its obligations pursuant to contract.

CONSEQUENTIAL DAMAGES Monetary compensation that may be recovered in order to compensate for injuries or losses sustained as a result of damages that are not the direct or foreseeable result of the act of a party, but that nevertheless are the consequence of such act and that must be specifically pled and demonstrated.

INCIDENTAL DAMAGES Those damages reasonably incurred and arising from the subject matter of a claim for actual damages; such damages generally arise from activities undertaken by the nonbreaching party as a result of the breach.

Brown Machine, Inc. v. Hercules, Inc.

Seller of trim press (P) v. Buyer (D)

Mo. Ct. App., 770 S.W.2d 416 (1989)

NATURE OF CASE: Appeal from award of damages for indemnification.

FACT SUMMARY: Hercules, Inc. (D), which purchased a trim press from Brown Machine, Inc. (Brown) (P) through an exchange of boilerplate forms, refused to indemnify Brown (P) in a lawsuit brought by a Hercules (D) employee who was injured while using the trim press, claiming that Brown's (P) boilerplate language of indemnification was only a counteroffer.

RULE OF LAW

An offeree's reply that purports to accept an offer but makes acceptance conditional on the offeror's assent to terms not contained in the original offer is a counteroffer rather than an acceptance.

FACTS: During negotiations for sale of a trim press to Hercules, Inc. (D), Brown Machine, Inc. (Brown) (P) submitted a proposal to which it attached a boilerplate form containing an indemnity provision. Hercules (D) then sent a written purchase order on its own boilerplate form, which contained no indemnity provision. After Hercules (D) purchased the machine from Brown (P), an employee of Hercules (D), who sustained injuries while operating the trim press, filed suit against Brown (P). Brown (P) demanded that Hercules (D) defend the suit, but Hercules (D) refused. Brown (P) filed suit against Hercules (D) for indemnification of the settlement amount paid, claiming that a condition of the original sales contract for the trim press required that Hercules (D) indemnify Brown (P) for any claims arising from operation or misuse of the trim press. The jury awarded damages plus interest to Brown (P), and Hercules (D) appealed.

ISSUE: Is an offeree's reply that purports to accept an offer but makes acceptance conditional on the offeror's assent to terms not contained in the original offer a counteroffer rather than an acceptance?

HOLDING AND DECISION: (Stephan, J.) Yes. An offeree's reply that purports to accept an offer but makes acceptance conditional on the offeror's assent to terms not contained in the original offer is a counteroffer rather than an acceptance. The general rule is that a price quotation is not an offer but rather an invitation to enter negotiations or a mere suggestion to induce offers by others. However, a price quote, if sufficiently detailed, can amount to an offer creating the power of acceptance; to do so, it must reasonably appear from the price quote that assent to the quote is all that is needed to ripen the offer into a contract. In this case Hercules, Inc. (D) could not have reasonably believed that Brown Machine, Inc.'s (Brown) (P) quotation was intended to be an offer but rather an offer to enter negotiations for the trim press. Even if the quotation were construed as an offer, there was no timely acceptance. Under these circumstances, the purchase order, not the price quotation, is treated as the offer since the purchase order did not create an enforceable contract. The question then was whether Brown's (P) acknowledgment containing the indemnity provision constituted a counteroffer or an acceptance of Hercules's (D) offer with additional or different terms. The general view held by the majority of states is that, to convert an acceptance to a counteroffer under Uniform Commercial Code (U.C.C.) § 2-207(1), the conditional nature of the acceptance must be clearly expressed in a manner sufficient to notify the offeror that the offeree is unwilling to proceed with the transaction unless the additional or different terms are included in the contract. Brown's (P) acknowledgment was not "expressly made conditional" on Hercules's (D) assent to the additional or different terms as provided for under § 2-207(1). Since Brown's (P) order acknowledgment was not a counteroffer, it operated as acceptance with additional or different terms from the offer since the purchase order contained no indemnity provision. Hercules's (D) purchase order here expressly limited acceptance to the terms of its offer. Given such an express limitation, the additional terms, including the indemnification provision, failed to become part of the contract between the parties. Reversed.

ANALYSIS

Under Uniform Commercial Code (U.C.C.) § 2-207(1), an offeree's response to an offer operates as a valid acceptance of the offer even though it contains terms additional to, or different from, the terms of the offer, unless the "acceptance is expressly made conditional" on the offeror's assent to the additional or different terms. Where the offeree's acceptance is made "expressly conditional" on the offeror's assent, the response operates not as an acceptance but as a counteroffer, which must be accepted by the original offeror. Under U.C.C. § 2-207(2), additional terms become a part of the contract between merchants unless (a) the offer expressly limits acceptance to the terms of the offer; (b) they

Continued on next page.

materially alter it; or (c) notification of objection to them has already been given or is given within a reasonable time after notice of them is given.

Quicknotes

ACCEPTANCE Assent to the specified terms of an offer resulting in the formation of a binding agreement.

COUNTEROFFER A statement by the offeree that has the legal effect of rejecting the offer deemed unsatisfactory and of proposing a new offer to the offeror.

U.C.C. § 2-207(1) Provides that a valid contract may exist where the acceptance contains additional or different terms not present in the offer, unless the offer specifically limits acceptance from including additional or different terms.

Paul Gottlieb & Co., Inc. v. Alps South Corp.

Fabrics producer (P) v. Medical device manufacturer (D)

Fla. Dist. Ct. App., 985 So. 2d 1 (2007)

NATURE OF CASE: Appeal from judgment for defendant/counterclaim plaintiff in action for contract damages.

FACT SUMMARY: Paul Gottlieb & Co., Inc. (Gottlieb) (P) contended that a limitation of liability clause on the back of its standardized finished goods contract did not materially alter the contract it had with Alps South Corp. (Alps) (D), so that the clause should not, as a matter of law, have been excluded from the contract, and, therefore, the clause served to limit Gottlieb's (P) liability to Alps (D) for consequential damages.

RULE OF LAW

Under Uniform Commercial Code § 2-207, a limitation of liability clause found on the back of a standardized contract for the sale of goods between merchants does not materially alter the contract where it does not, as a matter of law, cause unreasonable surprise or hardship.

FACTS: Paul Gottlieb & Co., Inc. (Gottlieb) (P) produced specialty fabrics. Alps South Corp. (Alps) (D) was a medical device manufacturer that produced liners that amputees used to attach prosthetic devices. Alps (D) began testing various high-tech fabrics to enhance the durability and stability of its liners; Gottlieb (P) supplied some of the fabrics. Eventually, Alps (D) settled on Gottlieb's (P) "Coolmax" fabric, which initially was well received by Alps's (D) customers. Six months later, however, Alps (D) rejected some fabric samples Gottlieb (P) submitted because of unacceptable inconsistencies in both color and texture. Alps (D) sent a letter promptly notifying Gottlieb (P) of the product deficiencies and stating that any future commercial relationship mandated that Gottlieb (P) provide a more consistent product. However, the letter failed to inform Gottlieb (P) of the possibility that Alps (D) could incur substantial additional costs as a result of using a different fabric. Also, Alps (D) did not disclose the specialized use of the fabric to Gottlieb (P). Gottlieb (P) agreed to rework the fabric before delivering it to Alps (D). Then, Gottlieb (P) exhausted the yarn used to make the Coolmax fabric, and, without notifying Alps (D), Gottlieb (P) substituted a similar fabric. The new fabric did not stretch nearly as well as the Coolmax fabric, but this defect was not easily detected by Alps (D), which eventually started receiving complaints from its customers about the liners using the substitute fabric. Eventually, Alps (D) was forced to recall and destroy the liners using the substitute fabric. After Alps (D) and Gottlieb (P) discovered that the cause of the defective products was the undisclosed substitute yarn, Alps (D) refused to pay Gottlieb (P) for a submitted bill. Gottlieb (P) then brought suit for damages due to the nonpayment. Alps (D) counterclaimed for damages it asserted were caused by Gottlieb's (P) breach of warranty. In regard to Alps's (D) counterclaim, Gottlieb (P) had used a standardized finished goods contract that had on its back a limitations-of-liability clause that purported to limit consequential damages (the contract was one of a series of six that had similar clauses on the forms). The trial court considered the language of this clause to be an affirmative defense to Alps's (D) counterclaim, but ultimately held that the clause materially altered the contract, so that the clause was excluded from the contract under Uniform Commercial Code § 2-207. The trial court awarded nonpayment damages (around $29,000) to Gottlieb (P) and consequential damages (around $695,000) to Alps (D). The state's intermediate appellate court granted review.

ISSUE: Under Uniform Commercial Code § 2-207, does a limitation of liability clause found on the back of a standardized contract for the sale of goods between merchants materially alter the contract where it does not, as a matter of law, cause unreasonable surprise or hardship?

HOLDING AND DECISION: (Casanueva, J.) No. Under Uniform Commercial Code (U.C.C.) § 2-207, a limitation of liability clause found on the back of a standardized contract for the sale of goods between merchants does not materially alter the contract where it does not, as a matter of law, cause unreasonable surprise or hardship. In reaching its decision to exclude the limitation of liability clause, the trial court reasoned that if the clause were given effect, the limitation of liability "would allow Gottlieb to substitute a product without notice to Alps that would affect the final marketability of the final product." This reasoning was flawed. Paul Gottlieb & Co., Inc.'s (Gottlieb) (P) substitution of fabric, resulting in a breach of the contract, is an undisputed fact that does not bear on the construction of the clause, and the trial court should have determined only whether the clause, as a matter of law, materially altered the contract. Under U.C.C. § 2-207(1), a timely acceptance serves as an acceptance notwithstanding that it states terms additional to or different from those offered or agreed upon, unless acceptance is expressly made conditional on assent to the additional or different terms. Where there are such additional terms, they become part of the contract unless, inter alia, they materially alter the contract. The only

Continued on next page.

issue before the court is whether the clause on the back of Gottlieb's (P) form contract materially altered the contract. The burden is on the party seeking to exclude the additional terms to prove material alteration, here, Alps South Corp. (Alps) (D). To determine whether an additional term materially alters a contract, courts typically use some alternative of a "surprise or hardship" test. Some courts have removed hardship from the analysis and look solely for surprise. As to surprise, Alps (D) must prove that, under the circumstances, it cannot be presumed that a reasonable merchant would have consented to the additional term. However, Alps (D) has not done so. The only surprise came to Alps (D) because it did not read the contract, which is never an excuse that lets a party out of a contract. Moreover, the type of clause at issue is not one that the U.C.C. deems as one that would involve unreasonable surprise. Alps (D) also failed to adduce evidence of hardship as a result of surprise. Gottlieb (P) never represented that, in the event of a breach, it would reimburse Alps (D) for any or all consequential damages it sustained resulting from the breach. Instead, Alps (D) previously had returned a sample of nonconforming fabric to Gottlieb (P) with a letter insisting on conforming goods. This letter did not mention or make claim for additional costs or damages resulting from Gottlieb's (P) prior breach of performance. Additionally, Alps (D) never informed Gottlieb (P) of any consequences other than discontinuing their relationship, or of the specific manner, in which the subject fabric would be used or what product would be crafted. Thus, Gottlieb (P) could not foresee the greater extent of its potential liability upon breach. Because Alps (D) failed to inform Gottlieb (P) of the larger consequences of the breach, Alps (D) cannot maintain that incorporating the limitation of liability clause would result in a severe economic hardship. Thus, Alps (D) failed to carry the burden of proof on material alteration, and the limitation of liability clause is part of the contract between the parties. That clause, however, limits only consequential damages, including lost profits. An additional ground for precluding lost profits damages is that Alps (D) failed to carry its burden of proving lost profits with reasonable certainty. Alps (D) may still pursue nonconsequential damages, such as direct and incidental damages, which the trial court should determine on remand. Reversed and remanded.

ANALYSIS

This dispute arises from the common, but risky, commercial practice where the seller and buyer negotiate a contract involving goods by exchanging one another's standardized forms. This practice is sometimes referred to as the "battle of the forms" and is governed by Uniform Commercial Code § 2-207, which is intended to end the battle by eliminating the uncertainty that often results from the exchange of conflicting purchase order forms and acknowledgment and acceptance forms. The battle lines are frequently created where, as here, the seller's form contains terms different from or additional to those set forth in the buyer's form. Despite the differences in the forms, the parties proceed with the commercial transactions and, as in this case, fight the battle in court after the transaction concludes.

Quicknotes

BURDEN OF PROOF The duty of a party to introduce evidence to support a fact that is in dispute in an action.

CONSEQUENTIAL DAMAGES Monetary compensation that may be recovered in order to compensate for injuries or losses sustained as a result of damages that are not the direct or foreseeable result of the act of a party, but that nevertheless are the consequence of such act and that must be specifically pled and demonstrated.

COUNTERCLAIM An independent cause of action brought by a defendant to a lawsuit in order to oppose or deduct from the plaintiff's claim.

DeFontes v. Dell, Inc.

Consumer (P) v. Computer seller (D)

R.I. Sup. Ct., 984 A.2d 1061 (2009)

NATURE OF CASE: Appeal from denial of motion to stay proceedings and compel arbitration in putative class action for violation of the Deceptive Trade Practices Act.

FACT SUMMARY: Dell, Inc. and various affiliates (collectively, Dell) (D) contended that consumers (P) who bought computers from Dell (D) were bound by the arbitration provisions in Dell's (D) terms and conditions, which Dell (D) contended the consumers (P) had accepted by accepting delivery of the computers. The consumers (P) countered that even though they had three separate opportunities to review the terms and conditions, none was sufficient to give rise to a contractual obligation.

RULE OF LAW

Terms and conditions included with consumer goods are not binding on consumers who accept the goods and do not return the goods where, because of the ambiguity of the terms and conditions requiring inferences on the part of the consumer, it would not be reasonably apparent to a reasonably prudent consumer that he or she could reject the terms and conditions simply by returning the goods.

FACTS: Consumers (P) who bought computers from Dell, Inc. and its affiliates (collectively, Dell) (D), brought a putative class action against Dell (D) for violation of the Deceptive Trade Practices Act on the grounds that Dell (D) had charged them a tax on service contracts they had purchased when no such tax was required by their state. Dell (D) moved to stay proceedings and compel arbitration on the grounds that the consumers (P) were bound by the arbitration provisions in Dell's (D) terms and conditions, which Dell (D) contended the consumers (P) had accepted by accepting delivery of the computers. Dell (D) asserted that the consumers (P) had three opportunities to review the terms and conditions: by selecting a hyperlink on the Dell (D) website, by reading the terms that were included in the acknowledgment/invoice that was sent to plaintiffs sometime after they placed their orders, or by reviewing the copy of the terms Dell (D) included in the packaging of its computer products. The trial court, applying Texas law and the Uniform Commercial Code (U.C.C.), held that the consumers (P) were not bound by Dell's (D) terms and conditions. The court found that the hyperlink on Dell's (D) website was inconspicuously located at the bottom of the webpage and insufficient to place customers on notice of the terms and conditions. As to the acknowledgments sent to the consumers (P) after their purchases and the copy of the terms included in the computer packaging, the court observed that courts will ordinarily enforce such "shrinkwrap" agreements provided they contain an express disclaimer that explains to consumers that they can reject the proposed terms and conditions by returning the product. Per the trial court, the crucial test is whether a reasonable person would have known that return of the product would serve as rejection of those terms. Looking at the language of the terms and conditions, the court concluded that it was insufficient to give a reasonable consumer notice of the method of rejection. The language admonished the consumers (P) to carefully read the terms and conditions; informed them that the terms and conditions contained a dispute resolution clause; informed them that they would be bound to the terms by accepting the computers; and informed them that the terms and conditions were subject to change without prior written notice at any time, in Dell's (D) sole discretion. The court found that Dell's (D) failure to include an express disclaimer meant that Dell (D) could not prove that the consumers (P) knowingly consented to the terms and conditions of the agreement. Accordingly, the court ruled that the consumers (P) could not be compelled to enter arbitration. The state's highest court granted review.

ISSUE: Are terms and conditions included with consumer goods binding on consumers who accept the goods and do not return the goods where, because of the ambiguity of the terms and conditions requiring inferences on the part of the consumer, it would not be reasonably apparent to a reasonably prudent consumer that he or she could reject the terms and conditions simply by returning the goods?

HOLDING AND DECISION: (Williams, C.J., ret.) No. Terms and conditions included with consumer goods are not binding on consumers who accept the goods and do not return the goods where, because of the ambiguity of the terms and conditions requiring inferences on the part of the consumer, it would not be reasonably apparent to a reasonably prudent consumer that he or she could reject the terms and conditions simply by returning the goods. This case, involving interstate commerce, invokes the Federal Arbitration Act (FAA), which requires enforcement of privately negotiated arbitration agreements "save upon such grounds as exist at law or in equity for the revocation of any contract." Thus, the question becomes whether, under state law (here, Texas) and

Continued on next page.

the Uniform Commercial Code (U.C.C.), the consumers (P) are bound by the terms and conditions agreement. Under U.C.C. § 2-204, contracts for the sale of goods may be formed in any manner sufficient to show agreement. The U.C.C. assumes that the buyer is the offeror and the seller is the offeree. However, the modern trend is to place the power of acceptance with the consumer, after he or she receives goods containing a standard form statement of additional terms and conditions, provided the buyer retains the power to accept or return the product. Judge Frank Easterbrook has authored what are widely considered to be the two leading cases on shrinkwrap agreements. In *ProCD, Inc. v. Zeidenberg*, 86 F.3d 1447 (7th Cir. 1996), the court challenged the traditional understanding of offer and acceptance in consumer transactions by holding that a buyer of software was bound by an agreement that was included within the packaging and later appeared when the buyer first used the software. In *ProCD*, Judge Easterbrook held that U.C.C. § 2-207, which addresses the treatment of additional terms in an exchange of forms between merchants, is inapplicable in the consumer setting because only one form is involved. He reasoned that under § 2-204 "[a] vendor, as master of the offer, may invite acceptance by conduct, and may propose limitations on the kind of conduct that constitutes acceptance. A buyer may accept by performing the acts the vendor proposes to treat as acceptance." Judge Easterbrook expanded this holding in *Hill v. Gateway 2000, Inc.*, 105 F.3d 1147 (7th Cir. 1997), beyond transactions involving software where the consumer is prompted to accept or decline the terms when he or she first uses the program. He determined that when a merchant delivers a product that includes additional terms and conditions, but expressly provides the consumer the right to either accept those terms or return the product for a refund within a reasonable time, a consumer who retains the goods beyond that period may be bound by the contract. Although not all courts have accepted *ProCD's* reasoning, it is clearly the majority position. The *ProCD* line of cases is better reasoned and more consistent with contemporary consumer transactions. It is simply unreasonable to expect a seller to apprise a consumer of every term and condition at the moment he or she makes a purchase. "A modern consumer neither expects nor desires to wade through such minutia, particularly when making a purchase over the phone, where full disclosure of the terms would border on the sadistic." Consumers are aware that with delivery comes a multitude of standard terms attendant to nearly every consumer transaction. Accordingly, formation occurs when the consumer accepts the full terms after receiving a reasonable opportunity to refuse them. Nonetheless, the seller has the burden of showing that the buyer accepted the seller's terms after delivery. Thus, the crucial question here becomes whether Dell, Inc. (D) reasonably invited acceptance by making clear in the terms and conditions agreement that by accepting its product the consumer (P) was accepting the terms and conditions contained within and that the consumer (P) could reject the terms and conditions by returning the product. Dell (D) has failed to do so. The language of its terms and conditions did not make clear a period beyond which the consumer would have indicated assent to those terms. "Acceptance of goods" has a technical meaning not easily discernable to the average consumer, and many consumers believe they are bound by the terms simply by opening the package. More significantly, the terms and conditions did not make clear that consumers could reject the terms simply by returning the goods. Here, there was no explicit disclaimer advising consumers of their right to reject the terms. Thus, it is possible that the consumers (P) were unaware of both their power to reject and the method with which to do so. Too many inferential steps were required of the consumers (P) and too many of the relevant provisions were left ambiguous. It is not clear that a reasonably prudent offeree would understand that by keeping the Dell (D) computer he or she was agreeing to be bound by the terms and conditions agreement and retained, for a specified time, the power to reject the terms by returning the product. Affirmed.

ANALYSIS

Those courts that reject the reasoning of *ProCD* and *Hill* find that a consumer's acceptance of goods and not returning them is consistent with a contract being formed at the time that the order was placed and cannot be construed as acquiescing in the terms and conditions later submitted to the consumer, whether they are included with the invoice or acknowledgment or with the packaging. The court reasons that if the contract was formed at the time the order was placed, the terms and conditions are additional terms of the contract under Uniform Commercial Code § 2-207. Thus, these terms and conditions do not become part of the contract but a proposal to add additional terms, which can only become part of the contract through the consumer's express agreement.

Quicknotes

CLASS ACTION A suit commenced by a representative on behalf of an ascertainable group that is too large to appear in court, shares a commonality of interests, and will benefit from a successful result.

INTERSTATE COMMERCE Commercial dealings between two parties located in different states or located in one state and accomplished through a point in another state or a foreign country; commercial dealings transacted between two states.

Long v. Provide Commerce, Inc.

Online shopper (P) v. Online retailer (D)

Cal. Ct. App., 245 Cal. App. 4th 855, 200 Cal. Rptr. 3d 117 (2016)

NATURE OF CASE: Appeal from denial of motion to compel arbitration in putative class action asserting claims for violations of consumer protection and unfair competition laws.

FACT SUMMARY: Provide Commerce, Inc. (Provide) (D), an online retailer, contended that the links on its website to its terms of use, which contained a mandatory arbitration provision, were sufficiently conspicuous to put Long (P), an online shopper, on constructive notice of those terms, so that any dispute Long (P) had with Provide (D) that arose from his use of the website should have been arbitrated, rather than litigated. Provide (D) also contended that even if Long (P) was not bound by the arbitration provision, he was bound by the forum selection clause contained in the terms of use.

RULE OF LAW

(1) An online user does not have constructive notice of a website's terms of use, so that the user may not be bound by those terms, where the terms are hyperlinked in a manner that is too inconspicuous to put a reasonably prudent Internet consumer on inquiry notice thereof.

(2) The presumptive validity of forum selection clauses does not relieve a party asserting the enforceability of a forum selection clause from proving the resisting party's objective manifestation of assent to the larger contract in which the forum selection clause is found.

FACTS: Provide Commerce, Inc. (Provide) (D), was an online retailer that owned and operated several websites, including ProFlowers.com, through which Provide (D) advertised and sold a variety of floral products. Long (P) purchased a floral arrangement on ProFlowers.com that had been depicted and advertised as a "completed assembled product," but which was delivered as a "do-it yourself kit in a box requiring assembly by the recipient." Based on this allegation Long (P) sued Provide (D), asserting claims for violations of state consumer protection and unfair competition laws on behalf of himself and a putative class of state consumers who purchased similarly advertised floral arrangements on ProFlowers.com. Provide (D) moved to compel arbitration, arguing Long (P) was bound by the Terms of Use for ProFlowers.com, including the dispute resolution provision contained therein. The Terms of Use were available via a capitalized and underlined hyperlink titled "TERMS OF USE" located at the bottom of each web page. The hyperlink was displayed in a light green typeface on the website's lime green background, and it was situated among 14 other capitalized and underlined hyperlinks of the same color, font, and size. Hyperlinks to the terms also appeared at the bottom of each page Long (P) encountered in a multipage checkout "flow." After Long (P) placed his order Provide (D) also sent a confirmatory email to Long (P) that contained numerous hyperlinks, along with hyperlinks to the Terms of Use. Long (P) averred that he had noticed neither a reference of any kind to ProFlowers Terms and Conditions nor a hyperlink thereto when he purchased flowers for delivery on ProFlowers.com. The trial court agreed with Long (P), concluding the hyperlinks were too inconspicuous to put a reasonably prudent Internet consumer on inquiry notice. Accordingly, the court denied Provide's (D) motion to compel arbitration. Provide (D) also argued, in the alternative, that even if Long (P) was not bound by the arbitration provision in the Terms of Use, he nevertheless was bound by its forum selection clause, since such clauses are presumptively valid. The trial court rejected this argument, again concluding that Long (P) had not assented, either expressly or constructively, to the Terms of Use, including the forum selection clause, because of the inconspicuous placement of the hyperlinks thereto. The state's intermediate appellate court granted review.

ISSUE:

(1) Does an online user have constructive notice of a website's terms of use, so that the user may be bound by those terms, where the terms are hyperlinked in a manner that is too inconspicuous to put a reasonably prudent Internet consumer on inquiry notice thereof?

(2) Does the presumptive validity of forum selection clauses relieve a party asserting the enforceability of a forum selection clause from proving the resisting party's objective manifestation of assent to the larger contract in which the forum selection clause is found?

HOLDING AND DECISION: (Jones, J.)

(1) No. An online user does not have constructive notice of a website's terms of use, so that the user may not be bound by those terms, where the terms are hyperlinked in a manner that is too inconspicuous to put a reasonably prudent Internet consumer on inquiry notice thereof. Although there is a strong policy favoring the enforcement of agreements to arbitrate disputes, there is no policy compelling persons

Continued on next page.

to accept the arbitration of controversies they have not agreed to arbitrate. To render such agreements enforceable, there must be an objective manifestation of assent thereto. Thus, an offeree is not bound by inconspicuous contract provisions of which the offeree was unaware. The type of contract at issue here is known as a "browsewrap" agreement, where a website's terms and conditions of use are posted on the site via hyperlink. This type of agreement does not require the user to expressly manifest assent to the terms and conditions. Instead, a user manifests assent simply by using the site. Because no affirmative action is required by the user to agree to the terms of a contract other than the use of the site, the determination of the validity of the browsewrap contract depends on whether the user has actual or constructive knowledge of the site's terms and conditions. Absent actual notice, the validity of a browsewrap agreement turns on whether the site puts a reasonably prudent user on inquiry notice of the terms of the contract. Here, based on the website's design and the design of the confirmation email, the hyperlinks to the terms of use were not sufficiently conspicuous to place a reasonably prudent Internet user on inquiry notice of those terms. Case law from the Ninth Circuit provides that where a website makes its terms of use available via a conspicuous hyperlink on every page of the site but otherwise provides no notice to users nor prompts them to take any affirmative action to demonstrate assent, even close proximity of the hyperlink to relevant buttons users must click on—without more—is insufficient to give rise to constructive notice. *Nguyen v. Barnes & Noble Inc.*, 763 F.3d 1171 (9th Cir. 2014). Provide Commerce, Inc. (Provide) (D) argues that case law from the Second Circuit, in *Specht v. Netscape Communications Corp.*, 306 F.3d 17 (2d Cir. 2002), suggests that a conspicuous hyperlink that provides immediately visible notice of a browsewrap agreement is sufficient, standing alone, to put a reasonably prudent Internet consumer on inquiry notice of the agreement's terms, and further argues that because the hyperlinks on its website were immediately visible, without scrolling, and were located next to several fields that the user was required to fill out and next to buttons the user had to click to complete the order, this placement was sufficient to put a user on inquiry notice of the terms. Provide's (D) arguments are unpersuasive. Here, the placement, color, size, and other qualities of the hyperlinks relative to the ProFlowers.com website's overall design are too inconspicuous to infer that a reasonable user would readily find them and be on inquiry notice of the terms to which they linked. Contrary to Provide's (D) characterization, the subject hyperlinks in the checkout flow are not "located next to" the fields and buttons a consumer must interact with to complete his or her order. Those fields and buttons are contained in a separate bright white box in the center of the page that contrasts sharply with the site's lime green background. To find a Terms of Use hyperlink in the checkout flow, a consumer placing an order must (1) remove attention from the fields in which the user is asked to enter information; (2) look below the buttons the user must click to proceed with the order; (3) look even further below a "VeriSign Secured" logo and notification advising that the "order is safe and secure," which itself includes a hyperlink to "Click here for more details"; (4) look still further below a thick dark green bar with a hyperlink for "SITE FEEDBACK"; and (5) finally find the "TERMS OF USE" hyperlink situated to the right of another hyperlink for the site's "PRIVACY POLICY," both of which appear in the same font and light green typeface that, to the unwary purchaser, could blend in with the site's lime green background. Also unpersuasive is Provide's (D) contention that the subsequent order confirmation e-mail provides the notice that was missing from the checkout flow. Unlike the hyperlink on some checkout flow pages, the hyperlink in the e-mail is located on a submerged page, requiring the customer to scroll below layers of order summary details, advertisement banners, other types of hyperlinks, several logos for Provide's (D) "Family of Brands," and customer service contact information to finally find a reference to "Terms" printed in grey typeface on a white background. This is not the sort of conspicuous alert that can be expected to put a reasonably prudent Internet consumer on notice to investigate whether disputes related to an order will be subject to binding arbitration. Affirmed as to this issue.

(2) No. The presumptive validity of forum selection clauses does not relieve a party asserting the enforceability of a forum selection clause from proving the resisting party's objective manifestation of assent to the larger contract in which the forum selection clause is found. Provide (D) argues the trial court's reasoning as to the forum selection clause was flawed, because forum selection clauses are presumptively valid. Thus Provide (D) maintains, though it had the burden to establish an enforceable arbitration agreement, the presumption in favor of forum selection clause enforcement shifted the burden to Long (P) to show why the provision should not be enforced. Provide's (D) reliance on the presumptive validity of forum selection clauses in otherwise enforceable contracts proves too much. Contrary to Provide's (D) implicit

Continued on next page.

premise, the presumption of validity is not a substitute for proof of the resisting party's objective manifestation of assent to the larger contract. If it were, a party would establish the existence of a binding contract simply by showing that the contract contained a presumptively valid forum selection clause—an obviously absurd result. The trial court was correct; because Long (P) was not bound by Provide's (D) Terms of Use (because the website's hyperlinks to the terms were inconspicuous), he also could not have been bound by the forum selection clause contained therein. Affirmed as to this issue. The order is affirmed. Long (P) is entitled to his costs.

ANALYSIS

The court stated its belief, without deciding the issue, that to establish the enforceability of a browsewrap agreement, a textual notice should be required to advise consumers that continued use of a website will constitute the consumer's agreement to be bound by the site's terms of use. In the court's opinion, the problem with merely displaying a hyperlink in a prominent or conspicuous place is that, without notifying consumers that the linked page contains binding contractual terms, the phrase "terms of use" may have no meaning or a different meaning to a large segment of the Internet-using public. In other words, a conspicuous "terms of use" hyperlink may not be enough to alert a reasonably prudent Internet consumer to click the hyperlink. Given the breadth of the range of technological savvy of online purchasers, the court observed that consumers cannot be expected to ferret out hyperlinks to terms and conditions to which they have no reason to suspect they will be bound, so that the onus must be on website owners to put users on notice of the terms to which they wish to bind consumers. The court added that such a bright line rule is necessary to ensure that Internet consumers are on inquiry notice of a browsewrap agreement's terms, regardless of each consumer's degree of technological savvy. Based on this view, online retailers would be well advised to include a conspicuous textual notice with their terms of use hyperlinks going forward.

Quicknotes

ACTUAL NOTICE The direct communication of information to a person.

INQUIRY NOTICE The communication of information that would cause an ordinary person of average prudence to inquire as to its truth.

PRESUMPTION A rule of law requiring the court to presume certain facts to be true based on the existence of other facts, thereby shifting the burden of proof to the party against whom the presumption is asserted to rebut.

CHAPTER 3

Liability in the Absence of Bargained-for Exchange: Reliance on Gratuitous Promises, Unaccepted Offers, and the Principle of Restitution

Quick Reference Rules of Law

Kirksey v. Kirksey

Sister-in-law (P) v. Brother-in-law (D)

Ala. Sup. Ct., 8 Ala. 131 (1845)

NATURE OF CASE: Appeal from verdict for plaintiff in action to recover damages for breach of a promise.

FACT SUMMARY: Kirksey (D) promised "Sister Antillico" (P), Kirksey's (D) widowed sister-in-law, a place to raise her family "if you come down and see me." She sought damages for breach of the promise after he required her to leave before she had raised her family.

RULE OF LAW

To be legally enforceable, an executory promise must be supported by sufficient, bargained-for consideration.

FACTS: Kirksey (D) wrote his widowed sister-in-law, "Sister Antillico" (P), a letter containing the following clause: "If you will come down and see me, I will let you have a place to raise your family." "Sister Antillico" (P) moved 60 miles to Kirksey's (D) residence, where she remained for more than two years in comfortable housing and with land to cultivate. Kirksey (D) then required her to leave, although her family was not yet "raised." "Sister Antillico" (P) contended that the loss that she sustained in moving was sufficient consideration to support Kirksey's (D) promise to furnish her with "a place" until she could raise her family. Verdict was rendered for "Sister Antillico" (P), and the state's highest court granted review.

ISSUE: To be legally enforceable, must an executory promise be supported by sufficient, bargained-for consideration?

HOLDING AND DECISION: (Ormond, J.) Yes. To be legally enforceable, an executory promise must be supported by sufficient, bargained-for consideration. The "loss and inconvenience" incurred by "Sister Antillico" (P) in moving to Kirksey's (D) could be deemed sufficient consideration to support a promise by Kirksey (D) to furnish her with a house and land until she finished raising her family. However, if, as the majority believes, Kirksey's (D) promise was a gratuity, an action for the breach of the promise will not lie. Reversed.

ANALYSIS

This well-known case demonstrates the court's insistence on finding a bargained-for exchange before it will enforce an executory promise. A promise to make a gift is generally not legally binding until it is executed. Compare Williston's famous hypothetical in which a benevolent man says to a tramp: "If you go around the corner to the clothing shop there, you may purchase an overcoat on my credit." This hypothetical highlights the conceptual problem of the present case in that it is unreasonable to construe the walk around the corner as the price of the promise, yet it is a legal detriment to the tramp to make the walk. Perhaps a reasonable (though not conclusive) guideline is the extent to which the happening of the condition will benefit the promisor. The present case might be decided differently today under the doctrine of promissory estoppel, which had not yet been developed in 1845, when *Kirksey* was decided.

Quicknotes

BARGAINED-FOR EXCHANGE A requirement for adequate consideration; the promise made by the offeror induces the return promise or performance on the part of the offeree and that the promise or performance on the part of the offeree induces the promise made by the offeror.

BREACH The violation of an obligation imposed pursuant to contract or law, by acting or failing to act.

CONSIDERATION Value given by one party in exchange for performance, or a promise to perform, by another party.

EXECUTORY PROMISE A promise to perform an action that has not yet been performed.

FORBEARANCE The act of refraining from doing something that one has the legal right to do.

PROMISE The expression of an intention to act, or to forbear from acting, granting a right to the promisee to expect and enforce its performance.

PROMISEE The party to whom a promise is made.

PROMISSORY ESTOPPEL A promise that is enforceable if the promisor should reasonably expect that it will induce action or forbearance on the part of the promisee, does in fact cause such action or forbearance, and is the only means of avoiding injustice.

Harvey v. Dow

Daughter (P) v. Parent (D)

Me. Sup. Jud. Ct., 962 A.2d 322 (2008)

NATURE OF CASE: Appeal from judgment for defendants in action to compel conveyance of land, or for damages.

FACT SUMMARY: Harvey (P), the Dows' (D) daughter, claimed that the Dows (D) were promissorily estopped from conveying a deed to a parcel of land on which she had built a house, contending that their general promises to transfer some of their land to her, as well as actions by her father, Jeffrey B. Dow, Sr. (D), including approving the site of her house, obtaining a building permit for it, and then building a substantial part of it himself at that location, supported a claim for promissory estoppel.

RULE OF LAW

When considering a claim of promissory estoppel, a court must consider the alleged promisor's conduct as well as any generalized promises the promisor has made in determining if all the promisor's actions, taken together, constitute a "promise" to the claimant.

FACTS: Ever since Harvey (P) was a child, her parents, the Dows (D), had been making general promises to her and her brother that the Dows (D) would at some point in the future convey some or all the Dows' (D) 125 acres of land to the children. After Harvey (P) got married, she and her husband decided to build a house on the Dows' (D) property, with the Dows' (D) permission. Initially, the financing was to come from the Dows' (D) home equity line of credit, but, after Harvey's (D) husband died in an accident, Harvey (D) decided to use the proceeds from the husband's life insurance policy. Harvey's father, Jeffrey B. Dow, Sr. (Jeffrey Sr.) (D), approved the site of the new house, obtained a building permit for it, and then built a substantial part of it himself at that location. Subsequently, the relationship between Harvey (P) and the Dows (D) began to deteriorate. After Harvey (P) moved into the house once it was completed, at around a $200,000 cost to her, she began to ask Jeffrey Sr. (D) for a deed so that she could obtain a mortgage to finance other projects. After a period of discussion, it became clear that the Dows (D) were not going to execute a deed. Harvey (P) brought suit to compel the Dows (D) to convey unspecified real property to her, or for damages, as well as other claims. One of her theories of recovery was promissory estoppel. The Dows (D) counterclaimed for a declaratory judgment that Harvey (P) had no rights in their property. At trial, there was conflicting evidence as to whether either of the Dows (D) had promised to deed any of their land to Harvey (P). The trial court concluded that Harvey (P) had failed to make out a claim of promissory estoppel, finding that the Dows' (D) statements were not promises that could be enforced even if they were the subject of detrimental reliance, as the promises were too indefinite and there was no agreement on basic elements such as the boundaries or size of the property involved. Harvey (P) appealed, arguing that the trial court had erred by failing to look beyond the Dows' (D) generalized statements to determine whether she had made out a promissory estoppel claim. The state's highest court granted review.

ISSUE: When considering a claim of promissory estoppel, must a court consider the alleged promisor's conduct as well as any generalized promises the promisor has made in determining if all the promisor's actions, taken together, constitute a "promise" to the claimant?

HOLDING AND DECISION: (Mead, J.) Yes. When considering a claim of promissory estoppel, a court must consider the alleged promisor's conduct as well as any generalized promises the promisor has made in determining if all the promisor's actions, taken together, constitute a "promise" to the claimant. Promissory estoppel applies to promises that are otherwise unenforceable, and it is used to enforce such promises to avoid injustice. Thus, a promise is an essential part of a promissory estoppel claim. Here, the trial court was correct in finding that the Dows (D) had made only generalized promises to Harvey (P) to convey land to her, and that those promises were not enforceable express promises due to indefinites as to key terms, such as identification of a specific parcel's size, boundaries, etc. If that is all the Dows (D) did, the trial court would have been correct in concluding that Harvey's (P) promissory estoppel claim had to fail. However, the Dows (D) did more than just make generalized promises to convey unspecified land at some unspecified point in time. They also acquiesced in, supported, and encouraged Harvey's (P) construction of a house on their property. Against the backdrop of the parties' general understanding that Harvey (P) would one day receive property as a gift or inheritance from her parents, Jeffrey Sr. (D) agreed to the location, obtained a building permit to allow construction at that site, and not only acquiesced in the house being built, but built a large portion of it himself. In a promissory estoppel analysis, the promise relied on by the promisee need not be express but may be implied from a party's conduct. Here, such a

Continued on next page.

promise could be implied from Jeffrey Sr.'s (D) conduct. Given that Harvey's (P) reliance on such a promise, if proved, has resulted in her owning an immobile $200,000 asset on the Dows' (D) land, refusal to enforce the promise would work an injustice on Harvey (P). Accordingly, such a promise can be enforced despite the lack of consideration. The Restatement (Second) of Contracts (the Restatement) supports this position, defining a promise as "a manifestation of intention to act or refrain from acting in a specified way," where such a manifestation justifies the promisee's comprehending that the promisor has made a certain commitment. Here, Jeffrey Sr.'s (D) actions could be construed as a manifestation of his intent to confirm his general promise to convey land to Harvey (P) and to direct it to that specific parcel. As regards promises to make a gift, the Restatement provides that such promises are enforceable only where it is foreseeable and reasonable that the promisee will rely on the promise. Here, given the Dows' (D) generalized statements and actions, it is arguable that Harvey's (P) reliance on these manifestations of intention to act was eminently foreseeable and reasonable. Accordingly, the trial court erred in failing to consider the Dows' (D) actions, in conjunction with their generalized statements, in determining whether the existence of promissory estoppel was established on these facts. The case is remanded to the trial court to make such considerations. Vacated and remanded.

ANALYSIS

On remand, the trial court again found for the Dows (D). The trial court did not make any new findings, and concluded that the Dows' (D) actions, as well as their generalized promises, were insufficient to support a claim of promissory estoppel. Harvey (P) appealed again, and the state's highest court, while concluding that the trial court had all the facts it needed for a proper promissory estoppel analysis, held that the trial court's legal conclusion was erroneous. The court held that, as a matter of law, the Dows' (D) acquiescence, support, and encouragement of Harvey's construction of a house on a parcel of their land conclusively demonstrated their intention to make a present conveyance of that property. Accordingly, the court vacated the trial court's judgment and remanded for entry of a judgment in favor of Harvey (P) but remanded once again for a determination of the appropriate remedy, admonishing the trial court to keep in mind that a promise binding under promissory estoppel is a contract, and full-scale enforcement by normal remedies is often appropriate.

Quicknotes

COUNTERCLAIM An independent cause of action brought by a defendant to a lawsuit in order to oppose or deduct from the plaintiff's claim.

DAMAGES Monetary compensation that may be awarded by the court to a party who has sustained injury or loss to his or her person, property, or rights due to another party's unlawful act, omission, or negligence.

DECLARATORY JUDGMENT A judgment of the court establishing the rights and other legal relations of the parties in a controversy.

DEED A signed writing transferring title to real property from one person to another.

DETRIMENTAL RELIANCE Action by one party, resulting in loss, which is based on the conduct or promises of another.

FORBEARANCE The act of refraining from doing something that one has the legal right to do.

PROMISE The expression of an intention to act, or to forbear from acting, granting a right to the promisee to expect and enforce its performance.

PROMISEE The party to whom a promise is made.

PROMISOR The party who promises to render an obligation to another in the future.

PROMISSORY ESTOPPEL A promise that is enforceable if the promisor should reasonably expect that it will induce action or forbearance on the part of the promisee, does in fact cause such action or forbearance, and is the only means of avoiding injustice.

REAL PROPERTY Land, an interest in land, or anything attached to the land that is incapable of being removed.

King v. Trustees of Boston University

Estate administratrix (P) v. Charity (D)

Mass. Sup. Jud. Ct., 420 Mass. 52, 647 N.E.2d 1196 (1995)

NATURE OF CASE: Appeal from a judgment for defendant in suit alleging conversion.

FACT SUMMARY: Coretta Scott King (P), in her capacity as administratrix of the estate of her late husband, Dr. Martin Luther King, Jr., sued Boston University (BU) (D) for conversion, alleging that the estate (P), and not BU (D), held title to Dr. King's papers housed in BU's (D) library.

RULE OF LAW

Where donative intent is sufficiently clear, the court will give effect to that intent to the extent possible without abandoning basic contract principles such as reliance.

FACTS: Coretta Scott King (P) sued Boston University (BU) (D) for conversion of papers that Dr. Martin Luther King, Jr., an alumnus of BU (D), had deposited with BU (D). The jury determined that Dr. King made a promise to give absolute title to his papers to BU (D) in a letter signed by him, and that the promise was enforceable as a charitable pledge supported by consideration or reliance. The jury also determined that the letter promising the papers was not a contract. The trial court denied King's (P) motion for judgment notwithstanding the verdict. King (P) appealed, alleging that BU (D) could not reasonably rely on his statement of donative intent because of Dr. King's initial retention of legal ownership, and that one statement in the letter amounted to a will and was therefore unenforceable because it failed to comply with formal requirements for a will.

ISSUE: Where donative intent is sufficiently clear, will the court give effect to that intent to the extent possible without abandoning basic contract principles such as reliance?

HOLDING AND DECISION: (Abrams, J.) Yes. Where donative intent is sufficiently clear, the court will give effect to that intent to prevent the extent possible without abandoning basic contract principles such as reliance. The bailor-bailee relationship established in the letter could be viewed by a rational factfinder as a security for the promise to give a gift in the future of the bailed property, and thus as evidence in addition to the statement in the letter of an intent of the donor to be bound. The statute of wills does not prevent a person from making a contract or a promise to take effect at his or her death. The letter could have been read to contain a promise supported by consideration or reliance and the issue of the transfer of ownership was properly submitted to the jury. Affirmed.

ANALYSIS

A pledge is defined as a bailment of personal property to secure an obligation of the bailor. To enforce a charitable subscription or a charitable pledge in Massachusetts, a party must establish that there was a promise to give some property to a charitable institution and that the promise was supported by consideration or reliance. This court reviewed whether there was sufficient evidence for the case to have been properly submitted to the jury.

Quicknotes

BAILEE Person holding property in trust for another party.

BAILOR Person who delivers property to be held in trust.

BAILMENT The delivery of property to be held in trust and that is designated for a particular purpose, following the satisfaction of which the property is either to be returned or disposed of as specified.

CONSIDERATION Value given by one party in exchange for performance, or a promise to perform, by another party.

DONATIVE INTENT Donor's intent to make a gift.

PROMISE The expression of an intention to act, or to forbear from acting, granting a right to the promisee to expect and enforce its performance.

PROMISEE The party to whom a promise is made.

WILL An instrument setting forth the distribution to be made of an individual's estate upon his or her death; since a will is not effective until the death of its maker, it is revocable during his or her life.

Katz v. Danny Dare, Inc.

Employee (P) v. Employer (D)

Mo. Ct. App., 610 S.W.2d 121 (1980)

NATURE OF CASE: Appeal from denial of pension benefits.

FACT SUMMARY: Danny Dare, Inc. (D) contended that Katz (P) did not give up anything of value in return for pension benefits, and that, thus, its promise to pay such benefits was unenforceable.

RULE OF LAW

The application of the doctrine of promissory estoppel does not require the relinquishment of a legal interest.

FACTS: Katz (P) had worked for Danny Dare, Inc. (Dare) (D) for more than 25 years. He suffered personal injuries and became ineffective in his job. Dare (D), through its president, sought to induce Katz's retirement by paying him pension benefits. Katz (P) could accept the pension or be fired, and after 13 months of negotiations, he retired. The retirement was specifically in reliance upon the promise to pay the pension. Dare (D) paid the pension for a period of time and then unilaterally reduced, then eliminated it. Katz (P) sued, contending Dare (D) was estopped from denying the enforceability of the agreement. Dare (D) contended Katz (P) did not give up anything by retiring, as his alternative was to be fired. The trial court denied recovery, and Katz (P) appealed.

ISSUE: Does the application of the doctrine of promissory estoppel require the relinquishment of a legal interest?

HOLDING AND DECISION: (Turnage, P.J.) No. The application of the doctrine of promissory estoppel does not require the relinquishment of a legal interest. It requires a promise, detrimental reliance, and that injustice cannot be otherwise avoided. In this case, admittedly, a promise to pay benefits was made, and Katz relied on such promise in retiring. Danny Dare, Inc. (Dare) (D) could have terminated him yet chose to negotiate for more than a year over the pension. Thus, the retirement was voluntary. Therefore, Dare (D) is estopped from failing to recognize its obligations. Reversed and remanded.

ANALYSIS

The general understanding is that all promises must be supported by consideration to be enforceable. However, other promises may be enforceable in the absence of consideration based upon promissory estoppel. In this case, it was the detrimental reliance reasonably based on the promise to pay that enforced the pension agreement. Clearly, no consideration was given by Katz (P) for the promise.

Quicknotes

DETRIMENTAL RELIANCE Reliance by one party that is based on the conduct or promises of another, resulting in loss to the party.

FORBEARANCE The act of refraining from doing something that one has the legal right to do.

PROMISE The expression of an intention to act, or to forbear from acting, granting a right to the promisee to expect and enforce its performance.

PROMISEE The party to whom a promise is made.

PROMISSORY ESTOPPEL A promise that is enforceable if the promisor should reasonably expect that it will induce action or forbearance on the part of the promisee, does in fact cause such action or forbearance, and is the only means of avoiding injustice.

Aceves v. U.S. Bank, N.A.

Mortgagor (P) v. Mortgagee (D)

Cal. Ct. App., 192 Cal. App. 4th 218, 120 Cal. Rptr. 3d 507 (2011)

NATURE OF CASE: Appeal from judgment for defendant in action, inter alia, for promissory estoppel and to set aside the sale of a foreclosed house.

FACT SUMMARY: Aceves (P), who defaulted on her mortgaged house, contended that the mortgagee, U.S. Bank, N.A. (U.S. Bank) (D), was promissorily estopped from foreclosing on her house because, in detrimental reliance on U.S. Bank's (D) promise to work with her to reinstate and modify her loan, she forwent the opportunity to save her home by converting a chapter 7 bankruptcy case to a chapter 13 case. Instead, U.S. Bank (D) foreclosed on the house without ever commencing negotiations toward a possible loan solution.

RULE OF LAW

A mortgagor in default states a claim of promissory estoppel where the mortgagor has, in reliance on the mortgagee's promise to reinstate and modify the mortgage, forgone the opportunity to save the mortgagor's home by converting a chapter 7 bankruptcy case to a chapter 13 case.

FACTS: Aceves (P) mortgaged her house with a lender, and the lender, in turn, transferred its entire interest under the mortgage to U.S. Bank, N.A. (U.S. Bank) (D). Aceves (P) became unable to pay the mortgage payments and shortly thereafter filed for bankruptcy protection under chapter 7 of the Bankruptcy Code, imposing an automatic stay on the foreclosure proceedings. Aceves (P) contacted U.S. Bank (D) and was told that, once her loan was out of bankruptcy, the bank "would work with her on a mortgage reinstatement and loan modification." She was asked to submit documents to U.S. Bank (D) for its consideration, which she did. Aceves (P) intended to convert her chapter 7 bankruptcy case to a chapter 13 case and to rely on the financial resources of her husband "to save her home" under chapter 13. In general, chapter 7 permits a debtor to discharge unpaid debts, but a debtor who discharges an unpaid home loan cannot keep the home. However, under chapter 13, a homeowner in default is permitted to reinstate the original loan payments, pay the arrearages over time, avoid foreclosure, and retain the home. U.S. Bank (D) filed a motion in the bankruptcy court to lift the stay so it could proceed with a nonjudicial foreclosure. When Aceves (P) approached the company servicing the loan about modifying the loan, she was told they could not speak to her before the motion to lift the bankruptcy stay had been granted. In reliance on U.S. Bank's (D) promise to work with her to reinstate and modify the loan, Aceves (P) did not oppose the motion to lift the bankruptcy stay and decided not to seek bankruptcy relief under chapter 13. The bankruptcy court lifted the stay, and, five days later, although neither U.S. Bank (D) nor the servicing company had contacted Aceves (P) to discuss the reinstatement and modification of the loan, U.S. Bank (D) scheduled Aceves's home for public auction a month later. A day later, Aceves (P) sent documents to the servicing company related to reinstating and modifying the loan. Around two weeks later, the servicing company informed Aceves (P) that a "negotiator" would contact her on or before a date that was four days after the scheduled auction of her house. Although the negotiator called, neither the servicing company nor U.S. Bank (D) ever worked with Aceves (P) to reinstate and modify her loan. The auction took place as scheduled, and U.S. Bank (D) bought the house. Two months later, U.S. Bank (D) served Aceves (P) with a three-day notice to vacate the premises and, a month later, filed an unlawful detainer action against her and her husband. Apparently, Aceves (P) and her husband vacated the premises during the eviction proceedings. Aceves (P) brought suit against U.S. Bank (D), claiming, inter alia, promissory estoppel and seeking to set aside the foreclosure sale of her house and to void the deed upon the sale of the home. The trial court entered judgment for U.S. Bank (D), and the state's intermediate appellate court granted review.

ISSUE: Does a mortgagor in default state a claim of promissory estoppel where the mortgagor has, in reliance on the mortgagee's promise to reinstate and modify the mortgage, forgone the opportunity to save the mortgagor's home by converting a chapter 7 bankruptcy case to a chapter 13 case?

HOLDING AND DECISION: (Mallano, P.J.) Yes. A mortgagor in default states a claim of promissory estoppel where the mortgagor has, in reliance on the mortgagee's promise to reinstate and modify the mortgage, forgone the opportunity to save the mortgagor's home by converting a chapter 7 bankruptcy case to a chapter 13 case. All the elements necessary to state a claim of promissory estoppel are present: (1) a promise clear and unambiguous in its terms; (2) reliance by the party to whom the promise is made; (3) the reliance must be both reasonable and foreseeable; and (4) the party asserting the estoppel must be injured by his or her reliance. As to the first element, U.S. Bank, N.A. (U.S. Bank) (D) agreed to work with Aceves (P) on a mortgage reinstatement and loan modification if she no longer pursued relief in the bankruptcy court. This

Continued on next page.

was a clear and unambiguous promise that indicated that U.S. Bank (D) would not foreclose on Aceves's (P) home without first engaging in negotiations with her to reinstate and modify the loan on mutually agreeable terms. U.S. Bank's (D) promise was to negotiate with Aceves (P), not necessarily to reach agreement on a reinstated loan. U.S. Bank (D) failed to fulfill its unambiguous promise by failing to negotiate. As to the second element, Aceves (P) relied on U.S. Bank's (D) promise by declining to convert her chapter 7 bankruptcy proceeding to a chapter 13 proceeding, and by not opposing U.S. Bank's (D) motion to lift the bankruptcy stay. As to the third element, Aceves (P) reasonably relied on U.S. Bank's (D) promise, as modification of her loan would have been more beneficial to her than pursuing chapter 13 bankruptcy protections. By promising to work with Aceves to *modify* the loan in addition to reinstating it, U.S. Bank (D) thus presented Aceves (P) with a compelling reason to opt for negotiations with the bank instead of seeking bankruptcy relief. Aceves's (P) reasonable reliance was thus also foreseeable and expected by U.S. Bank (D). As to the fourth element, Aceves (P) detrimentally relied on U.S. Bank's (D) promise because she gave up an opportunity to avoid foreclosure on her residence. Under chapter 13, a debtor gets to keep the residence only if he or she cures the default by making the payments required under the loan; the loan is reinstated, but not modified. Therefore, the mortgagee's interests are not diminished under chapter 13. Aceves (P) gave up various chapter 13 rights, including reinstating the loan to predefault conditions; obtaining a maximum of five years to make up the arrearages; and preventing U.S. Bank (D) from foreclosing on the property (by using her husband's resources). Accordingly, Aceves (P) has stated a claim for promissory estoppel. U.S. Bank (D) argues that an oral promise to postpone either a loan payment or a foreclosure is unenforceable. While this general principle is true, a written contract may be modified by oral agreement or promissory estoppel. Finally, a promissory estoppel claim generally entitles a plaintiff to the damages available on a breach of contract claim. Because Aceves (P) did not pay the funds needed to reinstate the loan before the foreclosure, promissory estoppel does not provide a basis for voiding the deed of sale or otherwise invalidating the foreclosure. Additionally, the elements of fraud are similar to the elements of promissory estoppel, with the additional requirements that a false promise is made and that the promisor knows of the falsity when making the promise. Aceves (P) has adequately pleaded the facts necessary to make out a claim of fraud. Reversed as to claims of promissory estoppel and fraud; affirmed as to all remaining claims. Affirmed in part and reversed in part.

ANALYSIS

In this case, the reliance element of promissory estoppel was strong, and the court ruled that Aceves's (P) reliance was both reasonable and foreseeable. Instances of reliance will be deemed neither foreseeable nor reasonable where a plaintiff's misguided belief or guileless action results in reliance on a statement on which no reasonable person would rely; the conduct of the plaintiff in light of his or her own intelligence and information is manifestly unreasonable; or where the plaintiff has a mere hopeful expectation. None of these instances can be equated with justifiable reliance, and no relief will be granted.

Quicknotes

CHAPTER 7 BANKRUPTCY A legal proceeding whereby a debtor, who is unable to pay his or her debts as they become due, is relieved of the obligation to pay creditors by liquidation and distribution of his or her remaining assets.

CHAPTER 13 BANKRUPTCY Debtor may modify plan at any time before the completion of the payments under such plan.

DETRIMENTAL RELIANCE Reliance by one party that is based on the conduct of another, resulting in loss to the party.

EVICTION The removal of a person from possession of property.

FORBEARANCE The act of refraining from doing something that one has the legal right to do.

INTER ALIA Among other things.

PROMISE The expression of an intention to act, or to forbear from acting, granting a right to the promisee to expect and enforce its performance.

PROMISEE The party to whom a promise is made.

PROMISOR The party who promises to render an obligation to another in the future.

PROMISSORY ESTOPPEL A promise that is enforceable if the promisor should reasonably expect that it will induce action or forbearance on the part of the promisee, does in fact cause such action or forbearance, and is the only means of avoiding injustice.

Berryman v. Kmoch

Owner of land (D) v. Real estate agent (P)

Kan. Sup. Ct., 221 Kan. 304, 559 P.2d 790 (1977)

NATURE OF CASE: Appeal from summary judgment denying the validity of an option contract.

FACT SUMMARY: Kmoch (P) claimed his expenditures of time and money in attempting to attract buyers constituted consideration to support the enforceability of an option on Berryman's (D) land.

RULE OF LAW

An agreement that lacks consideration may be enforceable based on promissory estoppel when (1) the promisor reasonably expected the promisee to rely on the promise; (2) the promisee reasonably relied on the promise; and (3) a failure to enforce the promise would result in perpetuation of fraud or result in other injustice.

FACTS: Berryman (D) entered into an agreement giving Kmoch (P), a real estate agent who wrote the agreement, option to purchase his land, yet the recited consideration was never paid. Berryman (D) expressed to Kmoch (P) his desire to be released from the agreement and sold the property to a third party. Subsequently, Kmoch (P) sought to exercise the option, and Berryman (D) sued to have the option declared void for lack of consideration. Kmoch (P) contended his expenditures of time and money in attempting to find a buyer for the land constituted detrimental reliance and the failure to enforce the promise will perpetuate fraud or result in other injustice on the agreement rendering it enforceable without consideration based on promissory estoppel. The trial court entered summary judgment for Berryman (D), and Kmoch (P) appealed.

ISSUE: May an agreement that lacks consideration be enforceable based on promissory estoppel when (1) the promisor reasonably expected the promisee to rely on the promise; (2) the promisee does in fact act in reliance on the promise; and (3) the failure to enforce the promise will perpetuate fraud or result in other injustice?

HOLDING AND DECISION: (Fromme, J.) Yes. An agreement that lacks consideration may be enforceable based on promissory estoppel when (1) the promisor reasonably expected the promisee to rely on the promise; (2) the promisee reasonably relied on the promise; and (3) a failure to enforce the promise would result in perpetuation of fraud or result in other injustice. In this case, Kmoch (P) was a real estate agent and personally wrote the agreement. Therefore, he knew it was not a contract to sell, and he knew that unless the consideration was paid the agreement was merely a continuing offer subject to revocation at any time prior to acceptance. Therefore, he did not reasonably rely on the agreement as a contract to purchase the land in expending the time and money to attract buyers. Accordingly, promissory estoppel cannot be applied to enforce the option. The agreement was merely a revocable offer that was revoked by Berryman's (D) expressed desire to do so occurring prior to Kmoch's (P) acceptance. Affirmed.

ANALYSIS

The primary distinction between promises supported by promissory estoppel and those supported by consideration is that consideration is bargained for while promissory estoppel is not. The detriment suffered as a consequence of the promise does not induce the promise. Courts generally will analyze a contract for the presence of consideration, and only in its absence will the elements of promissory estoppel be determined. Some jurisdictions limit the applicability of promissory estoppel to certain types of fact patterns such as promises to make a gift of land, or charitable subscriptions. However, the modern view extends the doctrine to any case meeting the requirements of promissory estoppel.

Quicknotes

CONSIDERATION Value given by one party in exchange for performance, or a promise to perform, by another party.

FORBEARANCE The act of refraining from doing something that one has the legal right to do.

PROMISE The expression of an intention to act, or to forbear from acting, granting a right to the promisee to expect and enforce its performance.

PROMISEE The party to whom a promise is made.

PROMISOR The party who promises to render an obligation to another in the future.

PROMISSORY ESTOPPEL A promise that is enforceable if the promisor should reasonably expect that it will induce action or forbearance on the part of the promisee, does in fact cause such action or forbearance, and is the only means of avoiding injustice.

RELIANCE Dependence on a fact that causes a party to act or refrain from acting.

James Baird Co. v. Gimbel Bros., Inc.

Contractor (P) v. Linoleum supplier (D)

64 F.2d 344 (2d Cir. 1933)

NATURE OF CASE: Appeal from judgment for defendant in action for breach of a contract for the sale of goods.

FACT SUMMARY: Gimbel Bros., Inc. (Gimbel) (D) offered to supply linoleum to various contractors who were bidding on a public construction contract. James Baird Co. (Baird) (P), relying on Gimbel's (D) quoted prices, submitted a bid and later the same day received a telegraphed message from Gimbel (D) that its quoted prices were in error. Baird's (P) bid was accepted.

RULE OF LAW

(1) Where an offer is withdrawn before it is accepted, and the offer language does not indicate a contrary intention, a contract is not formed.

(2) The doctrine of promissory estoppel is not applicable where an offer is made for an exchanged act or promise, and no consideration has been received by the offeror.

FACTS: Gimbel Bros., Inc. (Gimbel) (D), having heard that bids were being taken for a public building, had an employee obtain the specifications for linoleum required for the building and submitted offers to various possible contractors, including James Baird Co. (Baird) (P), of two prices for linoleum depending upon the quality used. The offer was made in ignorance of a mistake as to the actual amount of linoleum needed, causing Gimbel's (D) prices to be about half the actual cost. The offer concluded as follows: "If successful in being awarded this contract, it will be absolutely guaranteed . . . and . . . we are offering these prices for reasonable [sic] prompt acceptance after the general contract has been awarded." Baird (P) received this on the 28th, the same day on which Gimbel (D) discovered its mistake, and telegraphed all contractors of the error, but the communication was received by Baird (P) just after Baird (P) submitted its lump sum bid relying on Gimbel's (D) erroneous prices. Baird's (P) bid was accepted on the 30th. Baird (P) received Gimbel's (D) written confirmation of the error on the 31st but sent an acceptance despite this, two days later. Gimbel (D) refused to recognize a contract.

ISSUE:

(1) Where an offer is withdrawn before it is accepted, and the offer language does not indicate a contrary intention, is a contract formed?

(2) Is the doctrine of promissory estoppel applicable where an offer is made for an exchanged act or promise, and no consideration has been received by the offeror?

HOLDING AND DECISION: (Hand, J.)

(1) No. Where an offer is withdrawn before it is accepted, and the offer language does not indicate a contrary intention, a contract is not formed. First, looking at the language of Gimbel Bros., Inc.'s (Gimbel) (D) offer, Gimbel's (D) use of the phrase "if successful in being awarded this contract" clearly shows Gimbel's (D) intent of not being bound simply by a contractor relying or acting upon the quoted prices. This is reinforced by the phrase "prompt acceptance after the general contract has been awarded." No award had been made at the time and reliance on the prices cannot be said to be an award of the contract. If a relying contractor had been awarded the contract and then repudiated it, Gimbel (D) would not have had any right to sue for breach, nor, had the relying contractor gone bankrupt, could Gimbel (D) have gone against his bankruptcy estate. The contractors could have protected themselves by insisting on a contract guaranteeing the prices before relying upon them. However, the court will not strain to find a contract in aid of one who fails to protect himself. Thus, based on the offer language, no bilateral contract was formed.

(2) No. The doctrine of promissory estoppel is not applicable where an offer is made for an exchanged act or promise, and no consideration has been received by the offeror. The theory of promissory estoppel is not available here. Ordinarily, it is appropriate in donative or charitable cases where harsh results to the promisee arising from the promisor's breaking his or her relied-upon promise are to be protected against. However, an offer for an exchange, either being an act or another promise, is not meant to become a promise until a consideration is received. Here, the linoleum was to be delivered for the contractor's acceptance, not his bid. Moreover, the offer could not be considered an option, giving James Baird Co. (Baird) (P) the right to accept the offer if its bid was accepted, but not binding it to do so if it could get a better price elsewhere. There was nothing in the offer language indicating that Gimbel (D) intended to be bound by such a one-sided deal. If it had so bound itself, promissory estoppel might

Continued on next page.

have been applicable, since in such an instance, Baird (P) could have claimed reliance on Gimbel's (D) offer. Affirmed.

ANALYSIS

Later cases have held the doctrine of promissory estoppel not to be as narrow. A majority of courts that have considered the issue hold that justifiable detrimental reliance on an offer renders it irrevocable. Naturally, the contractor must have something upon which to justifiably rely. The court in its decision notes that Restatement (Second) § 90 follows its view. However, Restatement (Second) § 90 has expanded the section so to enlarge its scope according to the more modern viewpoint. It must be shown that the offeror foresaw that his or her promise would reasonably induce forbearance or action. The first inkling of this doctrine probably arose in the well-known *Hamer v. Sidway*, 27 N.E. 256 (1891), where an uncle promised to pay his nephew $5,000 for refraining from the use of liquor, swearing, and other activities until his 21st birthday, and reached full maturity in J. Traynor's decision in *Drennan v. Star Paving Company*, 51 Cal. 2d 409, 333 P.2d 757 (1958). Generally, this case is a good example of the manner in which the court will examine the words and actions of the parties in order to determine their intent and, hence, the existence of a contract. It appears that Gimbel Bros., Inc. (D) could have used the defense of unilateral mistake based upon a clerical error as seen in *M.F. Kemper Construction Co. v. City of Los Angeles*, 235 P.2d 7 (1951).

Quicknotes

DETRIMENTAL RELIANCE Reliance by one party that is based on the conduct or promises of another, resulting in loss to the party.

FORBEARANCE The act of refraining from doing something that one has the legal right to do.

IRREVOCABLE OFFER An offer that may not be retracted by the promisor without the assent of the offeree.

PROMISE The expression of an intention to act, or to forbear from acting, granting a right to the promisee to expect and enforce its performance.

PROMISEE The party to whom a promise is made.

PROMISOR The party who promises to render an obligation to another in the future.

PROMISSORY ESTOPPEL A promise that is enforceable if the promisor should reasonably expect that it will induce action or forbearance on the part of the promisee, does in fact cause such action or forbearance, and is the only means of avoiding injustice.

UNILATERAL MISTAKE A mistake or misunderstanding as to the terms of a contract made by one party; it is generally not a basis for relief by rescission or reformation.

Drennan v. Star Paving Co.

General contractor (P) v. Subcontractor (D)

Cal. Sup. Ct., 51 Cal. 2d 409, 333 P.2d 757 (1958)

NATURE OF CASE: Appeal of an award of damages for breach of contract.

FACT SUMMARY: Drennan (P) sued Star Paving Co. (Star) (D) to recover damages when Star (D) could not perform the paving work at the price quoted in its subcontracting bid.

RULE OF LAW

Reasonable reliance on a promise binds an offeror even if there is no other consideration.

FACTS: In formulating a bid to the Lancaster School District, Drennan (P), a general contractor, solicited bids for subcontracting work. Star Paving Co. (Star) (P) submitted the lowest paving bid, and Drennan (P) used that bid in formulating its bid to the school district. Using Star's (D) subcontracting bid of $7,131.60, Drennan (P) was awarded the general contract. Star (D) then told Drennan (P) that it made a mistake and could not do the work for less than $15,000. Star (D) refused to do the work, and Drennan (P) found a substitute company that did the work for $10,948.60. Drennan (P) sued Star (D) for the difference, claiming that Drennan (P) had reasonably relied on Star's (D) offer. Star (D) claimed that it had made a revocable offer. The trial court ruled in favor of Drennan (P) on the grounds of promissory estoppel, and Star (D) appealed.

ISSUE: Does reasonable reliance on a promise bind the offeror if there no other consideration?

HOLDING AND DECISION: (Traynor, J.) Yes. Reasonable reliance on a promise binds the offeror even if there is no other consideration. Section 90 of the Restatement of Contracts provides that when a promise is made that induces action or forbearance of the promisee, the promissor is bound if injustice would result from nonenforcement. In the case of a unilateral offer, the offeror is bound to the promise if it produces reasonable reliance. Star Paving Co. (Star) (D) made a promise to Drennan (P) of a certain price. Star's (D) bid was the lowest, and Drennan (P) reasonably relied on it in formulating its bid and winning the contract. As a result, Drennan (P) was obligated to do the work at the price quoted and even had to put up a bond. Star (D) should have known such a result would occur if Star's (D) bid was accepted. The absence of consideration is not fatal to Star's (D) initial promise, as Drennan (P) substantially changed its position in reliance on Star (D). Injustice can be avoided only by the enforcement of Star's (D) subcontracting promise. Affirmed.

ANALYSIS

Such reasonable reliance cases are often called firm offers. Firm offers can sometimes be implied promises to hold an offer open and have received criticism on the grounds that one party (the subcontractor) is bound while the other party (the general contractor) is not. Nonetheless, the modern trend is to enforce such promises.

Quicknotes

CONSIDERATION Value given by one party in exchange for performance, or a promise to perform, by another party.

FIRM OFFER Under the Uniform Commercial Code, a signed, written offer to enter into a contract for the sale of goods that is irrevocable for a specified period of time, or if no time is stated, then for a reasonable time period not exceeding three months.

FORBEARANCE The act of refraining from doing something that one has the legal right to do.

PROMISE The expression of an intention to act, or to forbear from acting, granting a right to the promisee to expect and enforce its performance.

PROMISEE The party to whom a promise is made.

PROMISOR The party who promises to render an obligation to another in the future.

PROMISSORY ESTOPPEL A promise that is enforceable if the promisor should reasonably expect that it will induce action or forbearance on the part of the promisee, does in fact cause such action or forbearance, and is the only means of avoiding injustice.

RELIANCE Dependence on a fact that causes a party to act or refrain from acting.

REVOCABLE OFFER An offer that may be retracted by the promisor without the assent of the offeree.

Pop's Cones, Inc. v. Resorts International Hotel, Inc.

Franchisee (P) v. Lessor (D)

N.J. Super. Ct., App. Div., 307 N.J. Super. 461, 704 A.2d 1321 (1998)

NATURE OF CASE: Appeal from summary judgment for defendant in a suit seeking damages based on a theory of promissory estoppel.

FACT SUMMARY: Pop's Cones, Inc. (P), a TCBY franchisee operating in Margate, after discussions with Resorts International Hotel, Inc. (Resorts) (D) on the possibility of leasing space in its hotel, relied on Resorts' (D) assurances that the deal would be approved, and did not renew its lease on its Margate location.

RULE OF LAW

A promise that the promisor should reasonably expect to induce action or forbearance on the part of the promisee or a third person, and that does induce such action or forbearance, is binding if injustice can be avoided only by enforcement of the promise.

FACTS: Pop's Cones, Inc. (Pop's) (P), a vendor of frozen yogurt products, negotiated with Resorts International Hotels, Inc. (Resorts) (D) to lease a location in its resort hotel. Relying on (D) advice and assurances from Resorts (D) that an agreement had been reached, Pop's (P) ended its lease at its other location, placed its equipment in temporary storage, and retained an attorney to finalize the terms of the lease. When Resorts (D) later withdrew its offer, Pop's (P) could not return to its former location, which had been relet, and incurred further expenses until it found another suitable location one year later. Pop's (P) sued Resorts (D) for damages resulting from its detrimental reliance upon promises made during the contract negotiations. When the motion for summary judgment filed by Resorts (D) was granted, Pop's (P) appealed.

ISSUE: Is a promise that the promisor should reasonably expect to induce action or forbearance on the part of the promisee or a third person, and that does induce such action or forbearance, binding if injustice can be avoided only by enforcement of the promise?

HOLDING AND DECISION: (Kleiner, J.) Yes. A promise that the promisor should reasonably expect to induce action or forbearance on the part of the promisee or a third person, and that does induce such action or forbearance, is binding if injustice can be avoided only by enforcement of the promise. Recent cases relaxing the strict requirement of a "clear and definite promise" in making a prima facie case of promissory estoppel are persuasive. Whether Pop's Cones, Inc. (Pop's) (P) reliance upon the assurances from Resorts International Hotels, Inc. (D) was reasonable is a question for the jury. Since Pop's (P) is not seeking enforcement of the lease, nor speculative lost profits, but merely its out-of-pocket expenses, its complaint should not have been summarily dismissed. Reversed and remanded.

ANALYSIS

The court in this case overruled earlier New Jersey cases requiring a "clear and definite promise" for a promissory estoppel action. Since the contract itself was not involved, and Pop's Cones, Inc. (P) requested damages resulting only from its detrimental reliance on promises made, despite the ultimate failure of the contract negotiations, the court followed the Restatement (Second) of Contracts § 90 approach. Under this approach, a more equitable analysis designed to avoid injustice has eroded the earlier stricter adherence to proof of a clear and definite promise.

Quicknotes

DETRIMENTAL RELIANCE Reliance by one party that is based on the conduct or promises of another, resulting in loss to the party.

EQUITABLE Just; fair.

FORBEARANCE The act of refraining from doing something that one has the legal right to do.

PROMISE The expression of an intention to act, or to forbear from acting, granting a right to the promisee to expect and enforce its performance.

PROMISEE The party to whom a promise is made.

PROMISOR The party who promises to render an obligation to another in the future.

PROMISSORY ESTOPPEL A promise that is enforceable if the promisor should reasonably expect that it will induce action or forbearance on the part of the promisee, does in fact cause such action or forbearance, and is the only means of avoiding injustice.

SUMMARY JUDGMENT Judgment rendered by a court in response to a motion made by one of the parties, claiming that the lack of a question of material fact in respect to an issue warrants disposition of the issue without consideration by the jury.

Credit Bureau Enterprises, Inc. v. Pelo

Credit bureau (P) v. Debtor (D)

Iowa Sup. Ct., 608 N.W.2d 20 (2000) (en banc)

NATURE OF CASE: Appeal by debtor from judgment taken against him by creditor.

FACT SUMMARY: In the early morning of January 8, 1995, Russell Pelo (D) argued with his wife, left the home, and checked into a motel. Pelo (D) then called his wife and threatened to buy a gun and harm himself. Pelo (D) was later taken to a private hospital by the police. At the hospital Pelo (D) was asked, but refused, to sign a payment release form, although later, under duress, he signed the form. The hospital sought payment for the services provided to Pelo (D) during his stay, but Pelo (D) refused to pay.

RULE OF LAW

Requiring a patient who was involuntarily committed to a private hospital to pay for medical services the patient received does not violate the patient's right to due process or the constitutional right to contract.

FACTS: Russell Pelo (D) left his marital residence after having an argument with his wife and checked into a motel. Pelo (D) telephoned his wife "making threats of self harm" and purchased a shotgun. Pelo (D) was subsequently taken to a hospital by the police. Pursuant to statutory emergency hospitalization procedures, a magistrate found probable cause that Pelo (D) was seriously mentally impaired and likely to physically injure himself. The magistrate thus entered an emergency hospitalization order requiring that Pelo (D) be detained in custody at the hospital's psychiatric unit for examination and care. The hospitalization referee found that Pelo (D) suffered from bipolar disorder, an illness from which Pelo (D) had suffered for many years. In addition, the referee concluded that although Pelo (D) needed and would benefit from treatment for his serious mental illness, the required elements for involuntary hospitalization were lacking and that further involuntary hospitalization was not authorized. Pelo (D) was released from the hospital and court jurisdiction. Subsequently, the hospital sought compensation from Pelo in the amount of $2,775.79 for the medical services provided to him. Pelo (D) refused to pay the bill or authorize his health insurance carrier to do so. The hospital later assigned its claim to Credit Bureau Enterprises, Inc. (Credit Bureau) (D) for collection. Credit Bureau (P) sued Pelo (D) in district court, winning a judgment on the hospital bill, and Pelo (D) appealed.

ISSUE: Does requiring a patient who was involuntarily committed to a private hospital to pay for medical services the patient received violate the patient's right to due process or the constitutional right to contract?

HOLDING AND DECISION: (McGiverin, C.J.) No. Requiring a patient who was involuntarily committed to a private hospital to pay for medical services the patient received does not violate the patient's right to due process or the constitutional right to contract. Historically, quasi-contracts were not true contracts and, therefore, constitutional provisions concerning the right to contract did not apply. Here, Pelo (D) did not assert that the emergency hospitalization or involuntary commitment proceedings were constitutionally invalid, and preliminary factual findings of the magistrate and hospitalization referee found that Pelo (D) was, in fact, seriously mentally impaired so as to warrant the hospitalization. Pelo (D) was involuntarily committed to the private hospital based upon his threats of self-harm made to his wife and his purchase of a shotgun. Pelo (D) was liable for the payment of the hospital bill under the theory of contract implied in law, or quasi-contract, since the hospitalization was of medical benefit to him, and such services were provided by the hospital in good faith and not gratuitously. Pelo (D) did not challenge the factual basis for his hospitalization, nor was it likely that such a challenge would have been successful given the fact that the necessary probable cause findings concerning emergency hospitalization by the magistrate and involuntary commitment procedures by the hospitalization referee were made. These fact-finding requirements were in place to guarantee a patient's liberty and due process interests when the state exercises its authority through emergency hospitalization and involuntary commitment proceedings. Pelo (D) also did not challenge the hospitalization referee's finding that he suffered from bipolar disorder, nor did he challenge the district court's finding that $2,775.79 was the reasonable cost of services provided to him during his hospitalization. Affirmed.

ANALYSIS

As noted in the *Credit Bureau* decision, the Restatement of Restitution § 2 states that a person who officiously confers a benefit upon another is not entitled to restitution. Under this rule, recovery is denied so that one will not have to pay for a benefit forced upon one against one's will, or for which one did not request or knowingly accept. "Officiousness," as here used, means

Continued on next page.

interference in the affairs of others not justified by the circumstances under which the interference takes place. Restatement of Restitution § 2 cmt. a. In certain circumstances, however, restitution for services performed will be required even though the recipient did not request or voluntarily consent to receive such services. For example, § 116 of the Restatement of Restitution provides that a person who has supplied things or services to another, although acting without the other's knowledge or consent, is entitled to restitution from the other if (a) he or she acted unofficiously and with intent to charge therefor, and (b) the things or services were necessary to prevent the other from suffering serious bodily harm or pain, and (c) the person supplying them had no reason to know that the other would not consent to receiving them, if mentally competent, and (d) it was impossible for the other to give consent or, because of extreme youth or mental impairment, the other's consent would have been immaterial.

Quicknotes

RESTITUTION The return or restoration of some thing to its rightful owner to prevent unjust enrichment.

RIGHT TO CONTRACT Article 4 § 10 of the U.S. Constitution guarantees the right to contract and prohibits a state from passing any law that impairs this right, or impairs the obligations tendered by contractual agreement.

Commerce Partnership 8098 Limited Partnership v. Equity Contracting Co.

Property owner (D) v. Subcontractor (P)

Fla. Dist. Ct. App., 695 So. 2d 383 (1997) (en banc)

NATURE OF CASE: Appeal from judgment for plaintiff in a construction contract claim.

FACT SUMMARY: Equity Contracting Co. (P), a subcontractor on a construction job who was not paid by the general contractor, alleged that Commerce Partnership 8098 Limited Partnership (D) had been unjustly enriched and sought payment for the work it had performed.

RULE OF LAW

Where an owner has given consideration for the subcontractor's work by paying out the contract price for the work, an unpaid subcontractor's claim that the owner has been unjustly enriched must fail.

FACTS: Commerce Partnership 8098 Limited Partnership (Commerce) (D) contracted with a general contractor to perform improvements on its office building. Equity Contracting Co. (Equity) (P) was the stucco and surfacing subcontractor for the job, and completely performed its work. The general contractor did not pay Equity (P) for the work it had performed, and later filed for bankruptcy. Equity (P) then sued Commerce (D), alleging unjust enrichment. In an answer, Commerce (D) asserted that it had paid the general contractor in full. The trial court entered judgment in favor of Equity (P), and Commerce (D) appealed.

ISSUE: Where an owner has given consideration for the subcontractor's work by paying out the contract price for the work, must an unpaid subcontractor's claim that the owner has been unjustly enriched fail?

HOLDING AND DECISION: (Gross, J.) Yes. Where an owner has given consideration for the subcontractor's work by paying out the contract price for the work, an unpaid subcontractor's claim that the owner has been unjustly enriched must fail. A subcontractor's quasi-contract action against an owner must prove two elements to establish that the enrichment of the owner was unjust. The subcontractor must have exhausted all remedies against the general contractor and still remain unpaid, and the owner must not have given consideration to any person for the improvements furnished by the subcontractor. An unjust enrichment cannot exist where payment has been made for the benefit conferred. In this case, Equity Contracting Co. (Equity) (P) did not prove at trial that Commerce Partnership 8098 Limited Partnership (Commerce) (D) had not made payment to any party for the benefits conferred on the property by Equity (P). On remand, Equity (P) will bear the burden of proving that Commerce (D) did not pay the general contractor. Reversed and remanded.

ANALYSIS

Though valid, the holding in this case has been rejected by many other courts. Proof of unjust enrichment is necessary for recovery in restitution. Unjust enrichment is an equitable concept.

Quicknotes

MECHANICS' LIEN A lien enforceable pursuant to statute in structures and/or improvements constructed in order to secure payment for the value of labor performed or materials furnished.

RESTITUTION The return or restoration of some thing to its rightful owner to prevent the unjust enrichment.

UNJUST ENRICHMENT The principle of retaining a benefit given to one by another, without compensating the giver, in situations where compensation is reasonably expected.

Watts v. Watts

Cohabitant (P) v. Cohabitant (D)

Wis. Sup. Ct., 137 Wis. 2d 506, 405 N.W.2d 303 (1987)

NATURE OF CASE: Appeal from dismissal of action for unjust enrichment.

FACT SUMMARY: Sue Anne Watts (P), upon the termination of her nonmarital cohabitation with James Watts (D), sought an order for an accounting of the personal and business assets accumulated during the parties' cohabitation and a determination of her share of that property.

RULE OF LAW

Unmarried cohabitants may raise claims based upon unjust enrichment following the termination of their relationships where one of the parties attempts to retain an unreasonable amount of the property acquired through the efforts of both.

FACTS: Sue Anne Evans Watts (P) and James Watts (D) accumulated property during their nonmarital cohabitation relationship, which lasted 12 years and produced two children. She was 19 when they met, living with her parents, and working full time as a nurse's aide in preparation for a nursing career. Shortly after they met, he persuaded her to quit her job and move into an apartment paid for by him. During their relationship, she contributed child-care and homemaking services. Additionally, she contributed personal property to the relationship; worked in his office as a receptionist, typist, and assistant bookkeeper; and started a business from which he barred her after she moved out of their home. Sue Anne (P) sought an accounting of the personal and business assets accumulated during the cohabitation and to determine her share of those assets. Her claim was based on five theories, one of which was unjust enrichment. The trial court dismissed the action for failure to state a claim on which relief may be granted, and this appeal followed.

ISSUE: May unmarried cohabitants raise claims based upon unjust enrichment following the termination of their relationships where one of the parties attempts to retain an unreasonable amount of the property acquired through the efforts of both?

HOLDING AND DECISION: (Abrahamson, J.) Yes. Unmarried cohabitants may raise claims based upon unjust enrichment following the termination of their relationships where one of the parties attempts to retain an unreasonable amount of the property acquired through the efforts of both. A claim of unjust enrichment does not arise out of an agreement entered by the parties but is grounded on the moral principle that one who has received a benefit has a duty to make restitution where retaining such a benefit would be unjust. An action for unjust enrichment is based upon proof of three elements: (1) a benefit conferred on the defendant by the plaintiff, (2) appreciation or knowledge by the defendant of the benefit, and (3) acceptance or retention of the benefit by the defendant under circumstances making it inequitable for the defendant to retain the benefit. The facts alleged are sufficient to state a claim based upon unjust enrichment. Reversed and remanded.

ANALYSIS

The court noted that because no express or implied-in-fact agreement usually exists between the parties in cohabitation termination cases, recovery based upon unjust enrichment is sometimes referred to as "quasi-contract" (or "implied-in-law contract") rather than "implied in fact contract." Quasi-contracts are obligations created by law to prevent injustice. Many courts have recognized that when a court refuses to enforce contract and property rights between unmarried cohabitants, the result is that one party keeps all or most of the assets accumulated during the relationship, while the other party is deprived of property that he or she helped to accumulate. Such a result is contrary to the principles of equity.

Quicknotes

QUASI-CONTRACT An implied contract created by law to prevent unjust enrichment.

RESTITUTION The return or restoration of some thing to its rightful owner to prevent unjust enrichment.

UNJUST ENRICHMENT The principle of retaining a benefit given to one by another, without compensating the giver, in situations where compensation is reasonably expected.

Mills v. Wyman

Nurse-caretaker (P) v. Parent (D)

Mass. Sup. Jud. Ct., 20 Mass. (3 Pick.) 207 (1825)

NATURE OF CASE: Action on appeal to recover upon alleged promise.

FACT SUMMARY: Mills (P) took care of Wyman's (D) son without being requested to do so and for so doing was promised compensation for expenses arising out of the rendered care by Wyman (D). Wyman (D) later refused to compensate Mills (P).

RULE OF LAW

A moral obligation is insufficient as consideration for a promise.

FACTS: Mills (P) nursed and cared for Levi Wyman, the son of Wyman (D). Upon learning of Mills's (P) acts of kindness toward his son, Wyman (D) promised to repay Mills (P) his expenses incurred in caring for Levi Wyman. Later, Wyman (D) refused to compensate Mills (P) for his expenses. Mills (P) filed an action in the court of common pleas, where Wyman (D) was successful in obtaining a nonsuit against Mills (P). Mills (P) appealed.

ISSUE: Is a moral obligation sufficient consideration for a promise?

HOLDING AND DECISION: (Parker, C.J.) No. It is said a moral obligation is sufficient consideration to support an express promise. However, the universality of the rule cannot be supported. Therefore, there must be some other preexisting obligation that will suffice as consideration. Affirmed.

ANALYSIS

In cases such as this one, the nearly universal holding is that the existing moral obligation is not a sufficient basis for the enforcement of an express promise to render the performance that it requires. The general statement is that it is not sufficient consideration for the express promise. The difficulties and differences of opinion involved in the determination of what is a moral obligation are probably much greater than those involved in determining the existence of a legal obligation. This tends to explain the attitude of the majority of courts on the subject and justifies the generally stated rule.

Quicknotes

CONSIDERATION Value given by one party in exchange for performance, or a promise to perform, by another party.

EXPRESS PROMISE The expression of an intention to act, or to forbear from acting, granting a right to the promisee to expect and enforce its performance.

Webb v. McGowin

Good Samaritan (P) v. Estate (D)

Ala. Ct. App., 27 Ala. App. 82, 168 So. 196 (1935), *cert. denied*, 232 Ala. 374, 168 So. 199 (1936)

NATURE OF CASE: Action on appeal to collect on a promise.

FACT SUMMARY: Webb (P) saved the now deceased J. McGowin from grave bodily injury or death by placing himself in grave danger and subsequently suffering grave bodily harm. J. McGowin, in return, promised Webb (P) compensation. McGowin's executors (D) now refuse to pay the promised compensation.

RULE OF LAW

A moral obligation is a sufficient consideration to support a subsequent promise to pay where the promisor has received a material benefit.

FACTS: Webb (P), while in the scope of his duties for the W.T. Smith Lumber Co., was clearing the floor, which required him to drop a 75-lb. pine block from the upper floor of the mill to the ground. Just as Webb (P) was releasing the block, he noticed J. McGowin below and directly under where the block would have fallen. In order to divert the fall of the block, Webb (P) fell with it, breaking an arm and leg and ripping his heel off. The fall left Webb (P) badly crippled and incapable of either mental or physical labor. In return for Webb's (P) act, J. McGowin promised to pay Webb (P) $15 every two weeks for the rest of Webb's (P) life. J. McGowin paid the promised payments until his death eight years later. Shortly after J. McGowin's death, the payments were stopped, and Webb (P) brought an action against N. McGowin (D) and J.F. McGowin (D) as executors of J. McGowin's estate for payments due him. The executors (D) of the estate were successful in obtaining a nonsuit against Webb (P) in the lower court. Webb (P) appealed.

ISSUE: Is a moral obligation a sufficient consideration to support a subsequent promise to pay where the promisor has received a material benefit?

HOLDING AND DECISION: (Bricken, P.J.) Yes. It is well settled that a moral obligation is a sufficient consideration to support a subsequent promise to pay where the promisor has received a material benefit. However, there was no original duty or liability resting on the promisor. Reversed and remanded.

CONCURRENCE: (Samford, J.) The strict letter of the rule as stated by the judges would perhaps bar the plaintiff from recovery. As Chief Justice Marshall stated in *Hoffman v. Porter*, 2 Brock. 156, 159, however, "... [the] law ought [not] to be separated from justice, where it is most doubtful."

ANALYSIS

In most cases where the moral obligation is asserted, the court feels the promise ought not be enforced; instead of going into the uncertain field of morality, the court chooses to rely upon the rule that moral obligation is not sufficient consideration. On the other hand, in cases where the promise is one that would have been kept by most citizens and the court feels enforcement is just, a few courts will enforce the promise using the *Webb v. McGowin* rule. In general, the *Webb v. McGowin* rule is the minority rule and the *Mills v. Wyman* rule, Mass. Sup. Jud. Ct., 20 Mass. (3 Pick.) 207 (1825), is the majority rule.

Quicknotes

MATERIAL BENEFIT An advantage gained by entering into a contract that is essential to the performance of the agreement and without which the contract would not have been entered into.

MORAL OBLIGATION A duty not enforceable at law, but is consistent with ethical notions of justice.

CHAPTER 4

The Statute of Frauds

Quick Reference Rules of Law

Crabtree v. Elizabeth Arden Sales Corp.

Sales manager (P) v. Cosmetics company (D)

N.Y. Ct. App., 305 N.Y. 48, 110 N.E.2d 551 (1953)

NATURE OF CASE: Appeal from affirmance of judgment for plaintiff in action for damages for breach of an employment contract.

FACT SUMMARY: Crabtree (P) was hired by Elizabeth Arden Sales Corp. (D) to be the latter's sales manager. No formal contract was signed but separate writings pieced together showed Crabtree to have been hired for a two-year term with pay raises after the first and second six months. When he did not receive his second pay raise, Crabtree (P) sued for damages for breach.

RULE OF LAW

Separate writings, connected as to subject matter and occasion, may be pieced together to find an enforceable contract under the statute of frauds.

FACTS: In September 1947, Crabtree (P) began negotiating with Elizabeth Arden Sales Corp. (Arden) (D) for the position of the latter's sales manager. Being unfamiliar with the cosmetics business and giving up a well-paying, secure job, Crabtree (P) insisted upon an agreement for a definite term. He asked for three years at $25,000 per year. But Arden (D) offered two years, with $20,000 per year the first six months, $25,000 per year the second six months, and $30,000 per year the second year. This was written down by Arden's (D) personal secretary with the notation "2 years to make good." A few days later, Crabtree (P) telephoned Mr. Johns, Arden's (D) executive vice-president, his acceptance. Crabtree (P) received a "welcome" wire from Miss Arden (D). When he reported for work, a "payroll change" card was made up and initialed by Mr. Johns showing the above pay arrangement with a salary increase noted "as per contractual agreement." Crabtree (P) received his first pay raise as scheduled, but not his second one. Miss Arden (D) allegedly refused to approve the second increase, denying Crabtree (P) had been hired for any specific period.

ISSUE: May separate writings, connected as to subject matter and occasion, be pieced together to find an enforceable contract under the statute of frauds?

HOLDING AND DECISION: (Fuld, J.) Yes. Separate writings, connected as to subject matter and occasion, may be pieced together to find an enforceable contract under the statute of frauds. First, as it is alleged that the contract is for a period of two years, there must be written evidence of its terms to be enforceable as the two-year performance places it within the statute of frauds. The payroll cards, one initialed by Elizabeth Arden Sales Corp.'s (Arden) (D) executive vice-president and the other by its comptroller, unquestionably constituted a memorandum under the statute. It is enough they were signed with the intent to authenticate the information contained therein and such information does evidence the terms of the contract. The cards had all essential terms except for duration. But as the memorandum can be pieced together from more than one document, all that is required between the papers is a connection established simply by reference to the same subject matter or transaction. Parol evidence is permissible in order to establish the connection. As the note prepared by Arden's (D) personal secretary shows, it was made in Miss Arden's (D) presence as well as that of Johns and of Crabtree (P), the dangers of parol evidence are at a minimum. All the terms must be set out in writing and cannot be shown by parol. That memo, the paper signed by Johns, and the paper signed by the comptroller all refer on their face to the Crabtree (P) transaction. The comptroller's paper shows that it was prepared for the purpose of a "salary increase per contractual arrangements with Miss Arden" (D). That is, a reference to more comprehensive evidence and parol evidence can so explain. "2 years to make good" probably had no other purpose than to denote the duration of the arrangement and parol evidence may explain its meaning. Affirmed.

ANALYSIS

When there is more than one writing and all are signed by the party to be charged, and it is clear by their contents that they relate to the same transaction, there is little problem. When not all the documents are signed, difficulties obviously crop up. It becomes difficult to say the memorandum has been authenticated to the party to be charged. When the unsigned document is physically attached to the signed writing, the statute of frauds is satisfied. And, as illustrated by this case, this is true when the signed document by its terms expressly refers to the unsigned document. The cases conflict where the papers are not attached or fail to refer to the other. The minority holds that that is a failure to show sufficient authentication. The better view is that if the signed document does not expressly refer to the unsigned, it is sufficient if internal evidence refers to the same subject matter or transaction. If so, extrinsic evidence is admissible to help show the connection between the documents.

Continued on next page.

Quicknotes

PAROL EVIDENCE RULE Doctrine precluding parties to an agreement from introducing evidence of prior or contemporaneous agreements in order to repudiate or alter the terms of a written contract.

STATUTE OF FRAUDS A statute that requires specified types of contracts to be in writing in order to be binding.

Beaver v. Brumlow

Seller of land (P) v. Buyer of land (D)

N.M. Ct. App., 148 N.M. 172, 231 P.3d 628 (2010)

NATURE OF CASE: Appeal from judgment for defendants/counterclaim plaintiffs in action for ejectment.

FACT SUMMARY: The Beavers (P), who orally agreed to sell land to the Brumlows (D), but then reneged on the agreement, contended that the statute of frauds barred specific performance of the agreement because the Brumlows' (D) part performance was not "unequivocally referable" to the verbal agreement, and the verbal agreement was not certain as to the purchase price and time of performance.

RULE OF LAW

Specific performance of an oral contract for the sale of land is not barred by the statute of frauds where the terms of the contract other than the purchase price have been proved, there has been part performance by both parties to the agreement, the part performance refers unequivocally to the sale of land through possession and the making of improvements, and a remedy at law would be inadequate.

FACTS: The Beavers (P) agreed verbally to sell property to the Brumlows (D) on which the Brumlows (D) would site a house. Mr. Brumlow (D) worked for the Beavers (P) at the time the agreement was made. In reliance on the Beavers' (P) promise, and with the Beavers' (P) permission, the Brumlows (D) cashed out their retirement plans and bought and installed a mobile home on the property and then added permanent improvements to it. The cost to the Brumlows (D) of purchasing the house and making improvements was around $85,000. The Beavers (P) supported the Brumlows' (D) efforts and helped them obtain necessary permits and applications. Throughout this time, the Brumlows (D) requested that the Beavers (P) formalize the parties' agreement, but the Beavers (P) never did, although they promised to and consulted an attorney about drafting the necessary documents. The parties also never agreed on a price or a date of closing. The Beavers (P) let the Brumlows (D) quietly enjoy possession of the land for several years. Then, all that changed. Mr. Brumlow (D) terminated his employment with the Beavers (P), as he was going to work for their competitor. Hurt and angry, the Beavers (P) decided not to sell the agreed upon tract of land to the Brumlows (D). Instead they attempted to restructure the agreement as a "lease" by having the Brumlows (D) sign an agreement under which the Brumlows (D) would pay the Beavers (P) $400 per month, though the agreement used no language of a lease, so that the Brumlows (D) believed the agreement was for payment for the land. When the Brumlows (D) began writing "Land Payment" on the checks, the Beavers (P) stopped cashing the checks and alleged that the "agreement" was for rental. The Brumlows (D) attempted to amicably resolve the dispute by offering to pay cash in the amount of the fair market value for the property and to have the property surveyed at their expense. The Beavers (P) refused, and then filed an ejectment action, alleging that the Brumlows (D) were in violation of their "rental" agreement. The Brumlows (D) denied the existence of a rental agreement and affirmatively alleged that their occupancy was pursuant to an agreement to purchase the property. The Brumlows (D) also filed counterclaims that included claims for breach of contract, fraud, and prima facie tort. The Beavers (P) pleaded the statute of frauds as a defense, arguing that the Brumlows' (D) part performance was not "unequivocally referable" to the verbal agreement, and the verbal agreement was not certain as to the purchase price and time of performance. The trial court held that the parties had entered into an agreement for the sale of land, and that by reneging on that agreement, the Beavers (P) injured the Brumlows (D), so that they committed a prima facie tort, which they knew would harm the Brumlows (D). The court rejected the statute of frauds defense on the grounds that part performance of the contract by both parties was sufficient to remove the contract from the statute of frauds. The court gave the Brumlows (D) a choice: money damages for the tort or specific performance of the contract, with the purchase price to be determined by an independent appraisal of the fair market value of the property, payable in cash within 30 days. The Brumlows (D) chose specific performance. The state's intermediate appellate court granted review.

ISSUE: Is specific performance of an oral contract for the sale of land barred by the statute of frauds where the terms of the contract other than the purchase price have been proved, there has been part performance by both parties to the agreement, the part performance refers unequivocally to the sale of land through possession and the making of improvements, and a remedy at law would be inadequate?

HOLDING AND DECISION: (Vigil, J.) No. Specific performance of an oral contract for the sale of land is not barred by the statute of frauds where the terms of the contract other than the purchase price have been proved, there has been part performance by both parties

Continued on next page.

to the agreement, the part performance refers unequivocally to the sale of land through possession and the making of improvements, and a remedy at law would be inadequate. The statute of frauds generally bars actions on contracts for the sale of land or interests in land where there has been no written agreement for the sale signed by the party to be charged or the party's representative. However, a judicially created exception to this rule known as the doctrine of part performance—effected to overcome the harshness and injustice that might result from a literal and mechanical application of the rule—provides that where an oral contract not enforceable under the statute of frauds has been performed to such extent as to make it inequitable to deny effect thereto, equity may consider the contract as removed from operation of the statute of frauds and decree specific performance. Here, it is uncontested that the agreement was made, or even that the parties partially performed. The key objection by the Beavers (P) to application of the part performance doctrine is that the character of the Brumlows' (D) performance was not sufficiently indicative of an oral agreement to sell land to qualify as partial performance. To satisfy the part performance doctrine, part performance must be referrable to the contract. In other words, it must be shown that there was no other reason for the performance than performance under the contract. Here, the Beavers (P) argue that the Brumlows' (D) conduct was consistent with those taken by a person who needs a place to live and who is given an opportunity to reside on another person's property. The Beavers (P) argue that if there is an alternative explanation for the actions taken in reliance of the oral contract, those actions are not "unequivocally referable" to the contract, and application of the part performance doctrine is improper. This argument is rejected. First, the "unequivocally referable" concept does not mean that outside of the contract, there can be no other plausible explanation for the part performance. Instead, it means that an outsider, knowing all the circumstances of a case except for the claimed oral agreement, would naturally and reasonably conclude that a contract existed regarding the land, of the same general nature as that alleged by the claimant. In other words, the performance must lead an outsider to "naturally and reasonably" conclude that the contract alleged actually exists. Two indicators of such performance are taking possession of the property, and making valuable, permanent, and substantial improvements to the property. Here, the Brumlows (D) did both. In sum, the Brumlows' (D) reliance on the agreement and their part performance were sufficient to take the oral agreement outside of the statute of frauds. The Brumlows (D) also argue that the trial court impermissibly imposed on them a purchase price to which they had never agreed when the court ordered that the purchase price would be established by an appraisal and that the terms of the payment would be in cash payable within 30 days. Precedent provides that a claim for specific performance of a contract involving land will not fail for failure to specify a price where the contract is otherwise complete, and there has been part performance of the contract by a transfer of possession. In such situations, equity may imply a reasonable price to avoid inequity. Here, the contract was otherwise complete, and the Brumlows (D) relied on it to their detriment by taking possession and making improvements. Therefore, the trial court, in the exercise of its equitable powers, did not err in ordering that the purchase price be determined by an independent appraisal at fair market value. Significantly, the Beavers (P) do not challenge the fairness of the purchase price established by the trial court. Similarly, where a closing date has not been agreed to, equity may supply a reasonable time for performance. Finally, because it is well settled that land is unique and is assumed to have special value not replaceable in money, the Brumlows (D) did not have an adequate remedy at law. Affirmed.

ANALYSIS

As did the court in this case, the majority of courts, in deciding whether a promisee's performance is "unequivocally referable" to the contract, look for two key factors: (1) whether the party seeking enforcement has obtained possession of the property, and (2) whether that party has made valuable improvements to the property. If these two factors are present, the majority of courts will apply the part performance exception. For these courts, mere payment of money usually is not enough. The Restatement (Second) of Contracts does not use the "unequivocally referable" standard, but, instead, focuses on whether the party seeking enforcement has, in reliance on the contract, so changed his or her position that only specific performance can avoid injustice.

Quicknotes

BREACH OF CONTRACT Unlawful failure by a party to perform its obligations pursuant to contract.

COUNTERCLAIM An independent cause of action brought by a defendant to a lawsuit in order to oppose or deduct from the plaintiff's claim.

EJECTMENT An action to oust someone in unlawful possession of real property and to restore possession to the party lawfully entitled to it.

FAIR MARKET VALUE The price of particular property or goods a buyer would offer and a seller would accept in the open market following full disclosure.

Continued on next page.

FRAUD A false representation of facts with the intent that another will rely on the misrepresentation to his or her detriment.

PART PERFORMANCE Partial performance of a contract, promise or obligation.

PRIMA FACIE CASE An action where the plaintiff introduces sufficient evidence to submit the issue to the judge or jury for determination.

REMEDY AT LAW Compensation for violation of a right or injuries sustained that is available in a court of law, as opposed to a court of equity.

SPECIFIC PERFORMANCE An equitable remedy whereby the court requires the parties to perform their obligations pursuant to a contract.

STATUTE OF FRAUDS A statute that requires specified types of contracts to be in writing in order to be binding.

TORT DAMAGES Monetary compensation awarded by the court to a party injured as the result of the tortious act of another.

Alaska Democratic Party v. Rice

Employer (D) v. Former employee (P)

Alaska Sup. Ct., 934 P.2d 1313 (1997)

NATURE OF CASE: Appeal from damages award for plaintiff in suit based on misrepresentation and promissory estoppel.

FACT SUMMARY: When Rice (P) was promised a job that never materialized, she sued on a theory of promissory estoppel.

RULE OF LAW

A promise that the promisor should reasonably expect to induce action or forbearance on the part of the promisee or a third person and that does induce the action or forbearance is enforceable notwithstanding the statute of frauds if injustice can be avoided only by enforcement of the promise.

FACTS: The chair-elect of the Alaska Democratic Party (Party) (D) orally offered a job to Rice (P) as executive director of the Party (D) for two years. The resulting obligation fell into the statute of frauds because it could not be performed within one year. After quitting another job and moving to Alaska, Rice (P) was told she did not have the job. When Rice (P) sued on the alleged oral contract, the jury awarded her damages. The Party (D) appealed.

ISSUE: Is a promise that the promisor should reasonably expect to induce action or forbearance on the part of the promisee or a third person and that does induce the action or forbearance enforceable notwithstanding the statute of frauds if injustice can be avoided only by enforcement of the promise?

HOLDING AND DECISION: (Rabinowitz, J.) Yes. A promise that the promisor should reasonably expect to induce action or forbearance on the part of the promisee or a third person and that does induce the action or forbearance is enforceable notwithstanding the statute of frauds if injustice can be avoided only by enforcement of the promise. Section 139 (2) of the Restatement (Second) of Contracts (Restatement) enumerates factors to consider in making the determination of whether injustice can be avoided only by enforcement of the promise. A plaintiff's burden in overriding the statute is to establish the promisor's existence by clear and convincing evidence. This court joins those states that endorse the Restatement approach in employment disputes such as this one. The statute of frauds represents a traditional contract principle that is largely formalistic and does not generally concern substantive rights. The need to satisfy the clear and convincing proof standard to establish the making and the terms of the promise ensures that promissory estoppel will not render the statute of frauds superfluous in the employment context. The court adopts section 139 as the law of this jurisdiction. Affirmed.

ANALYSIS

The Restatement (First) of Contracts also contemplated the possibility that an estoppel could operate to override the statute of frauds' requirement of a written document. An estoppel might preclude a defendant's assertion of the statute of frauds as a barrier to enforcement only if detrimental reliance could be shown. Reliance could be based on a misrepresentation of fact or on a promise to make a memorandum if the statute would otherwise operate to defraud.

Quicknotes

CLEAR AND CONVINCING An evidentiary standard requiring a demonstration that the fact sought to be proven is reasonably certain.

PROMISE The expression of an intention to act, or to forbear from acting, granting a right to the promisee to expect and enforce its performance.

PROMISEE The party to whom a promise is made.

PROMISOR The party who promises to render an obligation to another in the future.

PROMISSORY ESTOPPEL A promise that is enforceable if the promisor should reasonably expect that it will induce action or forbearance on the part of the promisee, does in fact cause such action or forbearance, and is the only means of avoiding injustice.

STATUTE OF FRAUDS A statute that requires specified types of contracts to be in writing in order to be binding.

Buffaloe v. Hart

Buyer (P) v. Seller (D)

N.C. Ct. App., 114 N.C. App. 52, 441 S.E.2d 172 (1994)

NATURE OF CASE: Appeal from denial of defendants' motions for directed verdict and judgment notwithstanding the verdict in an action for breach of a contract for the sale of goods.

FACT SUMMARY: Buffaloe (P) alleged that an oral contract he had with the Harts (D) to purchase their barns was valid because it fell under the partial performance exception to the statute of frauds.

RULE OF LAW

A contract is taken out of the statute of frauds if there is sufficient evidence of part performance; that is, if the seller delivered the goods and the buyer accepted them.

FACTS: Buffaloe (P) sought damages for breach of a contract he allegedly had for the purchase of tobacco barns. The Harts (D) denied the existence of the contract and contended the alleged contract, made orally and with a handshake, was unenforceable because it violated the statute of frauds. Specifically, they argued that a check that Buffaloe (P) had presented to them in attempting to fulfill his part of the contract did not have their endorsement and therefore did not satisfy the state's statute of frauds. That statute requires for a check to constitute a writing sufficient to support a contract, it must be "signed by the party or the party's authorized agent against whom enforcement is sought." The jury found there was a valid contract and awarded Buffaloe (P) damages. The Harts (D) filed a motion for judgment notwithstanding the verdict, which was denied. The Harts (D) appealed, and the state's intermediate appellate court granted review.

ISSUE: Is a contract taken out of the statute of frauds if there is sufficient evidence of part performance, that is, if the seller delivered the goods and the buyer accepted them?

HOLDING AND DECISION: (Greene, J.) Yes. A contract is taken out of the statute of frauds if there is sufficient evidence of part performance; that is, if the seller delivered the goods and the buyer accepted them. To qualify under the partial performance exception, acceptance must be voluntary and unconditional and may be inferred from the buyer's conduct in taking physical possession of the goods or some part of them. Part payment may be made by money or check, accepted by the seller. In this case, the evidence established that Buffaloe (P) told several people about purchasing the barns, reimbursed the Harts (D) for insurance on the barns, paid for improvements, took possession, enlisted the aid of an auctioneer and the paper to sell the barns, and received deposits from three buyers on the barns. Buffaloe (P) also delivered a check for $5,000 to the Harts (D) and the check was not returned until several days later. These acts represented substantial relevant evidence that a reasonable mind might accept as adequate to support the conclusions reached by the jury. The trial court did not err in denying the Harts' (D) motion for directed verdict or motion for judgment notwithstanding the verdict. Affirmed.

ANALYSIS

The court in this case first considered whether the buyer's check represented a memorandum sufficient to satisfy the statute of frauds. But since the sellers never signed the check, it could not be enforced against them. Under the partial performance exception, a buyer is required to deliver something that is accepted by the seller as such performance. In this case, the $5,000 check served this purpose.

Quicknotes

BREACH OF CONTRACT Unlawful failure by a party to perform its obligations pursuant to contract.

MEMORANDUM A brief written note outlining the terms of a transaction or an agreement.

STATUTE OF FRAUDS A statute that requires specified types of contracts to be in writing in order to be binding.

CHAPTER 5

Express Terms of the Agreement: Principles of Interpretation and the Parol Evidence Rule

Quick Reference Rules of Law

Prochazka v. Bee-Three Development, LLC

Commercial property seller (D) v. Commercial property purchaser (P)

Ark. Ct. App., 2015 Ark. App. 384, 466 S.W.3d 448 (2015)

NATURE OF CASE: Appeal from grant of summary judgment to plaintiff in action for return of earnest money under agreement for the purchase of commercial real property, and from dismissal of defendant's counterclaim.

FACT SUMMARY: Bee-Three Development, LLC (Bee-Three) (P) contended that its agreement with the Prochazkas (D) for the purchase of commercial real property unambiguously granted to it the absolute right to terminate the agreement, so that it was entitled to a return of the earnest money it had paid to the Prochazkas (D). The Prochazkas (D) countered that the agreement was ambiguous, that Bee-Three (P) had breached the contract, and that they were entitled to retain the earnest money.

RULE OF LAW

Where a contract is patently ambiguous, thereby presenting a genuine issue of material fact, an action on the contract may not be disposed of on summary judgment.

FACTS: Bee-Three Development, LLC (Bee-Three) (P) entered into a written agreement to purchase a commercial lot from the Prochazkas (D). During the inspection period Bee-Three (P) terminated the agreement. According to Bee-Three (P), it had lined up a tenant for the property, and the prospective tenant merely changed its mind about leasing the property from Bee-Three (P), so that Bee-Three (P) no longer had a need to purchase the land. According to the Prochazkas (D), this purpose was never communicated to them, and Bee-Three (P) shrouded the true purpose of the transaction—including the existence of its anticipated end-user client—in secrecy. Bee-Three (P) demanded that the Prochazkas (D) return $7,000 in earnest money it had paid to them. The Prochazkas (D) refused, and Bee-Three (P) sued for the earnest money; the Prochazkas (D) counterclaimed for breach of contract and asked that the earnest money be forfeited to them as liquidated damages. Bee-Three (P) then moved for summary judgment, and the trial court granted the motion, concluding that one of the contract's three termination clauses, in Article 4 of the agreement, unambiguously gave Bee-Three (P) an "absolute" right to terminate the contract within the inspection period. Accordingly, the trial court also dismissed the Prochazkas' (D) counterclaim. Article 4 concerned "Inspection of Property." In Section 4.1, it gave Bee-Three (P) the right to conduct testing relating to such matters as "soil, engineering, environmental, geotechnical," and other similar aspects of the property, as well as to determine the availability of governmental licenses and permits "relating to Buyer's intended use of the Property." Section 4.3, titled "Right to Terminate," provided, in relevant part, that "If Buyer determines, in its sole and absolute discretion, that the Property is not suitable for Buyer's intended use, then Buyer may terminate this Agreement by notifying Seller in writing of its election to terminate on or before the last day of the Inspection Period." There were two other termination provisions in the agreement, each connected to the subject matter of the Articles in which they appeared. In its determination that the contract was unambiguous, the trial court concluded that there was no interdependence between the "right to inspect" section, and the "right to terminate" section. The Prochazkas (D) appealed, and the state's intermediate appellate court granted review.

ISSUE: Where a contract is patently ambiguous, thereby presenting a genuine issue of material fact, may an action on the contract be disposed of on summary judgment?

HOLDING AND DECISION: (Harrison, J.) No. Where a contract is patently ambiguous, thereby presenting a genuine issue of material fact, an action on the contract may not be disposed of on summary judgment. The dispute here centers on whether the purchase agreement unambiguously granted to Bee-Three Development, LLC (Bee-Three) (P) an absolute termination right. A contractual provision is ambiguous when there is doubt or uncertainty as to its meaning so that it is open to at least two reasonable interpretations. When construing a contract, a court strives to give the parties' words the meaning that they intended them to have, but also to give the words their plain and ordinary meaning. Additionally, the parties' intention must be gleaned from the agreement taken in its entirety. When a contract is unambiguous the trial court applies the plain language of the parties' terms and determines as a matter of law how to apply the contract. If an ambiguity is present, the trial court may nonetheless apply the contract as a matter of law if the ambiguity can be resolved by referring to the contract. If the contract's terms cannot clear up the initial uncertainty, then the court may look outside the contract, and must give considerable weight to how the parties themselves understood a contract's terms, as shown by their subsequent statements, acts, and conduct. The first step in determining whether the disputed term in Section 4.3

Continued on next page.

is ambiguous is to read it in the context of the entire agreement. At this point, extrinsic evidence is not considered, because such evidence may not be used to create an ambiguity within the contract where one may not exist. A reasonable view of the contract is that the termination clauses are anchored to the subject matter of the sections in which they appear. If that is so, then the termination clause in Section 4.3 does not empower Bee-Three (P), as a matter of law, to terminate for the reason it has provided. A material ambiguity exists because Bee-Three's (P) right to terminate the purchase agreement could be viewed as being as "absolute"—as the trial court and the dissent view the provision—or the disputed termination provision can be read to mean that Bee-Three's (P) exercise of its termination right under Section 4.3 must be substantially related to the purpose of the inspection period and the events and concerns expressed in Article 4. If that were not the case, such a provision would not be placed in an article that concerns inspection rights, but rather would be a standalone provision, unmoored from any other subject matter or context like an inspection period. Moreover, the contract in this case does not define the term "intended use." For these reasons, there is an ambiguity within the contract that cannot be resolved by the contract itself. Now extrinsic evidence may come in for the purpose of resolving the ambiguity. Here, however, the parties' respective affidavits, which conflict as to the intended operation of Section 4.3's termination clause, and whether Bee-Three's (P) "intended use" had ever been disclosed, instead of resolving the ambiguity, create a genuine issue of material fact about the intent of that provision. Therefore, the ambiguity should be resolved by a jury. Reversed and remanded.

CONCURRENCE: (Virden, J.) Although there was no ambiguity in the agreement regarding termination, there was a genuine issue of material fact as to Bee-Three Development, LLC's (P) "intended use" and whether the property was suitable for such use. Therefore, the case must be remanded for trial before a jury to resolve this issue.

DISSENT: (Gruber, J.) The agreement's language is clear and unambiguous as to the right to terminate. To find an ambiguity is to enlarge and extend the terms of the contract, because Section 4.1 allows the buyer, during the inspection period, to "determine generally the desirability and utility of the Property for Buyer's planned use of the Property." Section 4.3 specifies that the buyer's determination of unsuitability for intended use, in the buyer's "sole and absolute discretion," gives the buyer the right to terminate and to have its earnest money returned if written notice is given before expiration of the inspection period. Bee-Three Development, LLC (Bee-Three) (P) was not required to convey its intended use to lease the property to an anchor tenant to the Prochazkas (D) as a condition of buying. Bee-Three (P) determined the property to be unsuitable, as was allowed by both paragraphs, and exercised its absolute right to terminate.

ANALYSIS

As the court in this case emphasizes, the objective of interpretation in the general law of contracts is to carry out the understanding of the parties rather than to impose obligations on them contrary to their understanding, because it is a principle of contract law that the courts should not make a contract for the parties. Thus, the primary search by a court is for a common meaning of the parties, not a meaning imposed on them by the law. Ordinarily, therefore, the mutual understanding of the parties prevails even where the contractual term has been defined differently by statute or administrative regulation. Consequently, however, parties who used a standardized term in an unusual sense may run a strong risk that their agreement will be misinterpreted in litigation.

Quicknotes

BREACH OF CONTRACT Unlawful failure by a party to perform its obligations pursuant to contract.

EARNEST MONEY A payment made by a prospective buyer to a seller to evidence the intent to fulfill the obligations of a contract to purchase property.

EXTRINSIC EVIDENCE Evidence that is not contained within the text of a document or contract, but that is derived from the parties' statements or the circumstances under which the agreement was made.

ISSUE OF MATERIAL FACT An issue or dispute regarding a fact that is legally relevant to a claim or cause of action that will, as a matter of substantive law, make a difference to the outcome reached in a given case. Also stated as "material issue of fact."

LIQUIDATED DAMAGES An amount of money specified in a contract representing the damages owed in the event of breach.

SUMMARY JUDGMENT Judgment rendered by a court in response to a motion made by one of the parties, claiming that the lack of a question of material fact in respect to an issue warrants disposition of the issue without consideration by the jury.

Frigaliment Importing Co. v. B.N.S. International Sales Corp.

Chicken purchaser (P) v. Seller (D)

190 F. Supp. 116 (S.D.N.Y. 1960)

NATURE OF CASE: Action for breach of warranty of a contract for the sale of goods.

FACT SUMMARY: Frigaliment Importing Co. (Frigaliment) (P) ordered a large quantity of "chicken" from B.N.S. International Sales Corp. (B.N.S.) (D), intending to buy young chicken suitable for broiling and frying, but B.N.S. (D) believed, in considering the weights ordered at the prices fixed by the parties, that the order could be filled with older chicken, suitable for stewing only, and termed "fowl" by Frigaliment (P).

RULE OF LAW

The party who seeks to interpret the terms of the contract in a sense narrower than their everyday use bears the burden of persuasion to so show, and if that party fails to support its burden, it faces dismissal of its complaint.

FACTS: Frigaliment Importing Co. (Frigaliment) (P), a Swiss corporation, and B.N.S. International Sales Corp. (B.N.S.) (D), a New York corporation, made two almost identical contracts for the sale of chicken by the latter to the former as follows: U.S. fresh frozen chicken, Grade A, government inspected, eviscerated, all wrapped and boxed suitably for export, 75,000 lbs. 2–3 lbs. at $33.00 per 100 lbs. and 25,000 lbs. 1–2 lbs. at $36.50 per 100 lbs. The second contract was the same except for 25,000 lbs. less of the heavier chicken and a price of $37.00 per 100 lbs. for the lighter birds. B.N.S. (D), which was new to the poultry business, believed any kind of chicken could be used to fill the order including stewing chickens. Most of the order for heavier birds was filled with stewers because that was the only way B.N.S. (D) could make a profit on the contract.

ISSUE: Does the party who seeks to interpret the terms of the contract in a sense narrower than their everyday use bear the burden of persuasion to so show, and if that party fails to support its burden, does it face dismissal of its complaint?

HOLDING AND DECISION: (Friendly, J.) Yes. The party who seeks to interpret the terms of the contract in a sense narrower than their everyday use bears the burden of persuasion to so show, and if that party fails to support its burden, it faces dismissal of its complaint. Frigaliment Importing Co. (Frigaliment) (P) failed to support its burden. While cables leading up to negotiations were predominantly in German, the use of the English word "chicken" as meaning "young chicken" rather than the German word "Huhn" meaning broilers and stewers lost its force when B.N.S. International Sales Corp. (B.N.S.) (D) asked if any kind of chickens were wanted to which an affirmative answer meaning "Huhn" was given. B.N.S. (D), being new to the chicken trade, the other party must show the other's acceptance of the trade use of a term. Frigaliment (P) failed to offer such proof. There was conflicting evidence anyway as to the trade use of the word "chicken." B.N.S.'s (D) price of $33.00 per 100 lbs. for the larger birds was $2.00 to $4.00 less than for broilers. Frigaliment (P) could not say that the price appeared reasonable because it was closer to the $35.00 broiler price than the $30.00 stewer price. B.N.S. (D) could be expected not to sell at a loss. While the evidence is generally conflicting, overall it appeared that B.N.S. (D) believed it could comply by supplying stewing chicken. This did conform to one dictionary meaning, with the definition in the department of animal regulations to which at least there was a contractual reference and with some trade usage. This evidence must be relied upon as the contract language itself could not settle the question here. Dismissed.

ANALYSIS

In determining intent of the parties, the court will turn first to the language of the contract to see whether the meaning of the ambiguous term can be raised. If this is unsuccessful, the court must look to other evidence. Under Restatement (First) § 235, certain guidelines aid in determining meaning. First, the ordinary meaning of language throughout the country is given to words unless circumstances show that a different meaning is applicable. Also, all circumstances surrounding the transaction may be taken into consideration. Also, if after consideration of all factors, it is still uncertain what meaning should be given, a reasonable, lawful, and effective meaning to all manifestations of intention is preferred to an interpretation that leaves a part of such unreasonable, unlawful, or ineffective. Restatement (First) § 236(a). Even so, the principal apparent purpose of the parties should be given greater weight in determining the meaning to be given.

Quicknotes

AMBIGUITY Language that is capable of more than one interpretation.

COURSE OF DEALING Previous conduct between two parties to a contract that may be relied upon to interpret their actions.

C & J Fertilizer, Inc. v. Allied Mutual Insurance Co.

Insured company (P) v. Insurer (D)

Iowa Sup. Ct., 227 N.W.2d 169 (1975)

NATURE OF CASE: Appeal from judgment for defendant on action to recover for burglary loss.

FACT SUMMARY: C & J Fertilizer, Inc. (P) had an insurance policy with Allied Mutual Insurance Co. (Allied) (D) covering it for burglary loss. A burglary occurred, but Allied (D) refused to pay because there were no visible marks or physical damage to the building exterior at the place of entry, as required under the policy.

RULE OF LAW

Insurance policies contain an implied warranty of fitness for their intended purpose, and the reasonable expectations of the policyholder will be honored, with unconscionable clauses disallowed.

FACTS: C & J Fertilizer, Inc. (C & J) (P) had an insurance policy with Allied Mutual Insurance Co. (Allied) (D) covering burglary loss at its fertilizer plant. A burglary occurred, but Allied (D) refused to pay on the grounds that there were no visible marks or physical damage on the building exterior at the place of entry of the burglar. This requirement was included in the insurance policy under its definition of burglary. Its purpose was to prevent fraud and payments on "inside jobs." An interior door had been damaged when the burglar entered a separate room and stole chemicals. The lower court held for Allied (D), stating that the definition of burglary under the policy was unambiguous and not met in this case. C & J (P) relied on the theories of reasonable expectation, implied warranty of fitness for intended purpose, and unconscionability of the burglary definition. The trial court found that there had been no discussion of policy provisions between the parties at the time the policy was secured, and there was no evidence that C & J (P) knew the policy definition of burglary.

ISSUE: Do insurance policies contain an implied warranty of fitness for their intended purpose, and will the reasonable expectations of the policyholder be honored, with unconscionable clauses dishonored?

HOLDING AND DECISION: (Reynoldson, J.) Yes. Insurance policies contain an implied warranty of fitness for their intended purpose, and the reasonable expectations of the policyholder will be honored, with unconscionable clauses disallowed. Insurance policies, such as the one here, are mass-produced, standardized adhesion policies. The policyholder should not be bound to unknown terms that are beyond the range of reasonable expectation. Here, nothing led C & J Fertilizer, Inc. (C & J) (P) to reasonably anticipate that it would have no coverage unless the exterior of the premises was marked or damaged. Further, Allied Mutual Insurance Co. (Allied) (D) breached an implied warranty that the policy would be reasonably fit for its intended purpose. There is no reason why this doctrine should not apply to insurance policies as well as the sale of tangible goods, as it now does. Finally, C & J (P) should prevail because the liability-avoiding provision in the definition of burglary is, in these circumstances, unconscionable, based on the standardized nature of the contract, the unequal bargaining positions, and the unreasonably favorable terms of the definition to Allied (D). Reversed and remanded.

DISSENT: (LeGrand, J.) The definition of burglary as contained in the policy was unambiguous, and its purpose was to omit coverage for "inside jobs." Contracts that clearly state their meaning should not be disturbed simply because the meaning is disliked.

ANALYSIS

There is a definite trend in recent cases to disallow unconscionable terms in adhesion contracts, especially insurance contracts. The courts will either deny enforcement of the contract as a whole or as to the unconscionable terms only. The term "unconscionable" is derived from the Uniform Commercial Code, § 2-302, and refers to terms in a contract that are so manifestly unfair as to be oppressive.

Quicknotes

ADHESION CONTRACT A contract that is not negotiated and is usually prepared by the dominant party on a "take it or leave it" basis.

BOILERPLATE Standard language commonly appearing in documents having a definite meaning in the same context without variation.

UNCONSCIONABILITY Rule of law whereby a court may excuse performance of a contract, or of a particular contract term, if it determines that such term(s) are unduly oppressive or unfair to one party to the contract as a result of disparity in bargaining power during the formation of the contract.

Thompson v. Libby

Seller of logs (P) v. Purchaser (D)

Minn. Sup. Ct., 34 Minn. 374, 26 N.W. 1 (1885)

NATURE OF CASE: Appeal from denial of motion for new trial in action for breach of contract.

FACT SUMMARY: Thompson (P) brought an action to enforce a written contract for the sale of logs. Libby (D) defended on an oral warranty.

RULE OF LAW

Where a contract is complete on its face, parol testimony is inadmissible to vary its terms, such as warranties of quality.

FACTS: Thompson (P) and Libby (D) entered into a contract for the sale of logs. The contract contained all necessary terms. Libby (D) later refused to pay for the logs. Thompson (P) brought a suit for the contract price and Libby (D) defended on basis of a parol contemporary warranty that was allegedly breached by Thompson (P). At trial, the court allowed the introduction of evidence concerning the warranty of quality orally given at the time of sale. It found for Libby (D) on this basis. The state's highest court granted review.

ISSUE: Where a contract is complete on its face, is parol testimony admissible to vary its terms, such as warranties of quality?

HOLDING AND DECISION: (Mitchell, J.) No. Where a contract is complete on its face, parol testimony is inadmissible to vary its terms, such as warranties of quality. In the case of a sale of personal property a warranty of quality is considered a part of the contract and not a collateral contract. The contract contains all necessary terms and is complete on its face. The parol evidence rule provides that contemporaneous parol evidence may not be admitted to contradict or vary the terms of a written contract that is complete on its face. Since a warranty is considered a contract term, it must be included in the contract. Parol evidence cannot be admitted to show that the contract is not a complete statement of the parties' agreement. The judge must determine whether the contract, based on its terms, represents the complete embodiment of the agreement. Since the contract here is complete on its face, the trial court was incorrect in allowing the parol evidence of the warranty to be admitted. Reversed.

ANALYSIS

Parol evidence of subsequent agreements may always be admitted. The parties are free to alter or modify the contract terms at any time. Separate collateral contracts may also be introduced. These do not alter or vary the terms of the written contract. However, it is necessary to show that the matter is collateral and would not normally have been included in the principal contract.

Quicknotes

BREACH OF CONTRACT Unlawful failure by a party to perform its obligations pursuant to contract.

PAROL Oral; unwritten.

PAROL CONTRACT A contract made orally or by a writing not under seal.

PAROL EVIDENCE RULE Doctrine precluding parties to an agreement from introducing evidence of prior or contemporaneous agreements in order to repudiate or alter the terms of a written contract.

Taylor v. State Farm Mutual Automobile Insurance Co.

Insured (P) v. Insurance company (D)

Ariz. Sup. Ct., 175 Ariz. 148, 854 P.2d 1134 (1993)

NATURE OF CASE: Review of a decision reversing a jury verdict in plaintiff's favor in a bad-faith insurance claim action.

FACT SUMMARY: Taylor (P) alleged that the court of appeals erroneously held that his insurance bad-faith claim was barred by a release he signed in 1981.

RULE OF LAW

A judge must first consider the offered evidence and, if he or she finds that the contract language is "reasonably susceptible" to the interpretation asserted by its proponent, admit the evidence to determine the meaning intended by the parties.

FACTS: State Farm Mutual Automobile Insurance Co. (State Farm) (D) insured Taylor (P), who was involved in an automobile accident with two other vehicles. The other parties to the accident obtained combined verdicts against Taylor (P) for approximately $2.5 million in excess of his insurance policy limits. The court of appeals affirmed those judgments. Taylor (P) sued State Farm (D) for bad-faith, seeking damages for the excess judgment, and claiming that State Farm (D) improperly failed to settle within policy limits. State Farm (D) moved for summary judgment, asserting that Taylor (P) had relinquished his bad-faith claim when he signed a release drafted by his attorney in exchange for State Farm's (D) payment of $15,000 in uninsured motorist benefits. The judge denied the motion, finding that the release was ambiguous and therefore parol evidence was admissible at trial to aid in interpreting the release. The jury returned a verdict in favor of Taylor (P) for compensatory damages of $2.1 million plus attorney's fees. The court of appeals reversed, holding that the release agreement was not ambiguous and should have been strictly enforced. Taylor (P) appealed.

ISSUE: Must a judge first consider the offered evidence and, if he or she finds that the contract language is "reasonably susceptible" to the interpretation asserted by its proponent, admit the evidence to determine the meaning intended by the parties?

HOLDING AND DECISION: (Feldman, C.J.) Yes. A judge must first consider the offered evidence and, if he or she finds that the contract language is "reasonably susceptible" to the interpretation asserted by its proponent, the evidence is admissible to determine the meaning intended by the parties. Taylor (P) argued that the bad-faith claim sounded in tort and was therefore neither covered nor intended to be covered by the language releasing "all contractual" claims. Because the legal character of bad faith was and is not universally established, the release reasonably could be interpreted as Taylor (P) asserts. The trial court, therefore, did not err in concluding that the text of the release did not necessarily cover claims for bad faith. The potential size of the bad-faith claim, the fact that the parties used limiting language in the release, and the recent authority characterizing the claim as a tort all support Taylor's (P) contention that the release language was not intended to release his bad-faith claim. Since interpretation was needed because the extrinsic evidence established controversy over what occurred and what inferences to draw from the events, the matter was properly submitted to the jury. The jury's resolution of the release issue in Taylor's (P) favor is left undisturbed. The decision of the court of appeals is vacated and the matter remanded for resolution of the remaining issues.

CONCURRENCE: (Corcoran, J.) Wavering and over-lapping lines of interpretation, rather than bright straight borders prevail in this area of contract interpretation. The problem with an amorphous rule is that ultimately it means that only this court must decide every contract dispute subject to its analysis.

ANALYSIS

The court in this case compared two views of the parol evidence rule. The "plain meaning" view of Professor Farnsworth holds that if a writing appears to be plain and unambiguous on its face, its meaning must be determined from the four corners of the instrument. Professor Corbin's view, which has been embraced by Arizona courts, holds that a court may consider surrounding circumstances and all the proffered evidence to determine its relevance to the parties' intent, and then apply the parol evidence rule to exclude only the evidence that contradicts or varies the meaning of the agreement.

Quicknotes

EXTRINSIC EVIDENCE Evidence not contained within the text of a document or contract but that is derived from the parties' statements or the circumstances under which the agreement was made.

FOUR CORNERS The express terms of a written document.

PAROL EVIDENCE RULE Doctrine precluding parties to an agreement from introducing evidence of prior or contemporaneous agreements in order to repudiate or alter the terms of a written contract.

Sherrodd, Inc. v. Morrison-Knudsen Co.

Construction subcontractor (P) v. General contractor (D)

Mont. Sup. Ct., 249 Mont. 282, 815 P.2d 1135 (1991)

NATURE OF CASE: Appeal from summary judgment for defendants in a suit for quantum meruit plus tort damages.

FACT SUMMARY: Sherrodd, Inc. (P), a construction subcontractor, alleged that the price provisions in the written construction contract should be set aside because of Morrison-Knudsen Co.'s (D) subcontractor's alleged fraud and breach of the covenant of good faith and fair dealing.

RULE OF LAW

A written contract may be altered only by a subsequent contract in writing or by an executed oral agreement.

FACTS: Sherrodd, Inc. (P), a family-owned construction company, subcontracted with the general contractors, Morrison-Knudsen Co. (D), to do certain earth-moving work involved in the construction of new family housing. Sherrodd (P) contended that a representative of Morrison-Knudsen (D) told him there were 25,000 cubic yards of excavation to be performed on the job and that he based his bid on that representation. Morrison-Knudsen (D) denied that its representative made such a statement to Sherrodd (P). Sherrodd's (P) bid was accepted and he began work before a written contract was signed. While performing the work, Sherrodd (P) discovered that the quantity of work far exceeded 25,000 cubic yards. The written contract Sherrodd (P) later signed did not specify the quantity in cubic yards, and Sherrodd (P) later sued to set aside the price provisions in the contract and to recover in quantum meruit for the work performed. Sherrodd (P) also alleged both actual and constructive fraud and breach of the covenant of good faith and fair dealing. Morrison-Knudsen (D) moved for summary judgment, which was granted based on the parol evidence rule regarding modification of written contracts. Sherrodd (P) appealed.

ISSUE: May a written contract be altered only by a subsequent contract in writing or by an executed oral agreement?

HOLDING AND DECISION: (Turnage, C.J.) Yes. A written contract may be altered only by a subsequent contract in writing or by an executed oral agreement. Because the written agreement supersedes all previous oral agreements, the parol evidence rule prohibits admission of any evidence of the alleged fraudulent statement of Morrison-Knudsen Co.'s (D) representative. The compensation of Sherrodd, Inc. (P) is governed exclusively by the written contract and his claims are barred under the parol evidence rule. The parol evidence rule is the public policy of this state and it is clearly established by statute and court precedent. Affirmed.

DISSENT: (Trieweiler, J.) The result of the majority's decision will be a grave injustice insofar as no party with superior bargaining power will ever be held liable for fraudulent conduct relating to an oral contract where it has obtained a signature on a written agreement from the party with inferior bargaining power. Taking Sherrodd Inc.'s (P) assertions as true, he has adequately pled that Morrison-Knudsen Co.'s (D) agent engaged in fraud. An important exception to the parol evidence rule provides that evidence to explain fraud is not to be excluded, and the legislature has provided that parol evidence can be offered to establish that a contract was induced by fraud. There is no exception in the statute where the fraudulent oral agreement contradicts the written agreement.

ANALYSIS

The court in this case applied a rule from an old case that the dissent claimed led to a great injustice. In *Continental Oil v. Bell*, 95 Mont. 123 (1933), the court had held that parol evidence of fraud was not admissible when the oral promise directly contradicted a provision of the written contract. The dissent claimed that only fraudulent parties who are in a superior bargaining position stand to benefit from this rule, which totally defeated the purpose of the fraud exception. The dissent also contended that the majority's reliance on the case was misplaced because the case contradicted the current statute governing the issue.

Quicknotes

FRAUD A false representation of facts with the intent that another will rely on the misrepresentation to his or her detriment.

PAROL EVIDENCE RULE Doctrine precluding parties to an agreement from introducing evidence of prior or contemporaneous agreements in order to repudiate or alter the terms of a written contract.

Nanakuli Paving & Rock Co. v. Shell Oil Co.

Concrete purchaser (P) v. Seller (D)

664 F.2d 772 (9th Cir. 1981)

NATURE OF CASE: Appeal from judgment n.o.v. denying damages for breach of contract.

FACT SUMMARY: Shell Oil Co. (D) contended it had not breached a supply contract as its course of conduct established the unwritten terms of the agreement.

RULE OF LAW

Trade usage and past course of dealings between contracting parties may establish terms not specifically enumerated in the contract, so long as no conflict is created with the written terms.

FACTS: Nanakuli Paving & Rock Co. (Nanakuli) (P) entered into a contract to purchase its requirements of concrete from Shell Oil Co. (Shell) (D). The contract was in effect for several years and renewed several times. Nanakuli (P) sued over a one-year contract, contending Shell (D) had failed to protect it from price increases. It argued that although such protection was not enumerated in the contract, it was part of the trade usage in concrete and thus implied in the contract. Further, Shell (D) had previously performed this service. Shell (D) argued the contract did not call for such, and its past conduct did not constitute a practice of protection. Rather it was a temporary waiver of the contract price. The trial court granted Shell (D) judgment n.o.v., and Nanakuli (P) appealed.

ISSUE: May trade usage and past course of dealings between contracting parties establish terms not specifically enumerated in the contract, so long as no conflict is created with the written terms?

HOLDING AND DECISION: (Hoffman, J.) Yes. Trade usage and past course of dealings between contracting parties may establish terms not specifically enumerated in the contract, so long as no conflict is created with the written terms. There was substantial evidence that the jury could rely upon in finding a consistent course of conduct including price protection. As a result, the entry of judgment n.o.v. was improper. Reversed and remanded.

CONCURRENCE: (Kennedy, J.) Here, the case involves specific pricing practices, not an allegation of unfair dealing generally. Therefore, the court's opinion should not be interpreted to permit juries to read into contracts price protection terms that are derived from a concept of good faith unless the parties know from custom and usage, or are otherwise on notice, that such good faith is expected. Here, the evidence of custom and usage regarding price protection in the asphaltic paving trade was not contradicted, so the jury could find that the parties knew or should have known of the practice at the time of making the contract. This principle applies to either theory of the case, namely, interpretation of the contract based on how the contract was performed or finding that good faith required the seller to hold the price.

ANALYSIS

The Parol Evidence Rule precludes extraneous evidence of contract terms unless such terms are ambiguous. The price protection term was so prevalent in the concrete trade that it was reasonable to find that the parties impliedly incorporated it into the contract. This was supported by Shell Oil Co.'s (D) history of price protection.

Quicknotes

COURSE OF DEALING Previous conduct between two parties to a contract that may be relied upon to interpret their actions.

JUDGMENT NOTWITHSTANDING THE VERDICT (JUDGMENT N.O.V.) A judgment entered by the trial judge reversing a jury verdict if the jury's determination has no basis in law or fact.

REQUIREMENTS CONTRACT An agreement pursuant to which one party agrees to purchase all his or her required goods or services from the other party exclusively for a specified time period.

TRADE USAGE A course of dealing or practice commonly used in a particular trade.

CHAPTER 6

Supplementing the Agreement: Implied Terms, the Obligation of Good Faith, and Warranties

Quick Reference Rules of Law

Wood v. Lucy, Lady Duff-Gordon

Marketer and licensor of designs (P) v. Designer (D)

N.Y. Ct. App., 222 N.Y. 88, 118 N.E. 214 (1917)

NATURE OF CASE: Appeal from reversal of an order denying defendant's motion for judgment on the pleadings in action for damages for breach of a contract for an exclusive right.

FACT SUMMARY: Wood (P), in a complicated agreement, received the exclusive right for one year, renewable on a year-to-year basis if not terminated by 90 days' notice, to endorse designs with Lucy's (D) name and to market all her fashion designs for which she (D) would receive one-half the profits derived. Lucy (D) broke the contract by placing her endorsement on designs without Wood's (P) knowledge.

RULE OF LAW

If a promise may be implied from a writing even though it is imperfectly expressed, there is a valid contract.

FACTS: Lucy (D), a famous-name fashion designer, contracted with Wood (P) that for her granting to him an exclusive right to endorse designs with her name and to market and license all her designs, they were to split the profits derived by Wood (P) in half. The exclusive right was for a period of one year, renewable on a year-to-year basis, and terminable upon 90 days' notice. Lucy (D) placed her endorsement on fabrics, dresses, and millinery without Wood's (P) knowledge and in violation of the contract. Lucy (D) claimed that the agreement lacked the elements of a contract as Wood (P) allegedly was not bound to do anything. The trial court held for Wood (P), the state's intermediate appellate court reversed, and the state's highest court granted review.

ISSUE: If a promise may be implied from a writing even though it is imperfectly expressed, is there a valid contract?

HOLDING AND DECISION: (Cardozo, J.) Yes. If a promise may be implied from a writing even though it is imperfectly expressed, there is a valid contract. While the contract did not precisely state that Wood (P) had promised to use reasonable efforts to place Lucy's (D) endorsement and market her designs, such a promise can be implied. The implication arises from the circumstances. Lucy (D) gave an exclusive privilege, and the acceptance of the exclusive agency was an acceptance of its duties. Lucy's (D) sole compensation was to be one-half the profits resulting from Wood's (P) efforts. Unless he gave his efforts, she could never receive anything. Without an implied promise, the transaction could not have had such business efficacy as they must have intended it to have. Wood's (P) promise to make monthly accounting and to acquire patents and copyrights as necessary showed the intention of the parties that the promise has value by showing that Wood (P) had some duties. The promise to pay Lucy (D) half the profits and make monthly accounting was a promise to use reasonable efforts to bring profits and revenues into existence. Reversed.

ANALYSIS

A bilateral contract can be express, implied in fact, or a little of each. The finding of an implied promise for the purpose of finding sufficient consideration to support an express promise is an important technique of the courts in order to uphold agreements that seem to be illusory and to avoid problems of mutuality of obligation. This case is the leading case on the subject. It is codified in Uniform Commercial Code (U.C.C.) § 2-306(2), where an agreement for exclusive dealing in goods imposes, unless otherwise agreed, an obligation to use best efforts by both parties.

Quicknotes

BILATERAL CONTRACT An agreement pursuant to which each party promises to undertake an obligation, or to forbear from acting.

U.C.C. § 2-306 Permits the seller to refuse to deliver unreasonable amounts demanded by a customer under a requirements contract.

Leibel v. Raynor Manufacturing Co.

Area distributor (P) v. Product manufacturer (D)

Ky. Ct. App., 571 S.W.2d 640 (1978)

NATURE OF CASE: Appeal of summary denial of damages for breach of contract.

FACT SUMMARY: Raynor Manufacturing Co. (D), without notice, abrogated an exclusive distribution agreement with Leibel (P).

RULE OF LAW

Reasonable notification is required in order to terminate an ongoing oral agreement creating a manufacturer-distributor relationship.

FACTS: Raynor Manufacturing Co. (Raynor) (D) orally contracted with Leibel (P) for Leibel (P) to become an area-exclusive distributor of Raynor's (D) products. Raynor (D) subsequently became dissatisfied with Leibel (P) and sent Leibel (P) a notice of termination. Leibel (P) sued, contending that reasonable notice was not given prior to termination. The trial court granted summary judgment for Raynor (D) as to the breach of contract cause of action, and Leibel (P) appealed.

ISSUE: Is reasonable notification required in order to terminate an ongoing oral agreement creating a manufacturer-distributor relationship?

HOLDING AND DECISION: (Howerton, J.) Yes. Reasonable notification is required in order to terminate an ongoing oral agreement creating a manufacturer-distributor relationship. The threshold question is whether the Uniform Commercial Code applies. By its terms, Article 2 applies to transactions involving goods or merchandise. It is quite apparent that a contract between a manufacturer and a distributor involves goods or merchandise, and therefore Article 2 should apply. Section 2-309 provides that where successive performances over an indefinite period of time are involved, reasonable notification of termination is required. An exception is made where invocation of this rule would be unconscionable. However, in a situation such as that presented here, the distributor undoubtedly incurs expenses in reliance upon continuing the relationship. It is certainly not unconscionable to require reasonable notification. For this reason, a triable issue of fact exists regarding whether the termination was given with reasonable notice. Vacated and remanded.

ANALYSIS

"Reasonable time" is not defined in Uniform Commercial Code § 2-309. This is not surprising, as the issue will always turn on the facts of the case. Reasonable notice is to some extent coextensive with the standard of good faith and fair dealing.

Quicknotes

GOOD FAITH An honest intention to abstain from any unconscientious advantage of another.

IMPLIED WARRANTY An implied promise made by one party to a contract that the other party may rely on a fact, relieving that party from the obligation of determining whether the fact is true and indemnifying the other party from liability if that fact is shown to be false.

U.C.C. § 2-309 Provides that reasonable notification of termination be given if successive performances have come to be expected over an indefinite time period.

Seidenberg v. Summit Bank

Seller of business (P) v. Purchaser of business (D)

N.J. Super. Ct., App. Div., 348 N.J. Super. 243, 791 A.2d 1068 (2002)

NATURE OF CASE: Appeal from dismissal, for failure to state a claim, of an action for a breach of the implied covenant of good faith and fair dealing.

FACT SUMMARY: Seidenberg and Raymond (collectively, Seidenberg) (P) claimed that Summit Bank (D) breached the implied covenant of good faith and fair dealing that arose from a contract between the parties by engaging in a bad-faith course of conduct that thwarted Seidenberg's (P) reasonable expectations, relating to compensation, under the contract.

RULE OF LAW

(1) A claim of breach of the implied covenant of good faith and fair dealing is not precluded because the parties possessed equal bargaining power, because the plaintiff was not financially vulnerable during the contract's formation, and because the plaintiff negotiated the contract with the assistance of highly competent counsel.

(2) When a plaintiff asserts a claim of breach of the implied covenant of good faith and fair dealing, the parol evidence rule does not prevent the plaintiff from substantiating the plaintiff's claims that the plaintiff had reasonable expectations that arose from the contract, and that the defendant failed to perform the defendant's contractual obligations in good faith.

(3) A claim of breach of the implied covenant of good faith and fair dealing may not be dismissed where the complaint alleges facts that if proven true show that the defendant exercised a right to terminate in bad faith or used its discretionary rights to thwart the contract's purpose.

(4) Allegations of bad faith and ill motives are sufficient to survive dismissal where it is asserted that the plaintiff suffered from defendant's actions that were "wanton and willful and without privilege or right."

FACTS: Seidenberg and Raymond (collectively, Seidenberg) (P) owned brokerage firms, which they sold to Summit Bank (Summit) (D). As part of the transaction, Seidenberg (P) retained his position as executive of the brokerage firms and was to be placed in charge of the daily operations of any other employee benefits insurance business that might be acquired by Summit (D). Seidenberg's (P) employment agreements with Summit (D) acknowledged the parties' joint obligation to work together with respect to the future performance of the brokerage firms, as Seidenberg's (P) compensation was tied to the growth and success of the firms and this line of business at Summit (D). After Seidenberg (P) was terminated, he brought suit claiming, inter alia, that Summit (D) had breached the implied covenant of good faith and fair dealing by failing to support, and even by actively thwarting, the growth of the firms and business. Seidenberg (P) alleged that Summit's (D) conduct demonstrated that Summit (D) never had any intention of performing its side of the bargain and that Summit (D), from the start, was not committed to developing the business with Seidenberg (P), but rather simply wanted to acquire the business and seek out its own broker to run it or grow it. Summit (D) moved to dismiss this claim, and the trial granted Summit's (D) motion, finding that Seidenberg (P) was seeking to prove the existence (and obtain enforcement) of an oral agreement allegedly made beyond the four corners of the written transaction agreements in violation of the parol evidence rule, and that the respective parties had equal bargaining power. The state's intermediate appellate court granted review.

ISSUE:

(1) Is a claim of breach of the implied covenant of good faith and fair dealing precluded because the parties possessed equal bargaining power, because the plaintiff was not financially vulnerable during the contract's formation, and because the plaintiff negotiated the contract with the assistance of highly competent counsel?

(2) When a plaintiff asserts a claim of breach of the implied covenant of good faith and fair dealing, does the parol evidence rule prevent the plaintiff from substantiating the plaintiff's claims that the plaintiff had reasonable expectations that arose from the contract, and that the defendant failed to perform the defendant's contractual obligations in good faith?

(3) May a claim of breach of the implied covenant of good faith and fair dealing be dismissed where the complaint alleges facts that if proven true show that the defendant exercised a right to terminate in bad faith or used its discretionary rights to thwart the contract's purpose?

(4) Are allegations of bad faith and ill motives sufficient to survive dismissal where it is asserted that the plaintiff suffered from defendant's actions that were "wanton and willful and without privilege or right"?

Continued on next page.

HOLDING AND DECISION: (Fisher, J.)

(1) No. A claim of breach of the implied covenant of good faith and fair dealing is not precluded because the parties possessed equal bargaining power, because the plaintiff was not financially vulnerable during the contract's formation, and because the plaintiff negotiated the contract with the assistance of highly competent counsel. The bargaining power of the parties is not the only factor determinative of whether there has been a breach of the implied covenant. Here merely because the parties were all sophisticated, financially strong, and represented by competent counsel does not preclude a finding that the implied covenant was breached. Although these factors are significant, and must be weighed accordingly by a fact finder, they are not exclusively determinative of the issue.

(2) No. When a plaintiff asserts a claim of breach of the implied covenant of good faith and fair dealing, the parol evidence rule does not prevent the plaintiff from substantiating the plaintiff's claims that the plaintiff had reasonable expectations that arose from the contract, and that the defendant failed to perform the defendant's contractual obligations in good faith. The parol evidence rule does not even come into play until it is first determined what the true agreement of the parties is. Accordingly, the rule cannot inhibit the application of the implied covenant of good faith and fair dealing because that covenant is contained in all contracts as a matter of law. Because the key premise of the implied covenant is the enhanced status of the parties' reasonable expectations, a vigorous application of the parol evidence rule would extremely limit the opportunity to pursue such a claim. The implied covenant is applied in three situations: (1) where terms and conditions which have not been expressly set forth in the written contract need to be added to give effect to the parties' expectations; (2) where there has been the bad faith performance of an agreement even when the defendant has not breached any express term; and (3) where a party's exercise of discretion expressly granted by a contract's terms is in derogation of the parties' expectations. Here, the second and third situations are implicated, and the parol evidence rule potentially could come into play regarding either one, but it should not. The parol evidence rule is not impacted in a case such as this because the obligation to act with good faith and fair dealing is, by its very nature, "implied." The prohibition on parol evidence to alter or vary a written contract relates only to the creation of the contract. Seidenberg (P) does not seek to contradict or alter any express term in a written contract, but rather questions Summit Bank's (Summit) (D) bona fides in both its performance and termination of the contract. Therefore, there is no concern that the particular manner in which Seidenberg (P) would have the implied covenant applied would run afoul of the parol evidence rule. To determine whether there was good faith performance, the court must consider the expectations of the parties and the purposes for which the contract was made. It would be difficult, if not impossible, to make that determination without considering evidence outside the written contract. Therefore, in determining whether a breach of the covenant has occurred, a court must allow for parol evidence and a ruling that the need for parol evidence is fatal to the complaint is erroneous.

(3) No. A claim of breach of the implied covenant of good faith and fair dealing may not be dismissed where the complaint alleges facts that if proven true show that the defendant exercised a right to terminate in bad faith or used its discretionary rights to thwart the contract's purpose. As discussed above (in issue 2) these are two of the three facets of the implied covenant. The trial court's job is to determine whether a cause of action consistent with any of these categories has been sufficiently alleged. Here, the allegation by Seidenberg (P) that Summit (D) terminated in bad faith, despite having the express right to do so, and Seidenberg's (P) expectation of continued employment, sufficiently pleads a claim under the second facet. Allegations that Summit (D) failed to take action in discretionary areas sufficiently allege a claim under the third facet.

(4) Yes. Allegations of bad faith and ill motives are sufficient to survive dismissal where it is asserted that the plaintiff suffered from defendant's actions that were "wanton and willful and without privilege or right." A party exercising its discretionary right under a contract acts in bad faith if that party exercises its discretionary authority arbitrarily, unreasonably, or capriciously, with the objective of preventing the other party from receiving its reasonably expected fruits under the contract. Whether a defendant has acted in bad faith requires inquiry into the defendant's state of mind and the context in which the claim arose, and is, therefore, a fact-specific inquiry. Ultimately, the question of whether there was bad faith resides in the eye of the trier of fact, and, therefore, the issue cannot be resolved until the parties are at least given a full and fair opportunity for further investigation and discovery. Here, by claiming that he was injured by Summit's (D) actions that were "wanton and willful and without privilege or right," Seidenberg (P) has sufficiently pled bad faith for the issue to go to trial. Reversed and remanded.

Continued on next page.

ANALYSIS

It is important to keep in mind that the implied covenant of good faith and fair dealing is never used to override or alter an express contract term. Instead, the implied obligation of good faith can be viewed as a device for protecting the bargain that the parties themselves have made against later attempts by one side to undermine it.

Quicknotes

BREACH The violation of an obligation imposed pursuant to contract or law, by acting or failing to act.

IMPLIED COVENANT OF GOOD FAITH AND FAIR DEALING An implied warranty that the parties will deal honestly in the satisfaction of their obligations and without an intent to defraud.

PAROL EVIDENCE RULE Doctrine precluding parties to an agreement from introducing evidence of prior or contemporaneous agreements in order to repudiate or alter the terms of a written contract.

Morin Building Products Co. v. Baystone Construction, Inc.

Siding installer (P) v. Construction firm (D)

717 F.2d 413 (7th Cir. 1983)

NATURE OF CASE: Appeal of award of damages for breach of contract.

FACT SUMMARY: General Motors Corp. refused, for aesthetic reasons, to approve aluminum siding installed by Morin Building Products Co. (P), which was subsequently not paid.

RULE OF LAW

Acceptance of performance in a contract whose purpose is primarily functional will be based on an objective standard.

FACTS: As part of a construction project for General Motors Corp., Baystone Construction, Inc. (Baystone) (D) subcontracted with Morin Building Products Co. (Morin) (P) to install aluminum siding. General Motors retained final approval rights. General Motors' agent rejected the siding due to a minor aesthetic flaw. The purpose of the siding was strictly functional. Baystone (D) had another subcontractor redo the job and refused to pay Morin (P), which sued for breach. The trial court held that the standard of acceptability of Morin's (P) performance was objective, and the jury held it objectively adequate. Baystone (D) appealed.

ISSUE: Will acceptance of performance in a contract whose purpose is primarily functional be based on an objective standard?

HOLDING AND DECISION: (Posner, J.) Yes. Acceptance of performance in a contract whose purpose is primarily functional will be based on an objective standard. The majority rule is that where the contract in question involves performance of commercial quality, an objective, reasonable person standard will be used in determining whether performance was adequate. It is unreasonable to expect a party to such a contract to permit his or her financial outcome to depend on whim. Therefore, in the absence of explicit language to the contrary, only if performance is inadequate objectively will performance be considered inadequate. Affirmed.

ANALYSIS

Generally speaking, a party will not be held to an objective standard when assessing the adequacy of performance when the nature of the contract is aesthetic. Even then, the law usually does not grant unfettered discretion. A good-faith requirement will generally be read into the contract.

Quicknotes

BREACH OF CONTRACT Unlawful failure by a party to perform its obligations pursuant to contract.

CONDITION Requirement; potential future occurrence upon which the existence of a legal obligation is dependent.

Locke v. Warner Bros. Inc.

Actress (P) v. Film studio (D)

Cal. Ct. App., 57 Cal. App. 4th 354, 66 Cal. Rptr. 2d 921 (1997)

NATURE OF CASE: Appeal of grant of summary judgment to defendant in breach of contract action.

FACT SUMMARY: Locke (P) had a development deal with Warner Bros. Inc. (Warner) (D), but none of her projects were ever picked up and Warner (D) never hired her as a director. Locke claimed breach of contract on the grounds that Warner (D) frustrated the purpose of the development deal.

RULE OF LAW

Contracts contain an implied covenant of good faith and fair dealing such that one party cannot frustrate the other party's right to receive the benefit of the bargain.

FACTS: Sondra Locke (P) appeared with Clint Eastwood in a 1975 film. The two began a relationship that lasted over a decade. When the relationship ended, Locke (P) sued Eastwood on various grounds and the two reached a settlement. Part of the settlement included a development deal for Locke (P) with a film studio, Warner Brothers, Inc. (Warner) (D). Warner (D) would pay $1.5 million to Locke (P) over three years in exchange for a first look at her potential film projects and consideration of Locke (P) as a director. This deal was a so-called pay or play deal. Locke (P) was unaware that Eastwood promised to reimburse Warner (D) for payments to Locke (P) if Warner (D) did not develop any of Locke's projects. Locke (P) had an office on Warner's (D) lot and proposed multiple projects to Warner (D), but Warner (D) rejected all of them and did not hire Locke (P) to direct any films. Locke (P) sued Warner (D) on a breach of contract action based on Warner's (D) alleged frustration of Locke (P) receiving the benefit of the Locke–Warner agreement. Testimony showed that Warner (D) never intended to develop any of Locke's (P) projects and that the agreement was "Clint's deal." Warner (D) moved for summary judgment, which the court granted, finding Warner (D) did consider the projects and did not breach the contract by failing to produce any of Locke's (P) projects. The trial court's order specifically held that judicial review cannot apply to "subjective artistic and business decisions" such as deciding what projects to produce. Locke (P) appealed.

ISSUE: Do contracts contain an implied covenant of good faith and fair dealing such that one party cannot frustrate the other party's right to receive the benefit of the bargain?

HOLDING AND DECISION: (Klein, J.) Yes. Contracts contain an implied covenant of good faith and fair dealing such that one party cannot frustrate the other party's right to receive the benefit of the bargain. The trial court erred in holding that it could not review Warner Bros. Inc.'s(Warner) (D) decision not to produce any of Locke's (P) projects. Warner (D) had the right to refuse the projects, but the refusals must be in good faith. All contracts have the implied covenant of good faith and fair dealing. An issue of material fact exists as to whether Warner (D) had the good-faith intention of developing a Locke project when appropriate or if Warner (D), in bad faith, struck down all Locke projects across the board. Locke (P) presented testimony sufficient to raise an issue of material fact. Warner (D) argues that Locke (P) is seeking to ignore Warner's (D) discretionary power to reject her projects, but that is not the case. Warner (D) retains the power to reject her projects, but the rejection must be in good faith. Categorically refusing to work with Locke (P) raises a question of fact. Reversed in part; affirmed in part.

ANALYSIS

Warner Bros., Inc. (Warner) (D) could determine that all of Locke's (P) proposals were terrible and did not deserve development and the courts would not second-guess such subjective judgment. The triable issue is whether Warner (D) actually viewed Locke's (P) proposals as terrible or simply ignored all of her proposals. The court also noted Warner (D) had multiple agreements with other producers and directors that amounted to nothing, but the theory that Warner (D) entered the agreement with Locke (P) just to pacify Eastwood taints Warner's (D) claim that it gave considered thought to Locke's proposals. Warner's (D) purposes for entering the contract could not prevent it from living up to its spirit.

Quicknotes

BREACH OF CONTRACT Unlawful failure by a party to perform its obligations pursuant to contract.

IMPLIED COVENANT OF GOOD FAITH AND FAIR DEALING An implied warranty that the parties will deal honestly in the satisfaction of their obligations and without an intent to defraud.

ISSUE OF MATERIAL FACT An issue or dispute regarding a fact that is legally relevant to a claim or cause of action

Continued on next page.

that will, as a matter of substantive law, make a difference to the outcome reached in a given case. Also stated as "material issue of fact."

SUMMARY JUDGMENT Judgment rendered by a court in response to a motion made by one of the parties, claiming that the lack of a question of material fact in respect to an issue warrants disposition of the issue without consideration by the jury.

Geysen v. Securitas Security Services, USA, Inc.

Terminated at-will employee (P) v. Former employer (D)

Conn. Sup. Ct., 322 Conn. 385, 142 A.3d 227 (2016)

NATURE OF CASE: Cross-appeals from judgment for plaintiff former employee on claim asserting that former employer's commissions plan violated public policy, and from judgment for defendant former employer striking counts alleging breach of the implied covenant of good faith and fair dealing and wrongful termination in violation of public policy, respectively.

FACT SUMMARY: Geysen (P), who's at-will employment with Securitas Security Services, USA, Inc. (Securitas) (D), was terminated, contended he had viable claims that his termination was made in breach of the implied covenant of good faith and fair dealing and that his wrongful termination violated public policy, respectively. Securitas (D) contended its commissions plan, which provided commissions would be paid only if the work had been invoiced prior to termination of the employee who had procured a contract for that work, did not violate public policy or statutory wage laws.

RULE OF LAW

(1) An at-will employment agreement, providing that an employee's commissions will not be paid unless the employer has invoiced commissionable amounts to the client prior to the employee's termination, is not void as contrary to public policy.

(2) A claim for breach of the implied covenant of good faith and fair dealing is available to a terminated at-will employee who asserts that the termination was done with the intent to avoid the payment of commissions, in violation of the employee's reasonable expectations.

(3) A claim for wrongful termination is not available to a terminated at-will employee who cannot, as a matter of law, predicate the claim on a violation of a public policy.

FACTS: Geysen (P) worked as an at-will sales manager for Securitas Security Services, USA, Inc. (Securitas) (D), earning a weekly base salary and, pursuant to a sales incentive plan, commissions on contracts he procured. The incentive plan provided, in part, that upon a manager's termination of employment, all commissions ceased, except that any commissionable amounts that had been invoiced to a client prior to the manager's termination date would still be paid commission as part of the terminated manager's final pay. Securitas (D) terminated Geysen's (P) employment after he had been with the company for about three years. Geysen (P) sued Securitas (D), alleging that Securitas (D) violated the state's wage law, breached his employment contract by violating the implied covenant of good faith and fair dealing, and wrongfully discharged him in violation of public policy. He also alleged that Securitas's (D) reasons for his termination were false and a pretext for nonpayment of owed commissions. Securitas (D) moved to strike count two, alleging breach of the implied covenant of good faith and fair dealing, and count three, alleging wrongful discharge in violation of public policy. The trial court granted Securitas's (D) motion to strike both counts because it believed Geysen (P) had an adequate statutory remedy under the wage law, and the court rendered a partial judgment for Securitas (D) on the two stricken counts. However, the trial court determined that, because Geysen's (P) right to commissions was not contingent upon his providing any further services to Securitas's (D) customers, he had fully earned his commissions when his employment was terminated. Thus, the trial court found that since the provision in the sales incentive plan deprived him of those earned commissions, resulted in forfeiture of wages, and applied even to an employee who was terminated for no cause, the provision was unenforceable because it violated two public policies: the first, which strongly favors the payment of wages, and the second, which disfavors forfeitures. Securitas (D) appealed from the judgment, and Geysen (P) cross-appealed. The state's highest court granted review.

ISSUE:

(1) Is an at-will employment agreement, providing that an employee's commissions will not be paid unless the employer has invoiced commissionable amounts to the client prior to the employee's termination, void as contrary to public policy?

(2) Is a claim for breach of the implied covenant of good faith and fair dealing available to a terminated at-will employee who asserts that the termination was done with the intent to avoid the payment of commissions, in violation of the employee's reasonable expectations?

(3) Is a claim for wrongful termination available to a terminated at-will employee who cannot, as a matter of law, predicate the claim on a violation of a public policy?

HOLDING AND DECISION: (Rogers, C.J.)

(1) No. An at-will employment agreement, providing that an employee's commissions will not be paid unless the employer has invoiced commissionable

Continued on next page.

amounts to the client prior to the employee's termination, is not void as contrary to public policy. Although it is well established that parties are free to contract for whatever terms on which they may agree, it is equally well established that contracts that violate public policy are unenforceable. The state has a strong policy that favors freedom of contract, and courts will not undo a bargain merely because it turns out to have been unwise. If a contract violates public policy, however, that is a reason not to enforce it. Here, if the commission provision acts to negate the wage statutes, it violates public policy. Therefore, as an initial matter, it must be determined whether the commission provision violates the wage statutes. The wage laws at issue do not contain substantive standards for determining the amount of wages that are payable but provide penalties to deter employers from deferring wage payments once they have accrued. They provide remedial protections for those cases in which the employer-employee wage agreement is violated. In prior cases involving the wage statutes, it was held that the wage statutes left the substantive standards for the determination of wages to the agreement between the employer and the employee. Precedent likewise has rejected arguments by commissioned employees that their wages accrued at the time they rendered their services by making sales, since, in contrast to the public policies of other states, there is no policy in this state as to when wages accrue, and, instead, the timing of accrual is left to the determination of the wage agreement between the employer and the employee. Accordingly, on basis of the clear language of the commission provision, invoicing prior to Geysen's (P) termination was a condition precedent to earning the commission, so that the commissions were not "due" within the meaning of the wage statutes because there was a condition precedent to their accrual that had not been satisfied. Nevertheless, Geysen (P) contends that the commission provision should not be enforceable because he did not have to provide any further services to Securitas's (D) customers and, therefore, he had fully earned his commissions under the wage statutes. This argument is rejected, since there is no case law supporting it, and since Geysen (P) assumed the risk that he could lose commissions on some sales in the agreement he entered with Securitas Security Services, USA, Inc. (Securitas) (D), pursuant to the sales incentive plan. The court will not undo the bargain he made merely because the employer adhered to it. Otherwise, the commission provision on its face does not negate laws enacted for the common good, and it is not designed to evade statutory requirements. Because Geysen (P) was not owed commissions under the express and enforceable terms of the agreement, and the agreement did not violate public policy, there was no violation of the wage statutes. Judgment for Securitas (D) as to this issue. Reversed as to this issue.

(2) Yes. A claim for breach of the implied covenant of good faith and fair dealing is available to a terminated at-will employee who asserts that the termination was done with the intent to avoid the payment of commissions, in violation of the employee's reasonable expectations. The duty of good faith and fair dealing is a covenant implied into every contract or contractual relationship that requires that neither party do anything that will injure the right of the other to receive the benefits of the agreement. This covenant presupposes that the terms and purpose of the contract are agreed upon by the parties and that what is in dispute is a party's discretionary application or interpretation of a contract term. To breach the covenant, a party must act, or fail to act, in bad faith, with some dishonest purpose. In the context of employment contracts, bad faith does not mean that an employer has terminated an employee without good cause. Other jurisdictions have held that where commissions are to be paid for work performed by the employee, a bad faith termination constitutes a breach of the employment contract. Thus, although an employer may terminate an at-will employee without good cause, the employer may not act in bad faith to prevent paying the employee commissions the employee reasonably expected to receive for services rendered under the contract. However, an employer does not act in bad faith solely by refusing to pay commissions on sales invoiced after an employee's termination if that obligation is an express contract term. Here, the trial court erroneously considered Geysen's (P) claim that the covenant was breached to be essentially the same as a wrongful discharge claim. A breach of the implied covenant of good faith and fair dealing contract claim, however, is different from a wrongful termination claim because the former focuses on the fulfillment of the parties' reasonable expectations rather than on a violation of public policy. Thus, although an at-will employee may not be able to recover for his or her termination per se under a theory of wrongful termination, the contract for payment of commissions creates rights distinct from the employment relation, and obligations derived from the covenant of good faith implicit in the commission contract may survive the termination of the employment relationship. In other words, a contract cannot be read to enable an employer to terminate an employee for the purpose of avoiding the payment of commissions that are otherwise owed. Accordingly, a terminated

Continued on next page.

employee may state a claim that the employer's termination action was specifically designed to cut off commissions that were coming due to the employee. Here, Geysen (P) alleged that Securitas (D) violated the implied covenant of good faith and fair dealing by failing to comply with his reasonable expectation that Securitas (D) would pay him commissions that he earned. If an employer can be shown to have interfered in bad faith with an employee's ability to secure his or her commissions, this would violate the reasonable expectation that the employer would not inhibit the employee's ability to earn commissions he or she worked for under the contract. Accordingly, on basis of the allegations in the complaint, Geysen (P) has stated a legally sufficient claim for breach of the implied covenant of good faith and fair dealing. Judgment for Geysen (P) as to this issue. Reversed as to this issue.

(3) No. A claim for wrongful termination is not available to a terminated at-will employee who cannot, as a matter of law, predicate the claim on a violation of a public policy. The public policy exception to the termination of at-will employment is narrow and applied only where an important public policy is violated by the termination. The question of whether a challenged discharge violates public policy is a question of law to be decided by the court. Here, the trial court, as well as this court, ruled that Geysen's (P) termination did not violate public policy. Contrary to Geysen's (P) argument, his termination did not violate the wage statutes, which promote a public policy favoring the payment of earned wages but should not be read to provide a broader public policy mandate to provide a remedy for unearned wages that were not due. Here, the commission provision is enforceable and does not violate the public policy embodied in the wage statutes. Therefore, Securitas's (D) termination of Geysen (P) did not violate a statutorily based public policy. Although Geysen (P) goes beyond statutorily based public policy in his complaint when he alleges that his employment was terminated "as a pretext to deprive him of the just fruits of his labor" and that this violates "the public policy of justly compensating employees for their work," the parameters of public policy regarding the payment of wages is reflected in the wage statutes. Thus, an employee cannot use the nonpayment of wages that have not accrued as the basis for a wrongful discharge claim, and it would be up to the legislature to decide if it wishes to expand this public policy to include unearned wages in this context. Consequently, the trial court did not err in striking this count. Judgment for Securitas (D) as to this issue. Affirmed as to this issue. Affirmed in part, reversed in part, and remanded.

ANALYSIS

As this case demonstrates, agreements that are contrary to public policy, i.e., those that negate laws enacted for the common good, are illegal and therefore unenforceable. Agreements that are legal on their face, yet are designed to evade statutory requirements, also are routinely held unenforceable. However, because of the inherent vagueness of the concept of public policy and the difficulty encountered when attempting to define precisely the contour of the public policy exception, courts ordinarily look to see whether a plaintiff has alleged a violation of any explicit statutory or constitutional provision, or any judicially conceived notion of public policy. In the at-will employment context, the public policy exception to the at-will employment rule attempts to balance the competing interests of the employer and the employee. Under the at-will employment rule, the employer is allowed, in ordinary circumstances, to make personnel decisions without fear of incurring civil liability, since an employer is entitled to be motivated by and to serve its own legitimate business interests, entitled to wide latitude in deciding whom it will employ in the face of the uncertainties of the business world, and entitled to flexibility in the face of changing circumstances. Accordingly, under the public policy exception to this rule, the employee has the burden of pleading and proving that his or her dismissal occurred for a reason violating public policy. Employee job security is thus protected, but only against employer actions that contravene public policy.

Quicknotes

AT-WILL EMPLOYMENT The rule that an employment relationship is subject to termination at any time, or for any cause, by an employee or an employer in the absence of a specific agreement otherwise.

CONDITION PRECEDENT The happening of an uncertain occurrence which is necessary before a particular right or interest may be obtained or an action performed.

FREEDOM OF CONTRACT A basic freedom that is guaranteed by Article I, § 10, cl. 1 of the U.S. Constitution and that may not be denied by the state.

IMPLIED COVENANT OF GOOD FAITH AND FAIR DEALING An implied warranty that the parties will deal honestly in the satisfaction of their obligations and without an intent to defraud.

Continued on next page.

PUBLIC POLICY Policy administered by the state with respect to the health, safety, and morals of its people in accordance with common notions of fairness and decency.

WRONGFUL DISCHARGE Unlawful termination of an individual's employment.

Bayliner Marine Corp. v. Crow

Boat manufacturer (D) v. Boat purchaser (P)

Va. Sup. Ct., 257 Va. 121, 509 S.E.2d 499 (1999)

NATURE OF CASE: Boat manufacturer's appeal from a judgment against it in a breach of warranty suit.

FACT SUMMARY: In the summer of 1989, John Crow (P) was invited by a sales representative for Tidewater Yacht Agency, Inc. (Tidewater) to ride on a new model sport fishing boat manufactured by Bayliner Marine Corp. (Bayliner) (D). Crow (P) was most interested in the speed of the boat, and after being given copies of "prop matrixes" and other promotional material, Crow (P) entered into a written contract for the purchase of the 3486 Trophy Convertible in which he had ridden. He took delivery in September 1989, and in 1992, filed suit for breached express warranties, implied warranties of merchantability, and fitness for a particular purpose (alleging lack of attainment of maximum speed).

RULE OF LAW

In assessing the merchantability of goods, the Uniform Commercial Code § 2-314(2)(a),(c) requirement that goods must be such as would "pass without objection in the trade" concerns whether a significant segment of the buying public would object to buying the goods, while the requirement that goods "are fit for the ordinary purposes for which such goods are used" concerns whether the goods are reasonably capable of performing their ordinary functions.

FACTS: John Crow (P) sought to purchase a fishing boat. When he asked the manufacturer, Bayliner Marine Corp. (Bayliner) (D), about the maximum speed, Bayliner's representative explained that he had no personal experience with the boat. Therefore, the representative consulted two documents described as "prop matrixes," which were included by Bayliner (D) in its dealer's manual. The representative gave Crow (P) copies of the "prop matrixes," which listed the boat models offered by Bayliner (D) and stated the recommended propeller sizes, gear ratios, and engine sizes for each model. The "prop matrixes" also listed the maximum speed for each model. The 3486 Trophy Convertible (the boat ultimately purchased) was listed as having a maximum speed of 30 miles per hour when equipped with a size "20 × 20" or "20 × 19" propeller. The boat Crow (P) purchased did not have either size propeller but, instead, had a size "20 × 17" propeller. At the bottom of one of the "prop matrixes" was the following disclaimer: "This data is intended for comparative purposes only and is available without reference to weather conditions or other variables. All testing was done at or near sea level, with full fuel and water tanks, and approximately 600 lb. passenger and gear weight." Crow (P) purchased the boat. During the next 12 to 14 months, Crow (P) made numerous repairs and adjustments to the boat in attempt to increase its speed capability. Despite these efforts, the boat consistently achieved a maximum speed of only 17 miles per hour, except for one brief period. Crow (P) sued the manufacturer Bayliner (D), arguing it had breached express warranties and implied warranties of merchantability and fitness for a particular purpose. Judgment was rendered for Crow (P), and Bayliner (D) appealed.

ISSUE: In assessing the merchantability of goods, does the Uniform Commercial Code § 2-314(2)(a),(c) requirement that goods must be such as would "pass without objection in the trade" concern whether a significant segment of the buying public would object to buying the goods, while the requirement that goods, "are fit for the ordinary purposes for which such goods are used" concern whether the goods are reasonably capable of performing their ordinary functions?

HOLDING AND DECISION: (Keenan, J.) Yes. In assessing the merchantability of goods, the Uniform Commercial Code (U.C.C.) § 2-314(2)(a),(c) requirement that goods must be such as would "pass without objection in the trade" concerns whether a significant segment of the buying public would object to buying the goods, while the requirement that goods "are fit for the ordinary purposes for which such goods are used" concerns whether the goods are reasonably capable of performing their ordinary functions. In order to prove that a product is not merchantable, the complaining party must first establish the standard of merchantability in the trade. Here, Bayliner Marine Corp. (Bayliner) (D) correctly noted that the record contained no evidence of the standard of merchantability in the offshore fishing boat trade. Nor did the record contain any evidence supporting a conclusion that a significant portion of the boat-buying public would object to purchasing an offshore fishing boat with the speed capability of the 3486 Trophy Convertible (the boat at issue). Crow (P), nevertheless, relied on his own testimony that the boat's speed was inadequate for his intended use, and another witness's opinion testimony that the boat took "a long time" to reach certain fishing grounds in the Gulf Stream off the coast of Virginia. However, this evidence failed to address the standard of merchantability in the trade or whether Crow's (P) boat failed to meet that standard. Thus, Crow (P)

Continued on next page.

failed to prove that the boat would not "pass without objection in the trade" as required by the U.C.C. As to whether the record supported a conclusion that Crow's (P) boat was not fit for its ordinary purpose as an offshore sport fishing boat, the evidence was uncontroverted that Crow (P) used the boat for offshore fishing, at least during the first few years after purchasing it, and that the boat's engines were used for 850 hours. While Crow (P) stated that many of those hours were incurred during various repair or modification attempts and that the boat was of little value to him, this testimony did not support a conclusion that a boat with this speed capability is generally unacceptable as an offshore fishing boat. Finally, the statement in the sales brochure that the model of boat bought by Crow (P) "delivers the kind of performance you need to get to the prime offshore fishing grounds" merely expressed Bayliner's (D) opinion concerning the quality of the boat's performance and did not create an express warranty that the boat was capable of attaining a speed of 30 miles per hour. Reversed.

ANALYSIS

In *Bayliner,* Crow (P) contended the "particular purpose" for which the boat was intended was as an offshore fishing boat capable of traveling at a maximum speed of 30 miles per hour. However, to establish an implied warranty of fitness for a particular purpose, the buyer must prove as a threshold matter that he or she made known to the seller the particular purpose for which the goods were required. In this regard, the *Bayliner* court noted that the record did not support a conclusion that Crow (P) had informed the manufacturer or the seller of this precise requirement. Although Crow (P) had informed them that he intended to use the boat for offshore fishing and discussed the boat's speed in this context, these facts did not establish that the seller actually knew on the date of sale that a boat incapable of travelling at 30 miles per hour was unacceptable to Crow (P). Accordingly, the *Bayliner* court concluded that the evidence failed to support the trial court's ruling that Bayliner (D) had breached an implied warranty of fitness for a particular purpose.

Quicknotes

EXPRESS WARRANTY An express promise made by one party to a contract that the other party may rely on a fact, relieving that party from the obligation of determining whether the fact is true and indemnifying the other party from liability if that fact is shown to be false.

Speight v. Walters Development Co.

Third-party homeowner (P) v. Home builder (D)

Iowa Sup. Ct., 744 N.W.2d 108 (2008)

NATURE OF CASE: Appeal from affirmance of summary judgment dismissal of action for breach of implied warranty of workmanlike construction.

FACT SUMMARY: The Speights (P), who purchased a home built by Walters Development Co. (D) after several homeowners had already occupied the home, contended the implied warranty of workmanlike construction should be extended to them as subsequent purchasers to cover construction defects in the home.

RULE OF LAW

(1) An implied warranty of workmanlike construction extends to subsequent, third-party, purchasers of a home.

(2) For purposes of the statute of limitations for a claim of breach of implied warranty of workmanlike construction, the action accrues when a defect in a house is discovered, rather than when construction of the house is completed.

FACTS: In 1995, Walters Development Co. (Walters) (D) custom built a home for the Roches, who then sold the home to the Rogers, who then sold it to the Speights (P) in 2000. At some point thereafter, the Speights (P) noticed water damage and mold, which was determined to have been caused by a defectively constructed roof and defective rain gutters. None of the previous owners had actual or imputed knowledge of these defects. The Speights (P) brought suit in 2005 against Walters (D) alleging, inter alia, a breach of the implied warranty of workmanlike construction. The parties cross-moved for summary judgment and the trial court granted summary judgment to Walters (D), concluding the implied warranty did not extend to subsequent purchasers. The state's intermediate appellate court affirmed. Both courts also agreed that, in any event, even if the implied warranty extended to subsequent purchasers, the Speights' (P) cause of action would be barred by the statute of limitations. The state's highest court granted review.

ISSUE:

(1) Does an implied warranty of workmanlike construction extend to subsequent, third-party, purchasers of a home?

(2) For purposes of the statute of limitations for a claim of breach of implied warranty of workmanlike construction, does the action accrue when a defect in a house is discovered, rather than when construction of the house is completed?

HOLDING AND DECISION: (Larson, J.)

(1) Yes. An implied warranty of workmanlike construction extends to subsequent, third-party, purchasers of a home. The implied warranty of workmanlike construction is a judicially created doctrine implemented to protect an innocent home buyer by holding the experienced builder accountable for the quality of construction. Given that homes are increasingly complex, and buyers are ill-equipped to discover defects in homes, many of which are latent defects, the implied warranty of workmanlike construction addresses the inequities between the buyer and the builder-vendor by requiring a building be constructed in a reasonably good and workmanlike manner and be reasonably fit for the intended purpose. In this state, the implied warranty has been applied to first purchasers of a home. The elements of an action asserting a breach of that warranty are these: (1) the house was constructed to be occupied by the buyer as a home; (2) the house was purchased from a builder-vendor, who had constructed it for the purpose of sale; (3) when sold, the house was not reasonably fit for its intended purpose or had not been constructed in a good and workmanlike manner; (4) at the time of purchase, the buyer was unaware of the defect and had no reasonable means of discovering it; and (5) by reason of the defective condition the buyer suffered damages. Here, the Speights (P) are asking the court to extend the warranty to subsequent purchasers who have no privity with the builder-vendor. Jurisdictions are split as to whether to extend this type of implied warranty to subsequent purchasers. Those that do not rely on traditional principles of contract and hold because there is a lack of privity between the subsequent purchaser and the builder-vendor, there is no reliance by the subsequent purchaser on any representations made by the builder-vendor regarding the quality of construction. Some courts have also concluded that the justifications for eliminating the privity requirement in products liability cases do not exist in the sale of real estate. Those states that do extend the warranty to subsequent purchasers rely on the public policy considerations supporting the warranty, namely, to protect innocent home buyers from latent defects, which are no more easily discovered

Continued on next page.

by subsequent purchasers than original purchasers. These states also rely on the purpose of the implied warranty of workmanlike construction, which is to ensure a home will be fit for habitation, a matter that depends upon the quality of the dwelling delivered rather than the buyer's status. In these jurisdictions, the lack of privity between the subsequent purchaser and the builder-vendor is not an impediment to extending the implied warranty, since the warranty exists independently of contract by its very nature. Additionally, in some of these jurisdictions, the same justifications used for eliminating the privity requirement in products liability cases are used for eliminating the privity requirement in home purchases, especially since our society is increasingly mobile, and as a result, a home's ownership is likely to change hands a number of times. A blanket rule prohibiting subsequent purchasers from recovering for a breach of the implied warranty of workmanlike construction would do injustice to those who purchase a home from a previous buyer shortly after the home was constructed when the subsequent purchaser later discovers the home was defectively constructed. Finally, one author posits the doctrine of assignment allows for the transfer to the subsequent purchaser of the original purchaser's right to sue for breach of the implied warranty of workmanlike construction. The latter, more modern approach, is the better one, and is now adopted in this state. Therefore, the implied warranty of workmanlike construction may extend to the Speights (P). Walters Development Co. (Walters) (D) contends adopting this approach would lead to increased costs for builders, increased claims, and increased home prices. However, builder-vendors are currently required to build a home in a good and workmanlike manner, and the implied warranty of workmanlike construction reasonably merely puts the risk of shoddy construction on the builder-vendor. That risk is not increased by allowing subsequent purchasers to recover for the same latent defects for which an original purchaser could recover. Moreover, the statute of repose extinguishes the possibility of unlimited liability for builder-vendors, since the period of repose starts upon completion of construction, and builder-vendors are not liable on an implied-warranty claim after the statute of repose has run, regardless of who owns the home. Judgment for the Speights (P) as to this issue.

(2) Yes. For purposes of the statute of limitations for a claim of breach of implied warranty of workmanlike construction, the action accrues when a defect in a house is discovered, rather than when construction of the house is completed. The appropriate statute of limitations for injuries to property is five years. The question, therefore, is when the Speights' (P) cause of action accrued. Walters (D) contends it accrued when the house was completed, in 1995, on basis of the Uniform Commercial Code, which provides the statute of limitations for causes of action for the sale of goods accrues when the goods are delivered, as opposed to when damage to the goods is discovered. However, a house is not "goods," and the appropriate timeframe for the accrual of a cause of action based on the implied warranty of workmanlike construction is when the defect in the house is actually discovered, or when the discovery may be imputed to the party asserting the warranty. Because the Speights (P) filed their suit in 2005, within five years of purchasing the house, they could not have gained actual or imputed knowledge of the defect in their home more than five years prior to commencing their action and their suit is therefore not time-barred. The appellate court decision is vacated; the trial court decision is reversed; and the action is remanded for further proceedings. Judgment for the Speights (P) as to this issue. We vacate the decision of the court of appeals, reverse the district court's judgment, and remand for further proceedings.

ANALYSIS

The court in this case joins a clear majority of jurisdictions that have recognized an implied warranty of quality in the sale of a new home by a builder-vendor. The warranty has different names in different jurisdictions, and may, in addition to being called an implied warranty of workmanlike construction, as in this case, may be called a warranty of habitability, a warranty of skillful construction, or a warranty of merchantability. As the decision notes, however, jurisdictions are split as to whether to extend such a warranty to subsequent purchasers.

Quicknotes

IMPLIED WARRANTY An implied promise made by one party to a contract that the other party may rely on a fact, relieving that party from the obligation of determining whether the fact is true and indemnifying the other party from liability if that fact is shown to be false.

STATUTE OF REPOSE A law prescribing the period of time in which an action can be commenced that begins to run upon the delivery of goods or the completion of performance.

CHAPTER 7

Avoiding Enforcement: Incapacity, Bargaining Misconduct, Unconscionability, and Public Policy

Quick Reference Rules of Law

12. *Valley Medical Specialists v. Farber.* In light of the public policy interest involved in restrictive covenants not to compete between physicians, each agreement will be strictly construed for reasonableness. *114*

13. *P.M. v. T.B.* A gestational surrogacy contract is legally enforceable in favor of the intended, biological father against a surrogate mother and her husband who are not the child's genetic parents. *116*

Dodson v. Shrader

Auto purchaser (P) v. Sellers of truck (D)

Tenn. Sup. Ct., 824 S.W.2d 545 (1992)

NATURE OF CASE: Appeal from award of rescission of contract.

FACT SUMMARY: Dodson (P) bought a car when he was 16 and, after it "blew up," wanted the purchase contract rescinded and refused to pay for depreciation to the truck while it had been in his hands.

RULE OF LAW

Even if a minor's contract is rescinded, the merchant may keep an amount equal to the decrease in value of the items returned rather than refund the full purchase price.

FACTS: Dodson (P), aged 16, bought a pickup truck from the Shraders (D) for $4,900. Although the truck developed a burnt valve nine months later, Dodson (P) drove it anyway until it "blew up." Parking the inoperable truck in his parents' yard, he contacted the Shraders (D) and demanded that his contract be rescinded and his money returned. The Shraders (D) refused. Dodson (P) filed suit, requesting rescission of his contract. When the general session court dismissed the case, Dodson (P) appealed. While his appeal was pending, he tendered the truck again. The Shraders (D) refused to take the truck unless Dodson (P) would pay for all the depreciation that had occurred while it had been in his hands. He refused. The circuit court held a new trial and granted rescission, ordering refund of the full purchase price. The Shraders (D) appealed on the ground that they were entitled to keep an amount for depreciation.

ISSUE: Even if a minor's contract is rescinded, may the merchant keep an amount equal to the decrease in value of the items returned rather than refund the full purchase price?

HOLDING AND DECISION: (O'Brien, J.) Yes. Even if a minor's contract is rescinded, the merchant may still keep an amount equal to the decrease in value of the items returned rather than refund the full purchase price. The rule permitting the contracts of minors to be rescinded exists to protect them from unscrupulous persons who would take advantage of their inexperience. However, a merchant who deals with a minor in good faith also should receive some protection. Therefore, if there has been no undue influence or fraud exercised on the part of the merchant, he or she may keep a reasonable compensation for the use and depreciation of and the willful or negligent damage to the item returned. This rule will prevent minors from taking advantage of merchants should they purchase an item, use it up, and then demand rescission. Reversed and remanded.

ANALYSIS

Generally, a minor's contracts are considered voidable, not void. This means the merchant cannot claim the contract is void, or, stated another way, the minor can elect to keep a contract if he or she so desires. Note that this rule has an exception: a minor's contracts for necessities such as food, clothing, and shelter are not voidable. Also, once the minor reaches majority, the minor must request rescission of an offensive contract within a reasonable amount of time, or the minor will be considered to have affirmed the contract as an adult. See, e.g., *Bobby Floars Toyota Inc. v. Smith*, 269 S.E.2d 320 (N.C. Ct. App. 1980) (no rescission of contract where minor kept car for 10 months after attaining majority).

Quicknotes

RESCISSION The canceling of an agreement and the return of the parties to their positions prior to the formation of the contract.

UNDUE INFLUENCE Improper use of power that deprives an individual of freedom of choice or substitutes another's choice for the individual's own choice.

VOIDABLE CONTRACT A valid contract that may be legally voided at the option of one of the parties.

Sparrow v. Demonico

Party to settlement agreement (P) v. Party to settlement agreement (D)

Mass. Sup. Jud. Ct., 461 Mass. 322, 960 N.E.2d 296 (2012)

NATURE OF CASE: Appeal from order denying enforcement of a settlement agreement.

FACT SUMMARY: Frances Sparrow (P), who had entered into a settlement agreement with her sister, Susan Demonico (Susan) (D), contended there was insufficient evidence Susan (D) was mentally incompetent at the time she entered into the agreement, and, therefore, the agreement should be enforced.

RULE OF LAW

Without medical evidence or expert testimony that a mental condition interfered with a party's understanding of a transaction, or with the party's ability to act reasonably in relation to it, the evidence will not be sufficient to support a conclusion of incapacity to contract.

FACTS: Frances Sparrow (Sparrow) (P) disagreed with her sister, Susan Demonico (Susan) (D), over the ownership of the family home, and Sparrow (P) brought suit against Susan (D) and Susan's (D) husband, David Demonico, to resolve the dispute. Prior to trial, Sparrow (P) and the Demonicos (D) entered into a settlement agreement pursuant to voluntary mediation, whereby the Demonicos (D) agreed to sell the property and to pay Sparrow (P) $100,000 from the proceeds of the sale. When Sparrow (P) sought an order enforcing the agreement, the Demonicos (D) claimed the agreement was unenforceable because Susan (D) had, in their view, experienced a mental breakdown during the mediation and thus lacked the capacity to authorize settlement. At an evidentiary hearing on the motion, the Demonicos (D) were the only witnesses, and no exhibits were admitted. The motion judge denied Sparrow's (P) motion on the basis "the purported agreement may have been the product of an emotionally overwrought state of mind on the part of Susan Demonico." The judge noted Susan's (D) testimony that she had been taking a medication, Zoloft, prior to the mediation, but that she had stopped taking the medication at some point before the mediation, and that she cried much of the day; he specifically credited Susan's (D) testimony that she "was out of control emotionally during the mediation" and found also that "she was not thinking rationally" on that day. The case proceeded to trial by jury before a different judge, who, at the close of evidence, allowed the Demonicos' (D) motion for a directed verdict on all counts. Sparrow (P) appealed from the judgment and the denial of her motion to enforce the mediated settlement agreement. The state's highest court granted review.

ISSUE: Without medical evidence or expert testimony that a mental condition interfered with a party's understanding of a transaction, or with the party's ability to act reasonably in relation to it, will the evidence be sufficient to support a conclusion of incapacity to contract?

HOLDING AND DECISION: (Duffly, J.) No. Without medical evidence or expert testimony that a mental condition interfered with a party's understanding of a transaction, or with the party's ability to act reasonably in relation to it, the evidence will not be sufficient to support a conclusion of incapacity to contract. Here, Susan (D) seeks to void the contract on the basis that she lacked the capacity to contract at the time of entering into the agreement, due to mental illness or defect. The Demonicos (D) bear the burden of proof on this issue. The modern test for mental incapacity, also known as the "cognitive" or the "volitional" test, recognizes competence may be lost, not only through cognitive disorders, but also through affective disorders that encompass motivation or exercise of will. Under this test, the controlling consideration is whether the transaction in its result is one a reasonably competent person might have made. Also relevant to the inquiry in these circumstances is whether the party claiming mental incapacity was represented by independent, competent counsel. The evidence required to support a finding of incapacity to contract does not necessarily have to demonstrate a party suffers from a mental illness or defect that is permanent, degenerative, progressive, or of significant duration. Instead, the focus is on a party's understanding or conduct only at the time of the disputed transaction. The Demonicos (D) claim Susan's (D) impairment was not permanent, but rather was limited to the time of the mediation session, and they argue this evidence was sufficient to support a conclusion of incapacity, despite the lack of medical evidence or expert testimony as to the nature of Susan's (D) mental impairment and its effect on her decision-making ability. The issue presented—whether medical or expert testimony is necessary to establish mental incapacity—is one of first impression in this jurisdiction. In prior decisions concerning the issue of incapacity to contract, however, evidence of mental illness or defect has been presented consistently through medical evidence, including the testimony of physicians and mental health providers or experts, in addition to lay testimony. Moreover, in other contexts, it has been held a lay witness is not competent to

Continued on next page.

give an opinion as to mental condition, and in such other contexts, the reliance on medical and expert evidence is routine when addressing issues of mental illness, capacity, and competence. Accordingly, medical evidence is necessary to establish a person lacked the capacity to contract due to the existence of a mental condition. The inquiry in contracts area is in contrast to other areas of the law, such as tort claims of emotional distress or mental anguish, where the inquiry is whether the evidence supports a plaintiff's claim to have experienced emotional distress or mental anguish, rather than on the impact of that state on the ability to comprehend. Nevertheless, even in such contexts, medical corroboration is often required as such corroboration not only guards against feigned or fraudulent claims of mental distress, but also alleviates the concern that even honest plaintiffs erroneously might convince themselves they suffer from emotional distress. These concerns apply with at least equal force where the question is the capacity to contract due to mental impairment. Applying these principles here, it is noted Susan's (D) testimony of her mental state was lay testimony, but no medical evidence was presented regarding a diagnosis that would have required her to take her medication, or how her discontinuation of her medicine might have impacted her mental capacity to contract. There also was no expert or medical testimony to explain the effect of Susan's (D) experiences or behavior on her ability to understand the agreement, to appreciate what was happening, or to comprehend the reasonableness of the settlement terms or the consequences to her of authorizing the settlement. Without such medical evidence, there was no basis to conclude she lacked the capacity to contract. Based on Susan's (D) own testimony, it is clear she understood the nature and quality of the transaction and grasped its significance. In addition, there was no evidence that the settlement agreement was unreasonable, or that a reasonably competent person would not have entered it. Therefore, the evidence did not support a conclusion Susan (D) lacked the mental capacity to authorize settlement on the day of the mediation. The trial court's order is vacated, and the case is remanded for entry of an order that the settlement agreement be enforced.

ANALYSIS

The traditional test for contractual incapacity, known as the "cognitive" test, focused on whether the party alleged to lack contractual capacity could not understand the nature and quality of the transaction or grasp its significance. The modern test was adopted to accommodate a greater understanding of mental incapacity and its many forms, and the modern test recognizes there may be circumstances when, although a party claiming incapacity has some, or sufficient, understanding of the nature and consequences of the transaction, the contract may still be voidable where, by reason of mental illness or defect, the person is unable to act in a reasonable manner in relation to the transaction and the other party has reason to know of his or her condition. The court in this case holds that, in the absence of medical evidence of mental incapacity, Susan (D) was unable to adduce sufficient evidence she suffered from mental incapacity to contract under either the traditional test or the modern test.

Quicknotes

CAPACITY TO CONTRACT The legal and physical ability to enter into a contractual agreement, typically characterized by the ability to understand the consequences of one's actions.

Totem Marine Tug & Barge, Inc. v. Alyeska Pipeline Service Co.

Construction materials transporter (P) v. Construction company (D)

Alaska Sup. Ct., 584 P.2d 15 (1978)

NATURE OF CASE: Appeal from denial of damages for breach of contract.

FACT SUMMARY: Totem Marine Tug & Barge, Inc. (Totem) (P) claimed that Alyeska Pipeline Service Co. (Alyeska) (D) had used economic duress to get Totem (P) to sign a binding release of all claims it had against Alyeska (D) after Alyeska (D) terminated a contract with Totem (P).

RULE OF LAW

A contract can be voided if it was entered as the result of economic duress.

FACTS: Totem Marine Tug & Barge, Inc. (Totem) (P) had contracted to transport pipeline construction materials from Houston, Texas, to a designated port in southern Alaska for Alyeska Pipeline Service Co. (Alyeska) (D). According to Totem (P), Alyeska's (D) failure to proceed in accordance with the terms and specifications in the contract caused considerable delays and occasioned the hiring of a second tug to handle the extra tonnage in materials that were waiting to be loaded when Totem (P) arrived in Houston. Alyeska (D) eventually terminated the contract without reason. When Totem (P) submitted invoices and began pressing for payment, it was in a serious cash-flow crisis and faced the possibility of bankruptcy. This, it maintained, led it to accept Alyeska's (D) offer of $97,500 in cash for settlement of all claims by Totem (P). Later, Totem (P), claiming economic duress, sought to recover in a contract action. A summary judgment was granted in favor of Alyeska (D).

ISSUE: Can a contract be voided if it was entered as the result of economic duress?

HOLDING AND DECISION: (Burke, J.) Yes. A contract can be voided if it was entered as the result of economic duress. Avoidance of a contract on these grounds is recognized by this and many other courts. According to Professor Williston, the party alleging economic duress must show that he has been the victim of a wrongful or unlawful act or threat and that such act or threat deprived him of his unfettered will. Thus, Totem Marine Tug & Barge, Inc. (Totem) (P) would have to show that wrongful acts or threats by Alyeska Pipeline Service Co. (Alyeska) (D) intentionally caused Totem (P) to involuntarily enter into the settlement agreement. This would mean showing that Totem (P) had no reasonable alternative to agreeing to Alyeska's (D) settlement terms. Certainly, the facts of this case are such as would lend themselves to such proof. It is up to Totem (P) to prove its allegations, but the facts indicate that a summary judgment was improper. Reversed and remanded.

ANALYSIS

Section 492 of the Restatement (First) of Contracts focused on the exercise of "free will and judgment" in defining duress, while the Restatement (Second) of Contracts looks to the victim's having "no reasonable alternative." At early common law, avoidance of a contract on the ground of duress was available only if a party could show that it was entered for fear of loss of life or limb, mayhem, or imprisonment.

Quicknotes

DURESS Unlawful threats or other coercive behavior by one person that causes another to commit acts that he or she would not otherwise do.

ECONOMIC DURESS A defense to an action that a party was unlawfully coerced into the performance of an action by another due to fear of imminent economic loss and was not acting in accordance with his or her own free volition in performing the action.

Odorizzi v. Bloomfield School District

Teacher (P) v. School district (D)

Cal. Dist. Ct. App., 246 Cal. App. 2d 123, 54 Cal. Rptr. 533 (1966)

NATURE OF CASE: Appeal from judgment dismissing action to rescind resignation based on undue influence.

FACT SUMMARY: Odorizzi (P) was arrested on homosexual charges. Immediately after his release the Bloomfield School District (D) convinced him to resign.

RULE OF LAW

When a party's will has been overborne, so that in effect the party's actions are not his or her own, a charge of undue influence may be sustained.

FACTS: Odorizzi (P) was arrested for criminal homosexual activities. At the time he was under contract as a teacher for the Bloomfield School District (District) (D). Immediately after he was released on bail, the District (D) convinced him to resign. Odorizzi (P) was subsequently acquitted of the charges, but he was refused reemployment by the District (D). He brought suit to rescind his resignation. He charged duress, menace, fraud, and undue influence. He claimed that the superintendent of the District (D) and the principal of his school came to his apartment immediately after his release. He had not slept in nearly 40 hours and was under severe emotional and physical stress. He was told that if he did not immediately resign the District (D) would be forced to suspend him and then dismiss him. This would occasion embarrassing and humiliating publicity. However, if he resigned, the matter would be kept quiet and his chance for future jobs would not be impaired. The trial court found nothing wrong with these actions, no confidential relationship existed, and the District (D) would have been forced by law to suspend Odorizzi (P).

ISSUE: When a party's will has been overborne, so that in effect the party's actions are not his or her own, may a charge of undue influence be sustained?

HOLDING AND DECISION: (Fleming, J.) Yes. When a party's will has been overborne so that in effect the party's actions are not his or her own, a charge of undue influence may be sustained. While none of Odorizzi's (P) allegations has any basis, he has made out a prima facie case of undue influence. In essence the charge involves the use of excessive pressures to persuade one vulnerable to such pressures to decide a matter contra to one's own judgment. Extreme weakness or susceptibility is an important factor in establishing undue influence. It is normally found in cases of extreme youth or age or sickness. While it normally involves fiduciary or other confidential relationships, they are not necessary to the action. Here, extreme pressures were leveled against Odorizzi (P). He had just gone through an arrest, booking, and interrogation procedure for a crime that, if well publicized, would subject him to public humiliation. He was threatened with such publicity if he did not immediately resign. He was approached at his apartment immediately after his release. He was not given the opportunity to think the matter over or to consult outside advice. He was told that in any event he would be suspended and dismissed. These factors present a jury issue. If Odorizzi (P) can establish that he wouldn't have resigned but for these pressures and the jury finds that they were unreasonable and overbore his will, Odorizzi (P) could rescind his resignation. Judgment reversed.

ANALYSIS

Many types of contracts may be rescinded for undue influence. Mortmain statutes are in effect in some states. These hold that bequests made to churches shortly before death and after a visit by religious leaders are void and unenforceable. Wills may be declared invalid where they were procured through undue influence. Contracts to sell land for far less than its value and transfers made in fear of civil or criminal prosecution are other examples.

Quicknotes

BEQUEST A transfer of property that is accomplished by means of a testamentary instrument.

MORTMAIN STATUTE A law limiting gifts and other dispositions of land to corporations (especially charitable corporations) and that prohibit corporations from holding land in perpetuity.

RESCISSION The canceling of an agreement and the return of the parties to their positions prior to the formation of the contract.

UNDUE INFLUENCE Improper use of power that deprives an individual of freedom of choice and substitutes another's choice for the individual's own choice.

Martinez-Gonzalez v. Elkhorn Packing Co. LLC

Foreign farm laborer (P) v. Employer (D)

25 F.4th 613 (9th Cir. 2022)

NATURE OF CASE: Appeal from denial of motion to compel arbitration in action for labor and wage law violations.

FACT SUMMARY: Dario Martinez-Gonzalez (Martinez-Gonzalez) (P), a Mexican citizen who had worked for Elkhorn Packing Co. LLC (Elkhorn) (D) as a farm laborer, sued Elkhorn (D) for violations of federal and state labor and wage laws. Elkhorn (D) moved to compel arbitration on the basis of arbitration provisions in employment contracts that Martinez-Gonzalez (P) had signed. Martinez-Gonzalez (P) contended that the arbitration provisions were unenforceable because he had signed them under economic duress and undue influence.

RULE OF LAW

(1) An agreement is not the product of economic duress, and, therefore, rescindable, where, although the agreement may result from hard bargaining, no wrongful act has been committed against the party seeking rescission, and the party seeking rescission has reasonable alternatives to entering into a coerced agreement.

(2) An agreement is not the product of undue influence, and, therefore, rescindable, where a dominating person or party has not applied excessive pressure on a servient person, who is particularly susceptible to such pressure, to take unfair advantage of the servient person to force his or her assent to the agreement.

FACTS: Elkhorn Packing Co. LLC (Elkhorn) (D), a U.S. farm labor contractor, hired Dario Martinez-Gonzalez (Martinez-Gonzalez) (P), a Mexican citizen, to perform farm labor under an agricultural worker visa. Martinez-Gonzalez (P) had a secondary-school education and was the bread winner for his family, for whom he provided housing and medical care. At the orientation for workers, which took place several days after the workers had already begun harvesting vegetables, Martinez-Gonzalez (P), along with around 150 other laborers, was asked to sign employment paperwork. To facilitate the signing of the paperwork, Elkhorn (D) representatives directed employees to form lines, where they stood—in at least one case for 40 minutes—and waited to sign the packages. Once at the front of the line, an Elkhorn (D) representative told each employee where to sign while flipping through the pages. Representatives urged employees to hurry so that others could have a chance to sign. The employment package included an arbitration agreement. The agreement required employees to resolve all disputes with Elkhorn (D) by arbitration. The agreement was written in Spanish, Martinez-Gonzalez's (P) native language. He signed the arbitration agreement without reading it. Elkhorn (D) representatives didn't explain the contents of the arbitration agreement to him, didn't give him a copy of the agreement, and didn't tell him he could consult an attorney before signing it. On the other hand, Martinez-Gonzalez (P) didn't ask for a copy of the agreement, attorney consultation, or time to read the agreement. Elkhorn (D) never expressly told him that he had to sign the agreement to keep working for the company. After working for Elkhorn (D) that season, Martinez-Gonzalez (P) returned to Mexico. The following year, he returned to work for Elkhorn (D), and again signed paperwork that contained an arbitration agreement. However, he quit mid-season and returned to Mexico. He then sued Elkhorn (D) in state court on behalf of himself and other similarly situated workers, alleging a failure to pay federal minimum wages under the Fair Labor Standards Act, and state-law claims related to meals, wages, rest periods, and privacy. Elkhorn (D) removed the case to federal district court and moved to compel arbitration under the two arbitration agreements. The district court concluded that the agreements resulted from undue influence and economic duress and denied the motion to compel arbitration. Elkhorn (D) appealed, and the Ninth Circuit Court of Appeals granted review.

ISSUE:

(1) Is an agreement the product of economic duress, and, therefore, rescindable, where, although the agreement may result from hard bargaining, no wrongful act has been committed against the party seeking rescission, and the party seeking rescission has reasonable alternatives to entering into a coerced agreement?

(2) Is an agreement the product of undue influence, and, therefore, rescindable, where a dominating person or party has not applied excessive pressure on a servient person, who is particularly susceptible to such pressure, to take unfair advantage of the servient person to force his or her assent to the agreement?

HOLDING AND DECISION: (Bumatay, J.)

(1) No. An agreement is not the product of economic duress, and, therefore, rescindable, where, although the agreement may result from hard bargaining, no wrongful act has been committed against the party

Continued on next page.

seeking rescission, and the party seeking rescission has reasonable alternatives to entering into a coerced agreement. Under state law, a contract may be rescinded if it was signed under economic duress. Economic duress occurs when one party commits a (1) "wrongful act" and (2) that act is sufficiently coercive to cause a reasonably prudent person faced with no reasonable alternative to agree to an unfavorable contract. Here, Elkhorn Packing Co. LLC (Elkhorn) (D) did not commit a wrongful act against Dario Martinez-Gonzalez (Martinez-Gonzalez) (P), who had reasonable alternatives to entering into the contracts that contained arbitration agreements. Therefore, the doctrine of economic duress is inapplicable. "Wrongful acts" in this context need not be unlawful or tortious, but require more than merely hard bargaining, and must be either coercive or taken in bad faith. Some examples of wrongful acts are the assertion of a false claim, a bad-faith threat to breach a contract, and a threat to withhold payment of an acknowledged debt. Martinez-Gonzalez (P) asserts that Elkhorn (D) committed a wrongful act by asking him to sign the arbitration agreement after he made the journey from Mexico to California, where he was dependent on Elkhorn (D) housing and had already started harvesting lettuce. This conduct, albeit not ideal, did not constitute a "wrongful act" under state law, as it did not impinge on freedom of contract or undermine the proper functioning of the economic system. To the contrary, the orientation's location served a practical business function, as a convenient place to gather hundreds of farm workers in a single orientation. For a court to hold that the orientation was wrongful would place courts in charge of determining business necessities and would encumber, rather than promote, freedom of contract. Elkhorn (D) did not ask Martinez-Gonzalez (P) to work for disproportionately low wages, to forgo earned wages, or to disclaim any claims against it, but merely asked him to sign a commonplace agreement to bring disputes to an arbitrator. Here, too, Martinez-Gonzalez (P) had reasonable alternatives to entering into the arbitration agreements. Although being forced into bankruptcy, financial ruin, or selling one's home are not reasonable alternatives, the need for a job and money by itself is not grounds for a finding of economic duress. The district court's finding that Martinez-Gonzalez (P) lacked reasonable alternatives to signing the arbitration agreements because his challenging financial situation required him to keep his job with Elkhorn (D) was clearly erroneous. He could have asked whether signing the arbitration agreements was necessary for him to keep his job. Additionally, the agreements did not say that they were mandatory, and no one at Elkhorn (D) told Martinez-Gonzalez (P) that refusing to sign the agreements was a cause for termination. Moreover, the fear of termination, even if justified, cannot be used to prove the lack of reasonable alternatives. Martinez-Gonzalez (P) could have revoked the agreements, which by their terms were revokable within ten days, and nothing prevented him from quitting, in the same manner he did during the middle of the second season he worked for Elkhorn (D).

(2) No. An agreement is not the product of undue influence, and, therefore, rescindable, where a dominating person or party has not applied excessive pressure on a servient person, who is particularly susceptible to such pressure, to take unfair advantage of the servient person to force his or her assent to the agreement. One who is particularly susceptible to pressure has a lessened capacity to freely enter a contract. It may be the result of mental incapacity, or it may be the consequence of a lack of full vigor owing to age, physical condition, emotional anguish, or a combination of such factors. The result is the inability to act with unencumbered volition. The district court did not make findings regarding this factor. However, the facts do not support a finding that Martinez-Gonzalez (P) was particularly susceptible to Elkhorn's (D) pressure. Notwithstanding his modest socioeconomic background, Martinez-Gonzalez (P) was able to support and take care of himself and his family, and his ability to quit his job when he became dissatisfied with it demonstrates he was not particularly susceptible to undue pressure. Given that Martinez-Gonzalez's (P) volition was not particularly encumbered, Elkhorn (D) would have had to have brought extraordinary force to bear against him for there to have been undue influence. That did not happen. Several factors tend to show that the dominant party exerted extraordinary force against the servient party. Here, for example, the district court found that (1) the time and place of the orientation was unusual—both because it was held after Martinez-Gonzalez (P) traveled to the United States and because it occurred in a hotel parking lot with no chairs; (2) there was a lack of time to read the agreement in advance or consult an attorney; (3) there was pressure to sign the agreements quickly after a long day's work; and (4) Elkhorn (D) supervisors made statements exhorting workers to follow the company's rules. First, although the circumstances of the orientation were less than ideal, none of the factors identified by the district court, when viewed in context, constitute excessive pressure. Although it may be atypical for workers to sign employment documents in a hotel parking lot, the parking lot was conveniently located at the workers' hotel. Also,

Continued on next page.

the business practicalities of employing over a hundred foreign workers easily explain why Elkhorn (D) waited for the workers to arrive in the United States before asking them to sign the employment packets. Nothing indicates that the orientation was a "high pressure" tactic—"a pressure which works on mental, moral, or emotional weakness"—aimed at extracting arbitration agreements. Second, regarding the lack of time to read the agreement in advance or consult an attorney, Elkhorn (D) did not interfere with Martinez-Gonzalez's (P) ability to use either option, and it did not preclude him from doing so. Third, Elkhorn (D) urged the workers to hurry in signing the paperwork, not out of some bad-faith pressure tactic, but to accommodate other employees also waiting to complete the forms. Fourth, Elkhorn (D) representatives' general statements to follow the company's rules and directions had nothing to do with the arbitration agreements but were part of the orientation where workers were encouraged to work hard and follow Elkhorn's (D) rules. These were standard first-day instructions, not oppressive extortions to sign an arbitration agreement. Accordingly, the district court clearly erred in finding otherwise. Reversed and remanded.

DISSENT: (Rawlinson, J.) The majority gives short shrift to the clear-error standard of review. Credibility determinations made by the judge presiding over a trial must be afforded "special deference." The district court determined that Dario Martinez-Gonzalez (Martinez-Gonzalez) (P) testified credibly regarding the signing of the arbitration agreements, and the majority should have deferred to the district court's factual finding unless such findings were illogical, implausible, or without support in the record. The majority should also have deferred to the district court's legal conclusions that were based on its detailed factual findings. Because the district court did not clearly err in concluding, after a bench trial, that the atmosphere surrounding the signing of the arbitration agreements rose to the level of a wrongful act, the majority was wrong to disagree with the district court's legal determination. State courts have increasingly recognized that the economic duress doctrine is equitable in nature, and that this doctrine should be applied to correct inequitable or unequal exchanges between parties of disproportionate bargaining power and a greater willingness not to enforce agreements that were entered into under coercive circumstances. In determining whether the party asserting economic duress had a reasonable alternative available, courts make a factual determination as to whether a reasonably prudent person would follow the alternative course, or whether a reasonably prudent person might submit. Based on the evidence presented during trial, the district court concluded that no reasonable migrant worker with Martinez-Gonzalez's (P) "significant financial obligations," and "without alternative employment prospects, an alternative place to live . . . and no practical way to return to Mexico," would have refused to sign the arbitration agreements. The majority simplifies the case, indicating that it finds Elkhorn Packing Co. LLC (Elkhorn) (D) did not commit a wrongful act when asking the workers to sign commonplace agreements. That oversimplification ignores the district court's detailed factual findings. Contrary to the majority's conclusion, this case is not simply one of hard bargaining. Instead, it is a prime example of the inequitable or unequal exchanges between parties of disproportionate bargaining power that the economic duress doctrine aims to rectify. In Mexico, Martinez-Gonzalez (P) earned the equivalent of $150 a week while financially supporting his wife, mother-in-law, mother, and stepfather. He could earn five times more in the United States. Elkhorn (D) knew that "behind every employee, there are three, five, even up to eight people from their families who depend on that worker." Therefore, it is not difficult to contemplate the desperate circumstances that would compel Martinez-Gonzalez (P) to leave his family, travel twelve hours by bus to another country, and work in a field six days a week for nine-plus hours. The majority is plainly wrong in stating that the district court did not find that Elkhorn (D) acted with a coercive purpose; to the contrary, the entire thrust of the district court's factual findings was that Elkhorn (D) created a "coercive environment" aimed at robbing Martinez-Gonzalez (P) and the other workers of the ability to say no to arbitration. Another indication that the majority turned a blind eye to the district court's factual findings is that it questions whether extracting an arbitration agreement can ever constitute a "wrongful act." This, however, is a red herring. Martinez-Gonzalez (P) did not argue that making him sign an arbitration agreement in and of itself was improper. Rather, he sought to invalidate the arbitration agreement on the basis that he signed it under economic duress and as a result of undue influence. Additionally, the majority's conclusion that Martinez-Gonzalez (P) failed to demonstrate a lack of reasonable alternatives to signing the arbitration agreements is belied by the evidence adduced at trial that of the thousands of employees hired, no employee had ever refused to sign the arbitration agreement. The majority's diminishing of Martinez-Gonzalez's (P) compelling situation as the need for "a job and . . . money," blatantly disregards the factual findings regarding Martinez-Gonzalez's (P) dire circumstances, as well as the realities of migrant workers. Moreover, each of the three points the majority makes in support of its conclusion that Martinez-Gonzalez (P) had reasonable alternatives seems to conveniently ignore the rest of the story told by the district's court's factual findings. The first majority point is that Martinez-Gonzalez

Continued on next page.

(P) was not told that refusing to sign the agreement was grounds for termination. However, this is contradicted by evidence that the workers were not told that signing the documents was optional, and testimony that the signing of the agreement was not voluntary, and, in fact, was a condition of the employment. The second majority point is that Martinez-Gonzalez (P) failed to ask if the agreement was mandatory and that he could have asked to review the documents. Additional evidence, however, shows that the workers were presented with a stack of papers, told where to sign, and rushed through the process. Although the majority is correct that Elkhorn (D) representatives testified that workers "were invited to ask questions about the documents," it fails to add that the district court did not credit this testimony because there was also evidence that even if workers asked about the agreement, Elkhorn (D) representatives were not allowed to explain the rights the workers would be waiving by signing the agreements. The third majority point is that the workers could revoke the agreements, but that fails to credit the district court's finding that there was no way that Martinez-Gonzalez (P) would have known about the revocation provision in the arbitration agreements, since he was not allowed to read the agreements, they were not explained to him, and he was never provided copies of the agreements. Because the documents were gathered up by the supervisors immediately after signing, there was no opportunity to request a copy to review later, particularly as the testimony reflected that the supervisors rushed the workers through the process, with no opportunity for questions. In sum, the district court's finding of economic duress is amply supported by the evidence developed during trial, whereas the majority's contrary finding is not. The district court's finding of undue influence is even stronger. State courts examine seven specific factors to determine the existence of excessive pressure resulting in the overbearing of one's will. The district court made specific factual findings directly corresponding to five of these in concluding that the force used by Elkhorn (D) to get the workers to sign the arbitration agreements was "excessive." The majority concedes that Elkhorn (D) hurried workers to sign the new-hire documents, but the majority mischaracterizes that fact as an accommodation to other workers waiting in line to sign rather than "some bad-faith pressure tactic." In doing so, the majority blatantly ignores the district court's finding that Elkhorn (D) manufactured the coercive atmosphere by urging tired and hungry workers to execute an unexplained stack of documents at the end of a long workday, in a hotel parking lot. In addition, the majority emphasizes that Elkhorn (D) did not expressly forbid Martinez-Gonzalez (P) from asking for time to review the documents or to consult an attorney. However, the district court found that Elkhorn (D) created an atmosphere that precluded and discouraged the ability to review documents, ask questions, and consult advisors. Of course, Elkhorn (D) did not expressly inform its workers: "sign these documents without reading them or consulting a lawyer or suffer termination." If employers openly displayed such coercive tactics, there would be no need to apply the multifactor test developed by the courts to determine coercion. The bottom line is that the district court's determination that Martinez-Gonzalez (P) was subjected to economic duress and undue influence was firmly tethered to its review of the witness testimony and evidence presented during trial and was in no way clearly erroneous. The majority, instead of deferring to the district court's findings, substitutes its own assessment of the facts for the district courts, but the majority's conclusions, unlike those of the district court, are not supported by the evidence.

ANALYSIS

In California, the seven factors that may show the presence of excessive pressure include: (1) discussion of the transaction at an unusual or inappropriate time, (2) consummation of the transaction in an unusual place, (3) insistent demand that the business be finished at once, (4) extreme emphasis on untoward consequences of delay, (5) the use of multiple persuaders by the dominant side against a single servient party, (6) absence of third-party advisers to the servient party, and (7) statements that there is no time to consult financial advisers or attorneys. Although excessive pressure usually involves several of these factors, there are no fixed definitions or inflexible formulas that determine whether a dominant party has exerted excessive pressure on a servient party. Instead, courts analyze the entire context in which an agreement was signed to determine whether the signer's will be overborne. In this regard, the majority indicated that it disagreed with the dissent that the inquiry regarding excessive pressure can be reduced to a simple box-checking exercise of these seven factors, and that notwithstanding that the district court made findings on five of the seven factors, the appellate court still must determine whether the facts can support a finding of undue influence. The dissent responded by saying that contrary to the majority's characterization, neither the dissent nor the district court engaged in a "simple box-checking exercise," but, instead, the district court applied the seven factors, and the dissent gave appropriate deference to the district court's application of those factors to the evidence presented at trial. The dissent also accused the majority of erasing all the boxes (i.e., ignoring the factors altogether), discarding the district court's factual findings,

Continued on next page.

and writing its own version of the facts based on a manufactured "totality of the circumstances" review.

Quicknotes

ARBITRATION An alternative resolution process where a dispute is heard and decided by a neutral third party, rather than through legal proceedings.

ECONOMIC DURESS A defense to an action that a party was unlawfully coerced into the performance of an action by another due to fear of imminent economic loss and was not acting in accordance with his or her own free volition in performing the action.

FAIR LABOR STANDARDS ACT Enacted in 1938, the statute regulates minimum wages, overtime pay, and the employment of minors.

FREEDOM OF CONTRACT A basic freedom that is guaranteed by Article I, § 10, cl. 1, of the U.S. Constitution and that may not be denied by the state.

UNDUE INFLUENCE Improper use of power that deprives an individual of freedom of choice and substitutes another's choice for the individual's own choice.

Syester v. Banta

Dance lesson purchaser (P) v. Dance studio owner (D)

Iowa Sup. Ct., 257 Iowa 613, 133 N.W.2d 666 (1965)

NATURE OF CASE: Action in damages for fraud and misrepresentation.

FACT SUMMARY: Syester (P) signed up for 4,057 hours of dancing lessons at a price of $29,174.

RULE OF LAW

Equity may, if fair to do so, relieve a party from the consequences of a release executed through a mistaken belief of fact and law.

FACTS: Syester (P) was talked into signing up for 4,057 hours of dancing lessons at a price of $29,174. Syester (P), a lonely and elderly 68-year-old widow, was continually flattered and induced into signing up for more and more lessons through a planned campaign of the school's staff. Syester (P) finally learned the truth about the operation and brought suit against the studio's owner Banta (D) to recover the payments. Various questionable means were used to persuade Syester (P) to drop the suit and to get her to distrust her attorney. Syester (P) executed a full release for $6,090, apparently without consulting her attorney. The suit was dropped. A second release with an unsigned note for $4,000 was executed subsequently. No payments were ever made on it. Syester (P) then brought suit alleging fraud and misrepresentation in the sale of lessons and in the obtaining of the two releases.

ISSUE: May equity, if fair to do so, relieve a party from the consequences of a release executed through a mistaken belief of fact and law?

HOLDING AND DECISION: (Snell, J.) Yes. Equity may, if fair to do so, relieve a party from the consequences of a release executed through a mistaken belief of fact and law. Where the other party's conduct has been egregious, equity may relieve a party of the consequences of a release signed under a mistaken belief of law and facts. There was sufficient evidence from which a jury could find overreaching influence, unconscionability, misrepresentation, and fraud throughout the course of dealings between Banta (D) and Syester (P). Under such circumstances a jury may relieve a party of unread or misunderstood contracts or releases. The original release for $6,090 was wholly inadequate and the second release was unenforceable since it was never signed by Banta (D). The judgment for Syester (P) is affirmed.

ANALYSIS

Syester is a very modern approach to equitable relief from mistakes. Most courts have, in the past, held that, absent fraud, a party will not be relieved from the consequences of a unilateral mistake. In *Syester* it was unnecessary for the court to reach the ultimate question of fraud, but it probably would have found that it was present under the unique set of facts herein.

Quicknotes

FRAUD A false representation of facts with the intent that another will rely on the misrepresentation to his or her detriment.

MISTAKE OF FACT An unintentional mistake in knowing or recalling a fact without the will to deceive.

MISTAKE OF LAW An error involving a misunderstanding or incorrect application of law.

Hill v. Jones

Real estate buyer (P) v. Real estate seller (D)

Ariz. Ct. App., 151 Ariz. 81, 725 P.2d 1115 (1986)

NATURE OF CASE: Appeal from summary dismissal of action for rescission of real estate purchase contract on grounds of misrepresentation and intentional nondisclosure of material facts.

FACT SUMMARY: Before buying the Joneses' (D) home, the Hills (P) asked whether it had been infested with termites, and the Joneses (D) denied that there had been previous infestations, despite firsthand knowledge of them. When the Hills (P) discovered that, in fact, there had been prior termite infestations, they sought to rescind the real estate purchase contract on grounds of misrepresentation and intentional nondisclosure.

RULE OF LAW

(1) A contract provision that is in the nature of an integration clause that purports to insulate a party from all liability, even for its own fraud in procuring the contract, is invalid as a defense to such fraud.

(2) Where the seller of a home knows of facts materially affecting the value of the property that are not readily observable and are not known to the buyer, the seller is under a duty to disclose them.

FACTS: During escrow for the purchase of the Joneses' (D) home, the Hills (P) expressed concern about a "ripple" in a parquet floor. The Joneses (D) claimed that the problem resulted from flooding from a broken water heater. Although the broken heater had necessitated repairs to certain areas of the floor, the damage the Hills (P) were concerned about had in fact been caused by termites. The Hills (P) asked that a termite inspection report be placed in escrow. The inspection failed to find instances of prior infestation resulting from strategic placement of boxes and plants designed to conceal such evidence. When the results of the termite report were revealed to the Hills (P), the Hills (P) closed escrow with the Joneses (D). After moving in, however, the Hills (P) found evidence of termites and prior infestations. They brought suit to rescind the purchase agreement, on theories of misrepresentation and intentional nondisclosure of the termite damage. Through the discovery process, the Hills (P) learned that the previous seller of the home had paid for termite guarantees and semiannual inspections when he sold the house to the Joneses (D). Despite previous infestations that had been treated during the Joneses' (D) ownership and occupancy of the house, the Joneses (D) had said nothing about termites to the Hills (P), their realtor, or the inspector. After investigating the second time, the inspector found termite damage and evidence of past treatment. The inspector indicated that it was customary to be given information about past termite infestations and treatments before he performed his inspection, and that it was atypical not to have received this information prior to the first inspection. Other evidence presented to the trial court was that during their numerous visits to the residence before close of escrow, the Hills (P) had unrestricted access to view and inspect the entire house, and both previously had seen termite damage and were therefore familiar with what it might look like. The trial court dismissed the claim for misrepresentation based upon a so-called integration clause in the parties' agreement. The trial court also granted summary judgment to the Joneses (D) on the "concealment" claim, concluding that they had no duty to disclose information pertaining to termite infestation. The state's intermediate appellate court granted review.

ISSUE:

(1) Is a contract provision that is in the nature of an integration clause that purports to insulate a party from all liability, even for its own fraud in procuring the contract, invalid as a defense to such fraud?

(2) Where the seller of a home knows of facts materially affecting the value of the property that are not readily observable and are not known to the buyer, is the seller under a duty to disclose them?

HOLDING AND DECISION: (Meyerson, J.)

(1) Yes. A contract provision that is in the nature of an integration clause that purports to insulate a party from all liability, even for its own fraud in procuring the contract, is invalid as a defense to such fraud. Any provision in a contract making it possible for a party to free itself from the consequences of that party's fraud in procuring its execution is invalid and necessarily constitutes no defense. Moreover, parol evidence is always admissible to show fraud, and this is true, even though it has the effect of varying the terms of a writing between the parties. Here, the claimed misrepresentation occurred after the parties executed the contract. Assuming, arguendo, that the integration clause would extend to statements made subsequent to the execution of the contract, the clause could not shield the Joneses (D) from liability should the Hills (P) be able to prove fraud. Judgment for Hills (P) as to this issue. Reversed as to this issue.

(2) Yes. Where the seller of a home knows of facts materially affecting the value of the property that are not

Continued on next page.

readily observable and are not known to the buyer, the seller is under a duty to disclose them to the buyer. Such a disclosure is necessary to prevent a previous assertion from being a misrepresentation or from being fraudulent or material, and such a duty is also necessary to correct mistakes of the purchaser as to a basic assumption on which the purchaser is making the contract and to protect the purchaser from misplaced trust in the vendor. The doctrine imposing a duty to disclose is akin to the well-established contractual rules pertaining to relief from contracts based upon mistake. Although the law of contracts supports the finality of transactions, over the years courts have recognized that under certain limited circumstances it is unjust to strictly enforce the policy favoring finality. Additionally, this doctrine arises from the judicial policy of promoting honesty and fair dealing in business relationships, which is expressed in the law of fraudulent and negligent misrepresentations. Where a misrepresentation is fraudulent or where a negligent misrepresentation is one of material fact, the policy of finality rightly gives way to the policy of promoting honest dealings between the parties. Moreover, under certain circumstances, as in sales of real estate, nondisclosure of a fact known to one party—the seller in a real estate sale transaction—may be equivalent to the assertion that the fact does not exist. Thus, nondisclosure may be equated with and given the same legal effect as fraud and misrepresentation. The existence of termite damage in a residential dwelling is the type of material fact that gives rise to the duty to disclose because it is a matter to which a reasonable person would attach importance in deciding whether or not to purchase such a dwelling. Here, the Joneses (D) failed to reveal the home's prior history of termite infestation, despite knowledge of such infestation and previous attempts to treat it. Allegations to this effect raise triable issues of material fact that must be determined by the trier of fact. Whether the Hills (P) were put on reasonable notice of the termite problem despite the Joneses' (D) nondisclosure or whether they exercised reasonable diligence in informing themselves about the termite problem should also be left to the trier of fact. Judgment for the Hills (P) as to this issue. Reversed and remanded.

ANALYSIS

The classic view was that a party to a business transaction was subject to the duty of caveat emptor, or buyer beware and, therefore, could not rescind a transaction because of the other party's nondisclosures. The court in this case departed from this historical view, noting that the doctrine of caveat emptor has increasingly lost its vitality, and that the modern view is that a vendor has an affirmative duty to disclose material facts in certain circumstances. This case is somewhat exceptional in that the court recognized a duty of disclosure between parties in an ordinary arm's-length, commercial transaction. More typically, courts will recognize a "duty to speak up" only in the presence of a confidential or fiduciary relationship. See, e.g., *Vai v. Bank of America Trust & Savings Association,* 15 Cal. Rptr. 71, 364 P.2d 247 (1961) (community property settlement set aside on grounds that husband had failed to disclose value of property involved to his wife). Beyond the existence of a confidential or fiduciary relationship, courts traditionally imposed a duty of disclosure between businesspeople only when necessary to correct a previous misstatement or mistaken impression.

Quicknotes

AFFIRMATIVE DUTY An obligation to undertake an affirmative action for the benefit of another.

CAVEAT EMPTOR Let the buyer beware; doctrine that a buyer purchases at his or her own risk.

ESCROW A written contract held by a third party until the conditions therein are satisfied, at which time it is delivered to the obligee.

MATERIAL FACT A fact without the existence of which a contract would not have been entered.

RESCISSION The canceling of an agreement and the return of the parties to their positions prior to the formation of the contract.

SUMMARY JUDGMENT Judgment rendered by a court in response to a motion made by one of the parties, claiming that the lack of a question of material fact in respect to an issue warrants disposition of the issue without consideration by the jury.

Park 100 Investors, Inc. v. Kartes

Lessor (P) v. Lessee (D)

Ind. Ct. App., 650 N.E.2d 347 (1995)

NATURE OF CASE: Appeal from judgment for defendant in an action to collect under a personal guarantee provision in a lease.

FACT SUMMARY: Park 100 Investors, Inc. (P) sought to collect unpaid rent from the Karteses (D) under a provision of the lease that was induced through fraudulent means.

RULE OF LAW

A contract of guaranty cannot be enforced by the guarantee, where the guarantor has been induced to enter into the contract by fraudulent misrepresentations or concealment on the part of the guarantee.

FACTS: The Karteses (D) negotiated with Park 100 Investors, Inc. (Park 100) (P) to lease space for their growing business in 1984. A lease agreement was signed that did not include any provisions for a personal guaranty of the lease and a personal guaranty was never mentioned. A representative of Park 100 (P) later had the Karteses (D) also sign a "lease agreement," but did not tell them that what they were signing was actually a personal guaranty of lease. The Karteses (D) called their attorney, who confirmed that he had examined and approved the lease agreement, and then signed. When the Karteses (D) later found out about the personal guaranty, they immediately disavowed the guaranty and refused to affirm that part of the tenant agreement. Park 100 (P) later brought suit to collect the unpaid rent from the Karteses (D) under the personal guaranty. The trial court found that Park 100 (P) obtained the signatures of the Karteses (D) on the personal guaranty of lease through fraudulent means, that the Karteses (D) had acted with ordinary care and diligence, and that they were not liable for any unpaid rent. Park 100 (P) appealed.

ISSUE: Can a contract of guaranty be enforced by the guarantee, where the guarantor has been induced to enter into the contract by fraudulent misrepresentations or concealment on the part of the guarantee?

HOLDING AND DECISION: (Barteau, J.) No. A contract of guaranty cannot be enforced by the guarantee, where the guarantor has been induced to enter into the contract by fraudulent misrepresentations or concealment on the part of the guarantee. Where one employs misrepresentation to induce a party's obligation under a contract, one cannot bind the party to the terms of the agreement. Whether fraud is present in a case is rooted in the surrounding facts and circumstances and is for the trial court to determine. The evidence supports the trial court's conclusion here; the findings support the judgment and are not clearly erroneous. Affirmed.

ANALYSIS

The court in this case found that Park 100 Investors, Inc. (Park 100) (P) used fraudulent means to procure the Karteses' (D) signature. The elements of fraud are these: a material misrepresentation of past or existing fact by the party to be charged, which was false; was made with knowledge or in reckless ignorance of the falsity; was relied upon by the complaining party; and proximately caused the complaining party injury. Park 100 (P) claimed that the third element of reliance was not proven, but the court found that the Karteses (D) had exercised ordinary care and diligence because they acted with reasonable prudence in calling their attorney before signing.

Quicknotes

FRAUD A false representation of facts with the intent that another will rely on the misrepresentation to his or her detriment.

GUARANTOR A party who agrees to be liable for the debt or default of another.

Williams v. Walker-Thomas Furniture Co.

Furniture buyer (D) v. Furniture company (P)

350 F.2d 445 (D.C. Cir. 1965)

NATURE OF CASE: Appeal from affirmance of judgment for furniture company in its suit to replevy goods for breach of contract.

FACT SUMMARY: Walker-Thomas Furniture Co. (P) sold to Williams (D) furniture burdened by a cross-collateral clause and, subsequent to Williams's (D) default, sought to replevy all goods previously purchased by Williams (D).

RULE OF LAW

The courts have the power to refuse enforcement of contracts found to be unconscionable.

FACTS: Walker-Thomas Furniture Co. (Walker-Thomas) (P) sold furniture to Williams (D) under a printed form contract containing a cross-collateral clause the effect of which was to keep a balance due on every item purchased until the balance due on all items, whenever purchased, was liquidated. As a result, Walker-Thomas (P) retained—by the terms of the contract—the right to repossess all items previously purchased in the event of any default. At the time Williams (D) made her last purchase, she had a balance of $164 still owing from her prior purchases, although she had already paid $1,400 toward clearing her account. Subsequently, Williams (D) defaulted on payment and now Walker-Thomas (P) sought to replevy all goods previously sold to Williams (D). The trial court held for Walker-Thomas (P) and an intermediate appellate court affirmed. Because the case was in the District of Columbia, the federal district court granted review.

ISSUE: Do the courts have the power to refuse enforcement of contracts found to be unconscionable?

HOLDING AND DECISION: (Wright, J.) Yes. The courts have the power to refuse enforcement of contracts found to be unconscionable. "Where the element of unconscionability is present at the time a contract is made, the contract should not be enforced. Unconscionability has generally been recognized to include an absence of meaningful choice on the part of one of the parties together with contract terms which are unreasonably favorable to the other party." Meaningfulness of choice is to be determined in light of all the circumstances—for example, gross disparity of bargaining power. Remanded to determine whether the contract was unconscionable.

DISSENT: (Danaher, J.) The judicial approach to issues raised by this case should be a cautious one that gives parties great leeway in making their own contracts. Any remedy to protect the public from exploitive contracts more appropriately resides with the legislature (in this case, Congress) since numerous public policy issues are implicated. Otherwise, the risk of decisions like the one handed down by the majority is that they will undo otherwise legitimate, nonexploitive installment credit contracts into which the parties thereto have knowingly entered.

ANALYSIS

The majority opinion, written by Judge Wright, relies heavily on Uniform Commercial Code § 2-302 to support its position. But the meaning and effect of § 2-302 has been hotly debated. Comment 1 to that provision defines "unconscionable ability" in terms of itself and says its principle is to prevent "oppression and unfair surprise," not to disturb the "allocation of risks because of superior bargaining power." Note that any court that declares a contract "substantively" unconscionable is dealing in the dangerous and tenuous business of substituting its own valuation of contract goods for that of the parties involved. This kind of paternalism should be approached with caution.

Quicknotes

UNCONSCIONABILITY Rule of law whereby a court may excuse performance of a contract, or of a particular contract term, if it determines that such term(s) are unduly oppressive or unfair to one party to the contract.

U.C.C. § 2-302 Provides that courts exercise their discretion to limit specific contract provisions that have unconscionable results.

Higgins v. Superior Court of Los Angeles County

Television show participant (P) v. Trial court (D)

Cal. Ct. App., 140 Cal. App. 4th 1238, 45 Cal. Rptr. 3d 293 (2006)

NATURE OF CASE: Petition for writ of mandate challenging a trial court's ruling.

FACT SUMMARY: The Higginses (P) contended that arbitration provisions of a written agreement and release compelling arbitration of claims arising from the production and broadcast of a television program were unconscionable.

RULE OF LAW

An arbitration clause in a written agreement may not be enforced if only the clause, as opposed to the entire agreement, is being challenged and the clause is unconscionable.

FACTS: Five siblings (the Higginses) (P), ranging in age from 14 to 21, whose parents were deceased, were living with the Leomitis. The Higginses (P) and the Leomitis were approached by the producers of the television program *Extreme Makeover: Home Edition (Extreme Makeover)* about making a show based on the loss of the Higginses' (P) parents and that they were now living with the Leomitis. Eventually, the Higginses (P) and the Leomitis were chosen to participate in the program in which the Leomitis' home would be completely renovated. The producers sent to the Higginses (P) and the Leomitis a contract that contained 24 single-spaced pages and 72 numbered paragraphs. Attached to it were several pages of exhibits, including an authorization for release of medical information, an emergency medical release, and, as exhibit C, a one-page document entitled "Release." The first page of the agreement warned potential signors not to sign unless they had read the agreement. Close to the end of the agreement, a paragraph stated that the signor had read the agreement and reviewed it with legal counsel or voluntarily declined such an opportunity. None of the last 12 numbered paragraphs contained a heading or title. Among these was paragraph 69, which required that all disputes or controversies arising under the agreement would be resolved by binding arbitration. There was nothing in the agreement that brought the reader's attention to this paragraph. The one-page release also contained a similar arbitration provision. No discussion took place between the Higginses (P) and the television producers or anyone else affiliated with the show, and the Higginses (P) did not participate in a meeting at the Leomitis' home where the agreement was presented. After this meeting, the Leomitis emerged with a packet of documents, which they handed to the Higginses (P), and Mrs. Leomitis instructed them to "flip through the pages and sign and initial the document where it contained a signature line or box," which they did without fully understanding what they were signing. Afterward, a representative from the show began to reconstruct the Leomitis' home, and the program featuring the Higginses (P) and the Leomitis was broadcast. After the show was broadcast, the Leomitis forced the Higginses (P) to leave. The Higginses (P) informed the producers of what had happened and requested help, but none was forthcoming. The show was rebroadcast. The Higginses (P) brought suit against various parties associated with the show (the "television defendants") (D), and also against the Leomitis. One of the claims was breach of contract. The television defendants (D) petitioned to compel arbitration. The Higginses (P) opposed on the ground that the arbitration provision was unconscionable. The trial court granted the petition, and the Higginses (P) filed a petition for writ of mandate challenging the trial court's ruling. The state's intermediate court of appeals granted review.

ISSUE: May an arbitration clause in a written agreement be enforced if only the clause, as opposed to the entire agreement, is being challenged and the clause is unconscionable?

HOLDING AND DECISION: (Rubin, J.) No. An arbitration clause in a written agreement may not be enforced if only the clause, as opposed to the entire agreement, is being challenged and the clause is unconscionable. Although the Federal Arbitration Act (FAA) governs the enforceability of arbitration clauses in contracts involving interstate commerce, state law treats arbitration agreements just like any other contract. If an arbitration agreement is unconscionable, it will not be enforced. A starting point of analyzing whether a contract is unconscionable is to determine whether it is a contract of adhesion—a standardized contract that is imposed and drafted by the party of superior bargaining strength and relegates to the other party "only the opportunity to adhere to the contract or reject it." If the contract is one of adhesion, the next step is to determine whether it is unconscionable. Unconscionability has both a procedural and a substantive element. The procedural element focuses on "oppression" or "surprise" due to unequal bargaining power. The substantive element focuses on "overly harsh" or "one-sided" results. Both elements must be present, but not necessarily in the same degree, for a court to refuse enforcement of the contract. The FAA does not permit a court to entertain a claim that an arbitration provision is unenforceable if the claim is in reality

Continued on next page.

a subterfuge for challenging the entire agreement. Thus, here, it must first be determined whether the Higginses (P) are challenging just the arbitration provisions or the agreement and release in toto, and if it is found that they are truly just challenging only the arbitration provisions, then it must be determined whether those provisions are unconscionable. Here, the Higginses' (P) opposition to arbitration was that the arbitration clause in particular, not the entire agreement or release, was unconscionable, and the Hinginses (P) devoted considerable attention to paragraph 69. The clause was not set out or made distinguishable in any manner and was not identified with a caption other than being one of several paragraphs grouped together in a section titled "miscellaneous." This addresses procedural unconscionability. As to substantive unconscionability, the Higginses (P) argued that the provision was one-sided, requiring only the Higginses (P) to submit to arbitration, not the television defendants (D). Also rejected is the trial court's reasoning that arbitration should be compelled because the Higginses (P) had a chance to read the contract before signing it. There is no rule that if a party reads an agreement, he or she is barred from claiming it is unconscionable. Because only the arbitration clauses were being challenged, and not the agreement and release in toto, the next question is whether those clauses were unconscionable. First, the agreement here was adhesive. It was a standardized contract drafted by the television defendants (D), who had more bargaining power than the Higginses (P). Finally, based on the fact that the Higginses (P) were not present at the meeting between the Leomitis and the television defendants (D), and that the documents had to be signed as a condition to their participation in the program, the agreement was presented to the Higginses (P) on a take-it-or-leave-it basis by the party with the superior bargaining position who was not willing to engage in negotiations. Second, the arbitration provisions in the agreement and release were procedurally unconscionable. This conclusion is supported by the fact that the arbitration clause appeared in one paragraph near the end of a lengthy, single-spaced document; that the Higginses (P) were known to the television defendants (D) to be young and unsophisticated and had recently lost their parents; that the clause was neither highlighted in any way nor set off by bold letters, large fonts, capitalization, or any other textual means; and that no box appeared next to the arbitration clause for the Higginses (P) to initial, unlike some of the other paragraphs. Although the top of the first page advised the reader to read the entire agreement before signing it and the second-to-last paragraph stated that the person signing acknowledged doing so, this language does not defeat the otherwise strong showing of procedural unconscionability. Third, the arbitration provisions were substantively unconscionable because the provision was one-sided, requiring only the Higginses (P) to submit their claims to arbitration, but not requiring the same of the television defendants (D). Under the agreement, the television defendants (D) could compel arbitration without fearing that doing so would preclude them from seeking injunctive or other equitable relief in court. Also, only the Higginses (P) were precluded from seeking appellate review of the arbitrator's decision or of a provision requiring arbitration in accordance with the rules of the American Arbitration Association, which provide that arbitration costs are to be borne equally by the parties. For these reasons, the arbitration provisions were unconscionable and, therefore, unenforceable. The petition for writ of mandate is granted.

ANALYSIS

A number of decisions have held that the fact a contract is adhesive is enough of itself to render a contract procedurally unconscionable. Other decisions, however, have held that something more must be shown before an adhesion contract can be found to be procedurally unconscionable. Such a showing could be that there was a lack of market alternatives.

Quicknotes

ARBITRATION AGREEMENT A mutual understanding entered into by parties wishing to submit to the decision-making authority of a neutral third party that is selected by the parties and charged with rendering a decision.

UNCONSCIONABILITY Rule of law whereby a court may excuse performance of a contract, or of a particular contract term, if it determines that such terms are unduly oppressive or unfair to one party to the contract as a result of disparity in bargaining power during the formation of the contract.

WRIT OF MANDATE The written order of a court directing a particular action.

De La Torre v. CashCall, Inc.

"Payday" loan borrower (P) v. "Payday" loan lender (D)

Cal. Sup. Ct., 5 Cal. 5th 966, 236 Cal. Rptr. 3d 353, 422 P.3d 1004 (2018)

NATURE OF CASE: Question certified from federal court to state supreme court in putative class action challenging the interest rate on certain "payday" loans as unconscionable.

FACT SUMMARY: Eduardo De La Torre (P) and other low-income borrowers who took out loans that exceeded $2500 from CashCall, Inc. (D), a California lender that specialized in making unsecured loans to low-income borrowers who needed to get money quickly (also known as "payday" loans), alleged that the rates of interest on the loans—which were either 96 percent or 135 percent—were unconscionable. CashCall, Inc. (D) contended that because the California legislature had not capped interest rates on loans exceeding $2500, the courts were precluded from deciding whether the interest rates on such loans were unconscionable.

RULE OF LAW

An interest rate on consumer loans exceeding a specified amount of principal may be deemed unconscionable, notwithstanding that the state's legislature has made the policy decision not to cap the interest rates on loans over that amount.

FACTS: Eduardo De La Torre (P) and other low-income borrowers took out loans from CashCall, Inc. (D), a California lender that specialized in making unsecured loans to low-income borrowers who needed to get money quickly. Such loans are also known as "payday" loans. The loans at issue were for $2600, payable over a 42-month period, and carrying an annual percentage rate of either 96 percent or 135 percent. People who took out such loans from CashCall (D) were "consumers with low credit scores," living "under financial stress." CashCall (D) attracted many such borrowers through its television advertisements, which capitalized on the viewer's need to get money quickly. De La Torre (P) and other borrowers brought a putative class action against CashCall (D) in federal district court, alleging, inter alia, that CashCall (D) violated California's Unfair Competition Law (UCL). Following class certification of certain claims, CashCall (D) moved for summary judgment. The District Court for the Northern District of California, initially denied the motion, but, after reconsideration, granted the motion and entered final judgment on the UCL claim, concluding that because the California legislature had decided that it would not cap interest rates on loans exceeding $2500, to decide the point at which CashCall's (D) interest rates crossed the line into unconscionability would be to second-guess the legislature and impermissibly intrude on its province to forge economic policy through legislation. On appeal, the Court of Appeals for the Ninth Circuit certified the question to the California Supreme Court as to whether interest rates on consumer loans of $2500 or more may render loans unconscionable. The certified question was: "Can the interest rate on consumer loans of $2500 or more governed by California Finance Code § 22303, render the loans unconscionable under California Finance Code § 22302?" The California Supreme Court accepted the certified question.

ISSUE: May an interest rate on consumer loans exceeding a specified amount of principal be deemed unconscionable, notwithstanding that the state's legislature has made the policy decision not to cap the interest rates on loans over that amount?

HOLDING AND DECISION: (Cuéllar, J.) Yes. An interest rate on consumer loans exceeding a specified amount of principal may be deemed unconscionable, notwithstanding that the state's legislature has made the policy decision not to cap the interest rates on loans over that amount. The doctrine of unconscionability reaches contract terms relating to the price of goods or services exchanged that are unreasonably and unexpectedly harsh. In determining whether a price term is unconscionable, all the circumstances are reviewed, not just the price term, and there is no reason that interest rates should be exempt from an unconscionability analysis. Although California Finance Code § 22303 sets maximum interest rates only on loans less than $2500, whether an interest rate is unconscionable is fundamentally a different inquiry from whether the rate exceeds a numerical cap. Unconscionability is a flexible standard in which the court looks not only at the complained-of term but also at the process by which the contractual parties arrived at the agreement and the larger context surrounding the contract, including its commercial setting, purpose, and effect. In contrast, an interest rate cap is a bright-line rule policing a single facet of loan agreement. As such, just because loans of at least $2500 are not subject to a numerical ceiling on the interest rate does not mean that they cannot be found unconscionable. Moreover, the legislature said as much, by keeping the unconscionability doctrine within § 22302 at the same time that it set $2500 as the amount of a loan with an uncapped interest rate in § 22303. Thus, De La Torre (P) has stated a cause of action. According to CashCall (D), because § 22303 expressly considers loans of $2500 or more and declares

Continued on next page.

that they are not subject to any rate cap, such loans cannot be unconscionable due to their rate. In essence, CashCall (D) argues that by stating that § 22303 does not apply to loans of $2500 or more, the legislature actually meant to say that § 22302 does not apply to interest rates. This, however, would stand § 22303 on its head. Unconscionability requires oppression or surprise—i.e., procedural unconscionability—along with the overly harsh or one-sided results that epitomize substantive unconscionability. Some measure of both procedural and substantive unconscionability must be present—although, given the sliding-scale nature of the doctrine, more of one kind mitigates how much of the other kind is needed. In considering the extent of either of these, a court must look at the context of the particular transaction; it is not enough for a court to consider only whether the price exceeds cost or fair value. These factors underscore why finding unconscionable a contract setting an interest rate is categorically different from imposing an unvarying cap on the interest rate. To declare an interest rate unconscionable means only that—under the circumstances of the case, taking into account the bargaining process and prevailing market conditions—a particular rate was "overly harsh," "unduly oppressive," or "so one-sided as to shock the conscience." *Sanchez v. Valencia Holding Co., LLC*, 61 Cal. 4th 899, 910 (2015). In other words, a reasonable legislature can lift an interest rate cap without also intending that unconscionability will never apply to an uncapped rate. There is a difference between not making an activity unlawful and making that activity lawful. The absence of a rate cap on loans of at least $2500 does not make all rates lawful, for all purposes, under all regulations. Here, contrary to the reasoning of the federal District Court, a court need not engage in complex economic regulation in the absence of legislative authority where the legislature has provided clear direction as to how to proceed. By making an unconscionable loan a violation of the California Financing Law and, therefore, actionable under California's Unfair Competition Law (UCL), the legislature made clear that courts must grapple with such actions. Accordingly, CashCall's (D) invitation for the court to abstain from deciding the case is rejected. Also rejected is CashCall's (D) argument that the court's involvement would supersede or interfere with the functions of the Department of Business Oversight (DBO), since nothing the court decides will interfere with DBO decisions or operation. Accordingly, California courts have the authority to decide whether contract provisions, including interest rates, are unconscionable. Although ad hoc court decisions about unconscionability may introduce some uncertainty into transactions and might disrupt some competition—which the California Financing Law is intended to foster—it must be remembered that the Financing Law is also intended to protect consumers. However, neither that uncertainty nor the fact that commerce depends on the enforceability, in most instances, of a duly executed written contract, has persuaded the legislature to decree that all duly executed written contracts must be enforced at all times. To the contrary, the legislature has enacted into statute the unconscionability doctrine, making it a limitation to the enforcement of contracts. In any event, the courts have exercised extreme restraint in this area, and there is a paucity of cases in the state declaring any interest rates unconscionable. In addition, because the UCL does not provide for damages or attorney's fees, the likelihood that there could be a flood of unmeritorious lawsuits merely because courts may declare certain interest rates unconscionable is slim.

ANALYSIS

Although some judicial remedies for unconscionable interest rates could conceivably operate in a manner that would approximate an impermissible across-the-board imposition of a cap on interest rates, a court could avoid rate-cap setting by ordering a lender to change its advertising practices; or the court could impose a "cool down" period before a lender could dispense loans; or the court could refuse to enforce a loan's terms so that a lender would be limited to the amount of interest it had recouped from the borrowers and no more. Along the same line, a court could also order restitution, so long as it tailored and justified its ruling based on the specific context of a case, taking into account such considerations as the borrowers' circumstances, the lenders' specific risks, and other terms in the contract (e.g., prepayment penalties, origination fees, or loan rollovers) that, in conjunction with the interest rate, could render the contract unduly oppressive and, therefore, unconscionable. In short, merely because judicial remedies routinely have some economic impact does not mean that courts are devoid of the power to issue properly fashioned remedies to mitigate unconscionability.

Quicknotes

CERTIFIED QUESTION A question of law previously unaddressed by the highest court for a jurisdiction that is submitted to that court to answer how it would rule on the question; questions can be certified from lower courts within the same state, from state courts outside the state, from federal courts to state courts, and from federal courts of appeals to the U.S. Supreme Court.

CLASS CERTIFICATION Certification by a court's granting of a motion to allow individual litigants to join as one plaintiff in a class action against the defendant.

UNCONSCIONABILITY Rule of law whereby a court may excuse performance of a contract, or of a particular contract term, if it determines that such terms are unduly oppressive or unfair to one party to the contract as a result of disparity in bargaining power during the formation of the contract.

Valley Medical Specialists v. Farber

Medical practice (P) v. Employee (D)

Ariz. Sup. Ct., 194 Ariz. 363, 982 P.2d 1277 (1999)

NATURE OF CASE: Appeal by a medical practice from an adverse judgment in suit to enforce a restrictive covenant in its shareholder/employment agreement with a physician.

FACT SUMMARY: In 1985, Dr. Steven Farber (D), an internist and pulmonologist, joined Valley Medical Specialists (VMS) (P). A few years later, Dr. Farber (D) became a shareholder and a minority officer and director, and entered into stock and employment agreements, which included restrictive covenants, with VMS. In 1994, Dr. Farber (D) left VMS and began practicing in the area defined by the restricted covenant. VMS brought suit to enforce the restrictive covenant.

RULE OF LAW

In light of public policy interest involved in restrictive covenants not to compete between physicians, each agreement will be strictly construed for reasonableness.

FACTS: In 1985, Valley Medical Specialists (VMS) (P), a professional corporation, hired Steven Farber, D.O. (D), an internist and pulmonologist who, among other things, treated AIDS and HIV-positive patients and performed brachytherapy, a procedure that radiates the inside of the lung in lung cancer patients. Brachytherapy can be performed only at certain hospitals that have the necessary equipment. A few years after joining VMS (P), Dr. Farber (D) became a shareholder and subsequently a minority officer and director. Subsequently, the three directors, including Dr. Farber (D), entered into new stock and employment agreements. The employment agreement contained a restrictive covenant, the scope of which was amended over time. In 1994, Dr. Farber (D) left VMS (P) and began practicing within the area defined by the restrictive covenant. VMS (P) filed a complaint against Dr. Farber (D) seeking, inter alia, to enjoin him from violating the restrictive covenant. The trial court denied the injunction, finding that the restrictive covenant violated public policy or, alternatively, was unenforceable because it was too broad. Specifically, the trial court found that any covenant over six months would be unreasonable; the five-mile radius from each of the three VMS (P) offices was unreasonable because it covered a total of 235 square miles; and the restriction was unreasonable because it did not provide an exception for emergency medical aid and was not limited to pulmonology. The intermediate appellate court reversed. Dr. Farber (D) appealed.

ISSUE: In light of public policy interest involved in restrictive covenants not to compete between physicians, will each agreement be strictly construed for reasonableness?

HOLDING AND DECISION: (Feldman, J.) Yes. In light of public policy interest involved in restrictive covenants not to compete between physicians, each agreement will be strictly construed for reasonableness. A covenant not to compete is invalid unless it protects some legitimate interest beyond the employer's desire to protect itself from competition. Despite the freedom to contract, the law does not favor restrictive covenants, and this disfavor is particularly strong concerning such covenants among physicians because the practice of medicine affects the public to a much greater extent. Each case in which a restrictive covenant is challenged must be decided on its own unique facts. Here, the restrictive covenant in Valley Medical Specialists' (VMS) (P) shareholder/employment agreement with Dr. Farber (D), prohibiting him from providing any and all forms of "medical care," including pulmonology, emergency medicine, brachytherapy treatment, and HIV-positive and AIDS patient care, for three years within a five mile radius of any office maintained or utilized by VMS (P) was unreasonable and unenforceable since VMS's (P) protectable interests were minimal compared to patients' rights to see the doctor of their choice, which was entitled to a substantial protection. Courts will sometimes "blue pencil" restrictive covenants, eliminating grammatically severable, unreasonable provisions. Here, the lower appellate court's modifications to the instant restrictive covenant in VMS's (P) shareholder/employment agreement with Dr. Farber (D) went further than cutting grammatically severable portions, but essentially and impermissibly rewrote the agreement in an attempt to make it enforceable; the lower appellate court determined that the covenant, which contained a severability clause, could be modified to allow the physician to provide emergency services within the restricted area, and allowed VMS (P) to stipulate that the physician could perform brachytherapy and treat AIDS and HIV patients. However, where the severability of an agreement is not evident from the contract itself, the court cannot create a new agreement for the parties to uphold the contract. Reversed in favor of Dr. Farber (D) and remanded.

Continued on next page.

ANALYSIS

In the *Valley Medical* decision, the court noted that although stopping short of banning restrictive covenants between physicians, the American Medical Association (AMA) "discourages" such covenants, finding they are not in the public interest. The Council on Ethical and Judicial Affairs discourages any agreement between physicians that restricts the right of a physician to practice medicine for a specified period of time or in a specified area upon termination of employment or a partnership or a corporate agreement. Such restrictive agreements are not in the public interest. In addition, the AMA recognizes that free choice of doctors is the right of every patient, and free competition among physicians is a prerequisite of optimal care and ethical practice. In line with this viewpoint, the *Valley Medical* court concluded that the doctor-patient relationship is special and entitled to unique protection, stating that it cannot be easily or accurately compared to other relationships in the commercial context.

Quicknotes

RESTRICTIVE COVENANT A promise (usually in a partnership contract, employment contract, or contract for the sale of a business) not to engage in the same type of business for a stated amount of time in the same market as the partner, employer, or purchaser of the business. Also called "noncompete covenant."

P.M. v. T.B.

Intended parent (P) v. Surrogate parent (D)

Iowa Sup. Ct., 907 N.W.2d 522 (2018)

NATURE OF CASE: Appeal from judgment for plaintiffs/intended parents upholding the enforceability of a gestational surrogacy contract in an action for breach of contract.

FACT SUMMARY: Intended parents (P) brought a breach of contract action against a surrogate mother and her husband after the surrogate mother (D) refused to deliver the baby to the intended parents (P) pursuant to a gestational surrogacy contract. The surrogate mother (D) and her husband (D) contended that the contract was unenforceable.

RULE OF LAW

A gestational surrogacy contract is legally enforceable in favor of the intended, biological father against a surrogate mother and her husband who are not the child's genetic parents.

FACTS: Intended parents (P), a married couple unable to conceive their own child, entered into a contract with a surrogate mother (D) and her husband (D), who, in exchange for future payments of up to $13,000 and medical expenses, agreed to have the surrogate mother (D) impregnated with embryos fertilized with the plaintiff-father's (P) sperm and the eggs of an anonymous donor. The surrogate couple (D) agreed to deliver the baby at birth to the intended parents (P). The surrogate mother (D) became pregnant with twins, but the couples' relationship started to deteriorate, and, after demanding additional payments, the surrogate mother (D) refused to honor the agreement. The babies were born prematurely, and one died, although the surrogate mother (D) did not inform the intended parents (P) of this. The intended parents (P), suspecting the birth had occurred, sued to enforce the contract and gain custody of the surviving child. The trial court, after genetic testing, ruled the contract was enforceable, terminated the presumptive parental rights of the surrogate couple (D), established paternity in the biological father (P), and awarded him permanent legal and physical custody. The surrogate couple (D) appealed, and the state's highest court granted review.

ISSUE: Is a gestational surrogacy contract legally enforceable in favor of the intended, biological father against a surrogate mother and her husband who are not the child's genetic parents?

HOLDING AND DECISION: (Waterman, J.) Yes. A gestational surrogacy contract is legally enforceable in favor of the intended, biological father against a surrogate mother and her husband who are not the child's genetic parents. Surrogacies are categorized as "traditional" or "gestational." In a traditional surrogacy, the surrogate is the genetic mother of the child and is artificially inseminated with the sperm of the intended father or a sperm donor. In a gestational surrogacy, the surrogate is not genetically related to the child; instead, "sperm is taken from the father (or from a donor) and an egg is taken from the mother (or from a donor), fertilization happens outside the womb (called in vitro fertilization or IVF), and the fertilized embryos are then implanted into the surrogate mother's uterus." *In re Paternity of F.T.R.*, 349 Wis.2d 84, 833 N.W.2d 634, 643 (2013) (quoting Thomas J. Walsh, *Wisconsin's Undeveloped Surrogacy Law*, 85-Mar. Wis. Law. 16, 17 (2012). The type of surrogacy at issue here is a gestational surrogacy. There is no uniformity among the states as to surrogacy laws. Some states outlaw surrogacy altogether, whereas others permit it but regulate or restrict different aspects of the surrogacy relationship, and the approaches taken by individual states are myriad and varied. In this state, the only legislation specifically mentioning surrogacy exempts traditional "surrogacy arrangements" from the criminal statute that prohibits selling babies. The surrogate couple (D) argues that the agreement they entered is unenforceable as inconsistent with statutory provisions and public policy. As to whether the agreement is inconsistent with statutory provisions, because surrogacy arrangements statutorily are exempted from criminal liability for selling children, not only do such agreements not violate statutory law, but they are, to the contrary, favored by the legislature. Legislative history shows that such statutory exemption of surrogacy agreements from criminal liability was enacted, in response to national events, to permit such arrangements, not prohibit them. Given the timing of the legislation, when IVF was in its infancy, it cannot be inferred that the legislature intended to criminalize gestational surrogacies while exempting traditional surrogacies, especially since in traditional surrogacies the mother's genetic relationship to the child raises more concerns than in gestational surrogacies. For these reasons, neither traditional nor gestational surrogacy contracts are statutorily prohibited. This conclusion is reinforced by state administrative regulations that specifically contemplate IVF gestational surrogacy agreements. Yet another reason the surrogacy agreement at bar does not violate any statutory provisions is that the surrogate mother (D) was paid for her gestational services, rather than for

Continued on next page.

her sale of a baby. Although the surrogate couple (D) argues that the agreement violates statutes aimed at giving birth mothers time before being permitted to place their babies up for adoption, those statutes are inapposite here, since here the surrogate mother (D) is not the child's genetic mother, and it is widely recognized that there is a significant difference between surrogacy arrangements and giving up one's own genetic child for adoption. And, in the surrogate parenting context, the agreement to bear the child is entered before conception. As to whether the surrogacy agreement violates public policy, the societal interest in freedom of contract between consenting adults outweighs other policy concerns that gestational surrogacy arrangements might raise. Prior cases have upheld embryo disposition contracts between a married couple but likewise have held that agreements entered at the time IVF is commenced are enforceable and binding on the parties, subject to the right of either party to change his or her mind about disposition up to the point of use or destruction of any stored embryo. This holding was based on the belief that judicial enforcement of an agreement between a couple regarding their future family and reproductive choices would be against the public policy of this state, even though embryo dispositional agreements remain enforceable as between the donors and the medical facility. However, there are important differences between an embryo disposition agreement signed by the egg and sperm donor during their marriage and the gestational surrogacy agreement at issue here. The former addresses disposition of the parties' own genetic material and assumes the marriage will continue, whereas here the surrogate mother (D) is not the biological or genetic mother of the baby. Therefore, the public policy considerations relating to embryo disposition agreements are inapposite. Rejected, too, is the surrogate couple's (D) argument that the surrogacy agreement violates public policy against the exploitation of women and turns surrogate mothers into breeding animals. Not only have such exploitation arguments been rejected by other jurisdictions, but the fact is that the surrogate mother (D) entered into the agreement voluntarily, without duress, in the absence of any unconscionable circumstances, and with full knowledge of pregnancy's effects. The argument that a woman cannot knowingly and intelligently agree to gestate and deliver a baby for intending parents carries overtones of the reasoning that for centuries prevented women from attaining equal economic rights and professional status under the law. To resurrect this view is both to foreclose a personal and economic choice on the part of the surrogate mother and to deny intending parents what may be their only means of procreating a child of their own genetic stock. Finally, surrogacy agreements do not undermine the state's public policy of favoring families. To the contrary, such agreements promote families by enabling infertile couples to raise their own children and help bring new life into this world through willing surrogate mothers. The enforcement of surrogacy agreements promotes stability and permanence in family relationships because it allows the intended parents to plan for the arrival of their child, reinforces the expectations of all parties to the agreement, and reduces contentious litigation that could drag on for the first several years of the child's life. For these reasons, the surrogacy agreement does not violate any public policies. [The court also held that a gestational surrogate does not fall within the statutory definition of a "biological parent." The court also rejected the surrogate mother's (D) argument that her emotional bond formed from acting as the baby's mother for the two months that she had physical custody after birth gave her greater legal rights than the biological father. The court also rejected constitutional law claims based on substantive due process and equal protection grounds.] Affirmed.

ANALYSIS

The first in vitro fertilization (IVF)-assisted human birth did not occur until 1978, and it was not until the mid- to late-1980s that doctors began to use gestational surrogates in conjunction with IVF procedures. Although IVF and other assisted reproductive technologies represent revolutionary biomedical advances and have enabled countless couples to conceive who otherwise could not have had children biologically, these advances are, as this case demonstrates, replete with complexities. IVF-assisted reproduction involving third-party egg donors and gestational surrogates raises moral and ethical issues that can affect multiple, and often divergent, interests – among them, those of biological fathers, egg donors, surrogate mothers, and the resulting embryos. Not surprisingly, as the court in this case observes, the states have approached IVF- and surrogacy-related issues in very different ways.

Quicknotes

IN VITRO FERTILIZATION The fertilization of a human egg using donor sperm in a controlled environment outside the womb.

PARENTAL RIGHTS Rights that accrue to a parent who demonstrates a full commitment to his or her parental responsibilities to the child. These rights cannot be waived as a parent's responsibilities to the child cannot be waived. These rights are secure absent a showing of unfitness as a parent. Parental rights are entitled to equal protection.

PRESUMPTION A rule of law requiring the court to presume certain facts to be true based on the existence of

Continued on next page.

other facts, thereby shifting, the burden of proof to the party against whom the presumption is asserted to rebut.

PUBLIC POLICY Policy administered by the state with respect to the health, safety, and morals of its people in accordance with common notions of fairness and decency.

SURROGACY AGREEMENT A contract pursuant to which a woman agrees to provide her uterus to carry an embryo throughout pregnancy, after which she is to surrender all of her parental rights to the other party to the agreement.

CHAPTER 8

Justification for Nonperformance: Mistake, Changed Circumstances, and Contractual Modifications

Quick Reference Rules of Law

Lenawee County Board of Health v. Messerly

County board (P) v. Property owners (D)

Mich. Sup. Ct., 417 Mich. 17, 331 N.W.2d 203 (1982)

NATURE OF CASE: Appeal from reversal of judgment against counterclaimant-defendants seeking rescission of contract.

FACT SUMMARY: When the Lenawee County Board of Health (P) found a defective sewage system shortly after the Pickleses purchased rental property from Mr. and Mrs. Messerly (D) and sought a permanent injunction proscribing human habitation, the Pickleses sought rescission of their contract on the grounds of mutual mistake.

RULE OF LAW

A mutual mistake of fact does not require rescission of a contract where the party seeking rescission has assumed the risk of loss.

FACTS: When Mr. Bloom owned the property on which there was a three-unit apartment building, he installed a septic tank without a permit and in violation of the applicable health code. This was not known to the Messerlys (D) when they subsequently bought it or to Barnes when he purchased it on a land contract from the Messerlys (D). After Barnes defaulted on the land contract, an arrangement was made whereby the land was quit-claimed back to the Messerlys (D), and they sold it on a new land contract to the Pickleses. About six days later, the Pickleses discovered raw sewage seeping out of the ground. The Lenawee County Board of Health (P) condemned the property and sought an injunction against human habitation until it was brought into compliance with the sanitation code. In resulting cross-actions, the Pickleses sought rescission of the contract on grounds of mutual mistake. Focusing on the "as is" clause in their land contract, the trial court denied rescission and awarded the Messerlys (D) a judgment against the Pickleses on the land contract. The court of appeals reversed, and the state's highest court granted review.

ISSUE: Does a mutual mistake of fact require rescission of a contract where the party seeking rescission has assumed the risk of loss?

HOLDING AND DECISION: (Ryan, J.) No. A mutual mistake of fact does not require rescission of a contract where the party seeking rescission has assumed the risk of loss. A mutual mistake that is the prerequisite for rescission is one that relates to a basic assumption of the parties, upon which the contract was made, and that materially affects the agreed performance of the parties. However, rescission need not be granted in every case where there is such a mistake. It cannot be ordered to relieve a party who has assumed the risk of loss in connection with the mistake. Furthermore, where both parties are innocent, as in this case, the court exercises its equitable powers to determine which blameless party should assume the loss. Here, the "as is" clause suggests it should be the Pickleses. Reversed.

ANALYSIS

According to Restatement (Second) of Contracts § 124, a party bears the risk of mistake if it is allocated to him by agreement of the parties, or he is aware at the time of contracting of his limited knowledge of the facts to which the mistake relates but treats his limited knowledge as sufficient, or the court allocates it to him because "it is reasonable in the circumstances to do so."

Quicknotes

MUTUAL MISTAKE A mistake by both parties to a contract, who are in agreement as to what the contract terms should be, but the agreement as written fails to reflect that common intent; such contracts are voidable or subject to reformation.

RESCISSION The canceling of an agreement and the return of the parties to their positions prior to the formation of the contract.

BMW Financial Services NA, LLC v. Deloach

Vehicle finance company (P) v. Vehicle lessee (D)

Cal. Ct. App., 2017 WL 1832250 (2017)

NATURE OF CASE: Appeal from an order granting a motion to compel acknowledgment of satisfaction of judgment in action for breach of lease and for odometer tampering.

FACT SUMMARY: BMW Financial Services NA, LLC (BMW Financial) (P) mistakenly sent Deloach's (D) account to a collection agency, which settled Deloach's (D) debt for far less than a default judgment BMW Financial (P) had obtained a few days earlier against Deloach (D) for breach of a car lease and for odometer tampering. When BMW Financial (P) learned of its mistake, it sought to rescind the settlement agreement on grounds of mistake.

RULE OF LAW

A party may not rescind a settlement agreement on the grounds of mistake where the party seeking rescission itself made the error, so that it bears the risk of that error, and where enforcement of the agreement would not otherwise be unconscionable.

FACTS: Deloach (D) leased a vehicle for which BMW Financial Services NA, LLC (BMW Financial) (P) provided the financing. At the time of the lease, the vehicle's odometer displayed 4,293 miles. Deloach (D) did not make his payments and the car was repossessed. At that time, the odometer displayed 94 miles, and inspection revealed that the odometer had been tampered with, in violation of state and federal laws. BMW Financial (P) received $25,000 for the vehicle at auction. BMW Financial (P) brought suit against Deloach (D) for breach of lease and for odometer tampering. Deloach (D) defaulted, and, on August 13, 2015, the trial court entered a default judgment in favor of BMW Financial (P) and against Deloach (D) for $114,677. Most of the judgment, $81,296, was for treble damages for the odometer tampering. Prior to the issuance of the default judgment, BMW Financial (P) mistakenly sent Deloach's (D) account to a collection agency that it used, Firstsource Advantage, LLC (Firstsource), because it failed, internally, to flag the account as in litigation. The account showed that approximately $24,000 was owing. After Firstsource contacted Deloach (D), his father, David Deloach, negotiated a settlement agreement with Firstsource whereby Firstsource agreed to accept $14,000 in satisfaction of the entire debt. Firstsource confirmed the settlement in writing on August 17, 2015, and thereafter confirmed, not only the receipt of the $14,000, but also "that our client [BMW Financial (P)] has agreed to accept less than the full balance due as settlement on the above-mentioned account." Firstsource had a preauthorized settlement authority range, and the ultimate settlement of $14,000 was within that range. BMW Financial (P), however, did not learn of this settlement agreement until around a month after the default judgment had issued. Counsel for BMW Financial (P) then contacted Deloach (D) on September 15, 2015, asserting that the August settlement was entered by mistake and purporting to rescind it by returning the $14,000. Deloach (D) countered with a motion to compel acknowledgment of satisfaction of judgment. The trial court granted the motion, finding that Firstsource, as BMW Financial's (P) agent, had acted within the scope of its authority and that the deal was reasonable, given that settlement amounts are routinely less than the actual debt. The court also concluded that rescinding the settlement agreement would be unconscionable, because there was no evidence of either sharp dealing by Deloach (D) or an overly harsh outcome. The state's intermediate appellate court granted review.

ISSUE: May a party rescind a settlement agreement on the grounds of mistake where the party seeking rescission itself made the error, so that it bears the risk of that error, and where enforcement of the agreement would not otherwise be unconscionable?

HOLDING AND DECISION: (Bedsworth, J.) No. A party may not rescind a settlement agreement on the grounds of mistake where the party seeking rescission itself made the error, so that it bears the risk of that error, and where enforcement of the agreement would not otherwise be unconscionable. The applicable test for rescission based on mistake of fact, which is derived from the Restatement (Second) of Contracts (Restatement), requires that the following facts must be established to qualify: (1) the party seeking rescission made a mistake regarding a basic assumption upon which it made the contract; (2) the mistake has a material effect upon the agreed exchange of performances that is adverse to that party; (3) the party seeking rescission does not bear the risk of the mistake; and (4) the effect of the mistake is such that enforcement of the contract would be unconscionable. Here, the first two factors are not disputed. As to the third factor, allocation of risk, the trial court found it was reasonable under the circumstances to allocate the risk to BMW Financial Services NA, LLC (BMW Financial) (P). BMW Financial (P) argues that the risk of the mistake may be allocated to it only if it neglected a legal duty,

Continued on next page.

and that its error in sending Deloach's (D) account to Firstsource Advantage, LLC (Firstsource) did not violate a legal duty. Neglect of a legal duty is not, however, the only circumstance under which a court may allocate risk. The Restatement, which addresses the allocation of risk issue, stresses reasonableness and observes that a court will consider the purposes of the parties and will have recourse to its own general knowledge of human behavior in bargain transactions. Here, under the circumstances, it is reasonable to allocate the risk of mistake to BMW Financial (P). The error was attributable solely to BMW Financial's (P) failure to tag Deloach's (D) account as being in litigation. BMW Financial (P) presented no evidence that Firstsource or either Deloach (D) or David Deloach knew about the default judgment when Firstsource and David Deloach entered into negotiations to settle the case. In other words, the mistake was BMW Financial's (P) and no one else's. Moreover, BMW Financial (P) waited nearly a month to inform Deloach (D) that it wanted to rescind. The hard fact is that someone must bear the risk of the mistake. Should it be the person who negotiated a reasonable settlement for actual damages with the agent for the other party and received confirmation that the settlement was a done deal, only to be told a month later that the settlement was off? Or should it be the party whose error caused the problem and who is nevertheless coming out roughly even? Again, the Restatement provides guidance. It provides that even though a mistaken party does not bear the risk of a mistake, that party may be barred from avoidance if the mistake was the result of the party's failure to act in good faith and in accordance with reasonable standards of fair dealing. Accordingly, BMW Financial (P) argues that it acted with good faith and fair dealing, so it should be entitled to rescind. However, good faith and reasonable standards of fair dealing in this context are not limited to an absence of cheating or of fraud. They include not disappointing the justifiable expectations of the other party. Deloach (D) was justified in expecting that Firstsource could settle his debt with BMW Financial (P), especially after receiving Firstsource's confirmatory letter. BMW Financial (P) had an opportunity to discover that the account was in litigation after it received notification of the settlement by Firstsource. Moreover, there is no evidence that David Deloach was pressing Firstsource to settle immediately, so BMW Financial (P) had time to check its records. As to the test's fourth factor, unconscionability, substantial evidence supports the trial court's conclusion that it would not be unconscionable to enforce the settlement agreement. BMW Financial (P) received $39,000 for the leased BMW—$25,000 from its sale at auction and $14,000 from the settlement. The balance on the Deloach (D) account when it was sent to Firstsource was $24,442; thus, BMW Financial's (P) actual loss was a little over $10,000. On the plus side, as is so often true of settlements, BMW Financial (P) had a $14,000 bird in the hand and did not have to spend money chasing after $24,000 it might never collect. Its recognition of this benefit is reflected in the fact that Firstsource was authorized to accept $14,000 to settle a $24,000 debt. An additional factor is that settlement agreements are favored under the state's law. Further, the large discrepancy between the amount of the settlement and the amount of the default judgment was, largely, the penalty awarded for odometer tampering. This amount did not reflect an actual loss to BMW Financial (P), nor was it intended to, since the purpose of punitive damages is to punish wrongdoers and thereby deter the commission of wrongful acts; such awards are not intended to compensate plaintiffs or make them whole. For these reasons, the district court did not err in granting the motion to compel acknowledgment of the settlement agreement. Affirmed.

ANALYSIS

Section 157 of the Restatement (Second) of Contracts (Restatement) provides that, "A mistaken party's fault in failing to know or discover the facts before making the contract does not bar him from avoidance . . . under the rules stated in this Chapter, unless his fault amounts to a failure to act in good faith and in accordance with reasonable standards of fair dealing." As the court observes in this case, the duty of good faith and fair dealing implied in every contract does not apply to precontract negotiations. However, under the Restatement approach, the failure to act in good faith or deal fairly will bar a mistaken party from relief based on a mistake that otherwise would not have been made, since during the negotiation stage each party is held to a degree of responsibility appropriate to the justifiable expectations of the other.

Quicknotes

DEFAULT Failure to carry out a legal obligation.

FAIR DEALING An implied warranty that the parties will deal honestly in the satisfaction of their obligations and without an intent to defraud.

MATERIALITY Importance; the degree of relevance or necessity to the particular matter.

RESCISSION The canceling of an agreement and the return of the parties to their positions prior to the formation of the contract.

SATISFACTION The performance of an agreement between two parties, one of which has a valid claim against the other, to settle the controversy.

Hemlock Semiconductor Operations, LLC v. Solarworld Industries Sachsen GmbH

Supplier (P) v. Component manufacturer (D)

867 F.3d 692 (6th Cir. 2017)

NATURE OF CASE: Appeal from grant of summary judgment to plaintiff in action for breach of contract.

FACT SUMMARY: Solarworld Industries Sachsen GmbH (Sachsen) (D) contended its breach of long-term supply agreements (LTAs) that it had entered with Hemlock Semiconductor Operations, LLC (Hemlock) (P) was excused on grounds, inter alia, of illegality, commercial impracticability and frustration of purpose, and in any event, that the LTAs' provision for the award of the full outstanding balance constituted an unenforceable penalty rather than permissible liquidated damages.

RULE OF LAW

(1) A motion to strike an illegality defense to a breach of contract action is properly granted where no state of the facts could be proved by the defendant in support of the defense.

(2) Significant changes in market conditions alone are insufficient to support a commercial impracticability defense to a breach of contract action.

(3) Significant changes in market conditions alone are insufficient to support a frustration-of-purpose defense to a breach of contract action where the purpose of the contract at issue is to provide stability of price in an otherwise fluctuating market.

(4) A liquidated damages clause in a contract is enforceable where the agreed amount is reasonably intended to compensate for injury suffered, it is not unconscionable or excessive, the potential damages from breach are uncertain and difficult to anticipate when the contract is made, and the contract expressly indicates that the damages are intended to cover costs incurred by the non-breaching party.

FACTS: Solarworld Industries Sachsen GmbH (Sachsen) (D), a German company manufacturing solar power components, entered into a series of long-term supply agreements (LTAs) with Hemlock Semiconductor Operations, LLC (Hemlock) (P), a U.S. company also in the solar power industry, for polycrystalline silicon (polysilicon) at fixed prices between 2006 and 2019. Although the market price for polysilicon was initially well above the LTA price, the market price plummeted after China began subsidizing its national production of the substance. In 2011, Sachsen (D) and Hemlock (P) agreed to temporarily lower the LTA price, but after that agreement expired in 2012, the price reverted to the original amount. Hemlock (P) then demanded that Sachsen (D) pay the original LTA price for the specified quantity of polysilicon for 2012, but Sachsen (D) refused. The LTAs required Sachsen (D) to purchase a specified quantity of polysilicon each year at a fixed price, and to pay that price even if it declined to take delivery (the "take-or-pay" provision). In the event Sachsen (D) failed to pay the specified amount for a given year, Hemlock (P) had the right to terminate the LTAs, and Sachsen (D) would then owe Hemlock (P) the full remaining balance of the LTA price, including amounts due for future years (the "liquidated-damages" provision). Hemlock (P) brought suit in federal district court for breach of contract, seeking the full amount due under the liquidated-damages provision. Sachsen (D) asserted numerous affirmative defenses, including illegality, commercial impracticability, and frustration of purpose. Upon Hemlock's (P) motion, the district court struck Sachsen's (D) illegality defense and denied Sachsen's (D) motion to reconsider this defense. The district court also granted summary judgment in favor of Hemlock (P) and awarded Hemlock (P) the amounts owing to Hemlock (P) under the liquidated-damages provision, which with interest came to around $800 million. The court of appeals granted review.

ISSUE:

(1) Is a motion to strike an illegality defense to a breach of contract action properly granted where no state of the facts could be proved by the defendant in support of the defense?

(2) Are significant changes in market conditions alone sufficient to support a commercial impracticability defense to a breach of contract action?

(3) Are significant changes in market conditions alone sufficient to support a frustration-of-purpose defense to a breach of contract action where the purpose of the contract at issue is to provide stability of price in an otherwise fluctuating market?

(4) Is a liquidated damages clause in a contract enforceable where the agreed amount is reasonably intended to compensate for injury suffered, it is not unconscionable or excessive, the potential damages from breach are uncertain and difficult to anticipate when the contract is made, and the contract expressly

Continued on next page.

indicates that the damages are intended to cover costs incurred by the non-breaching party?

HOLDING AND DECISION: (Gilman, J.)

(1) Yes. A motion to strike an illegality defense to a breach of contract action is properly granted where no state of the facts could be proved by the defendant in support of the defense. Solarworld Industries Sachsen GmbH (Sachsen) (D) argued that the long-term supply agreements (LTAs) were illegal under European Union (E.U.) and German antitrust law, and that the LTAs violated E.U. antitrust law by tying Sachsen's (D) predominant demand for polysilicon to a single seller—Hemlock Semiconductor Operations, LLC (Hemlock) (P). Although motions to strike are disfavored, they are properly granted when plaintiffs would succeed despite any state of the facts that could be proved in support of the defense. The promise to take-or-pay standing alone does not violate U.S. antitrust law; and enforcing this provision in the LTAs is consistent with E.U. and German antitrust law as well. The LTAs also do not violate E.U. regulations that prohibit long-term tying contracts. Accordingly, there was no illegality in the LTAs and, therefore, the district court did not err in striking Sachsen's (D) illegality defense. Judgment for Hemlock (P) as to this issue. Affirmed as to this issue.

(2) No. Significant changes in market conditions alone are insufficient to support a commercial impracticability defense to a breach of contract action. Under the commercial impracticability defense, though performance need not be impossible, performance must be rendered impracticable as a result of extreme and unreasonable difficulty, expense, injury, or loss. Additionally, the defense is viable only if an unforeseen event occurs, the non-occurrence of which was a basic assumption of the parties when they entered the contract. However, the expectation that current market conditions will continue for the life of the contract is not such a basic assumption, so shifts in market prices ordinarily do not constitute impracticability, and this is especially true when, as here, the parties have entered into a contract for the sale of goods at fixed prices, because such contracts are made for the very purpose of establishing a stable price despite a fluctuating market. Moreover, even relatively drastic changes in the market—as when a global recession occurs—are usually insufficient to trigger the impracticability defense. Here, Sachsen (D) argued that China's illegal actions caused the out-of-the-ordinary drop in polysilicon prices and gave rise to impracticability. The district court rejected this argument, reasoning that even if China's actions were illegal, such actions were irrelevant because their effect was simply to cause a shift in market pricing. The district court also concluded that Sachsen's (D) argument amounted to a claim of economic unprofitability—which does not support an impracticability defense. The district court's rulings were not erroneous, as there is no pertinent case law that supports the proposition that a third party's illegal actions can render the performance of a contract impracticable. Although the parties may not have specifically anticipated China's actions, the possibility that the market price for polysilicon could fluctuate significantly certainly would have been within their contemplation, since the purpose of the LTAs was to establish a stable price that would operate independently of the market. Not only would allowing Sachsen (D) to avoid its obligations under the LTAs be unfair to Hemlock (P), but it would also potentially open the flood gates to similar arguments based on allegedly illegal actions of third parties. Allowing parties to litigate the causes of market shifts would swallow the general rule that a contract's unprofitability does not warrant application of the impracticality defense. Judgment for Hemlock (P) as to this issue. Affirmed as to this issue.

(3) No. Significant changes in market conditions alone are insufficient to support a frustration-of-purpose defense to a breach of contract action where the purpose of the contract at issue is to provide stability of price in an otherwise fluctuating market. Sachsen (D) argues China's illegal actions frustrated Sachsen's (D) purpose in entering the LTAs. Frustration of purpose and impracticability are overlapping defenses, as both defenses require proof that an unforeseen event altered a basic assumption on which the contract was made. The frustration-of-purpose defense also requires that the unforeseen event thwart the parties' purpose in making the contract to such a degree that one party's performance becomes virtually worthless to the other. Like the impracticability defense, the frustration-of-purpose defense generally cannot be based on an argument that the continuation of existing market conditions was a "basic assumption" on which the contract was made, and courts usually will not assume that "mutual profitability" was a contract's primary purpose. Based on these principles, the frustration-of-purpose defense is inapplicable here because Sachsen (D) adduces no evidence that the primary purpose of the LTAs was anything other than the provision by Hemlock (P) to Sachsen (D) of a stable supply of polysilicon at a predictable price. Sachsen's (D) frustration-of-purpose argument boils down to a claim that "mutual profitability" was the purpose of the LTAs, but this argument is unconvincing given the LTAs establish a fixed price under which either party could suffer depending on the relationship of the market price

Continued on next page.

to the LTA price. Moreover, Sachsen (D) has failed to distinguish on procedural grounds another case that the district court found helpful to Hemlock (P), since its defenses fail as a matter of law for the same reasons that the court in the other case dismissed the defendant's counterclaims. Further, a case on which Sachsen (D) relies, where a party's impracticability and frustration-of-purpose defenses were permitted to proceed to trial, involved an index on which the contract relied in setting prices. In that case, third-party manipulation of the index rendered the index unreliable. That case is distinguishable from the one at bar because (1) the parties' very purpose in adopting the contract provision in that case was to use the index to allocate risks, and (2) that purpose was frustrated when the index ceased to accurately reflect the true market price. Here, the contract price was fixed specifically to avoid market fluctuations, just the opposite of the pricing mechanism in that case, so that case is readily distinguishable. In sum, the district court did not err in rejecting Sachsen's (D) impracticability and frustration-of-purpose defenses. Judgment for Hemlock (P) as to this issue. Affirmed as to this issue.

(4) Yes. A liquidated damages clause in a contract is enforceable where the agreed amount is reasonably intended to compensate for injury suffered, it is not unconscionable or excessive, the potential damages from breach are uncertain and difficult to anticipate when the contract is made, and the contract expressly indicates that the damages are intended to cover costs incurred by the non-breaching party. Sachsen (D) asserts that the liquidated damages provisions in the LTAs are unenforceable because they are unreasonable penalties, rather than permissible liquidated damages. Liquidated damages are enforceable where the agreed-upon amount is reasonably related to the possible injury suffered and is not unconscionable or excessive. Liquidated damages are especially appropriate where the damages that would result from a breach are uncertain and difficult to ascertain when the contract is executed, as courts determine the enforceability of liquidated-damages provisions based on the circumstances existing at the time that the contract was executed, not at the time of the breach. Also, courts should give effect to the parties' intent and enforce liquidated-damages provisions unless it is obvious from the contract that the principle of compensation has been disregarded. Here, the record indicates that it would have been difficult to measure actual damages at the time the LTAs were executed. Finally, the LTAs expressly noted that the liquidated damages provisions were intended to compensate Hemlock (P) for costs it incurred in expanding its capabilities in producing polysilicon. In light of this express language, the liquidated-damages provision can be interpreted as taking into account Hemlock's (P) expansion costs. For all these reasons, the district court did not err in concluding that the liquidated damages provisions were enforceable. Judgment for Hemlock (P) as to this issue. Affirmed as to this issue. Affirmed.

ANALYSIS

As a matter of contract drafting, Solarworld Industries Sachsen GmbH (Sachsen) (D) could have protected itself against a large drop in the market price of polysilicon during the 14-year term of the long-term supply agreements (LTAs) by requiring a renegotiation if the market price dropped a certain percentage or dollar amount below the contract price. However, no such condition was included in the LTAs, despite the sophistication of both the parties and their lawyers. Sachsen (D) thus knowingly assumed the unfiltered risk of a drop in the price for a high-tech product during a long-term, fixed-price contract.

Quicknotes

AFFIRMATIVE DEFENSE A manner of defending oneself against a claim not by denying the truth of the charge but by the introduction of some evidence challenging the plaintiff's right to bring the claim.

AFFIRMATIVE DEFENSES An assertion raised by the defendant in the answer, permitting the introduction of additional evidence to address or refute a plaintiff's allegations; affirmative defenses shift the burden of proof to the defendant to establish all the elements of the defense.

BREACH OF CONTRACT Unlawful failure by a party to perform its obligations pursuant to contract.

COMMERCIAL IMPRACTICABILITY A doctrine relieving the parties to a contract from liability for nonperformance of their duties thereunder if the subject matter of the contract ceases to exist.

FRUSTRATION OF PURPOSE A doctrine relieving the parties to a contract from liability for nonperformance of their duties thereunder when the purpose of the agreement ceases to exist due to circumstances not subject to either party's control.

IMPOSSIBILITY A doctrine relieving the parties to a contract from liability for nonperformance of their duties thereunder if the subject matter of the contract ceases to exist, a person essential to the performance of the contract is deceased, or the service or goods contracted for has become illegal.

Continued on next page.

IMPRACTICABILITY A doctrine relieving the parties to a contract from liability for nonperformance of their duties thereunder if the subject matter of the contract ceases to exist.

LIQUIDATED DAMAGES An amount of money specified in a contract representing the damages owed in the event of breach.

Mel Frank Tool & Supply, Inc. v. Di-Chem Co.

Landlord (P) v. Tenant (D)

Iowa Sup. Ct., 580 N.W.2d 802 (1998)

NATURE OF CASE: Tenant's appeal from a judgment in favor of the landlord for the breach of a lease.

FACT SUMMARY: Di-Chem Co. (D) signed a three-year lease to begin June 1, 1994, with Mel Frank Tool & Supply, Inc. (Mel Frank) (P) for a storage and distribution facility. Di-Chem (D) claimed it was going to be selling chemicals, but the use of the premises was limited to "storage and distribution." In July 1995, city officials inspected the premises and informed Di-Chem (D) that they had found Code violations (enacted after Di-Chem took occupancy) that had to be eliminated. Di-Chem (D) vacated the premises in October 1995, and Mel Frank (P) sued for breach of lease and damage to the property.

RULE OF LAW

A tenant is not relieved from the obligation to pay rent due to a subsequent governmental regulation that prohibits the tenant from legally using the premises for its originally intended purpose if there is a serviceable use still available consistent with the use provision in the lease, and the fact that the use of the premises is less valuable or less profitable or even unprofitable does not necessarily mean the tenant's use has been substantially frustrated.

FACTS: Di-Chem Co. (D), a chemical distributor, negotiated with Mel Frank Tool & Supply, Inc. (Mel Frank) (P) to lease a storage and distribution facility. Mel Frank's (P) real estate agent handled the negotiations. Mel Frank (P) asked Di-Chem (D) what it was going to be selling and was told chemicals. The lease limited Di-Chem's (D) use of the premises to "storage and distribution." Some of the chemicals Di-Chem distributes are considered "hazardous material." There was no testimony that Mel Frank (P) was aware of this at the time the three-year lease to commence June 1, 1994, was executed. In July 1995, city authorities informed Di-Chem (D) that it could no longer use its leased premises to store its hazardous chemicals because of a recently enacted ordinance, whereupon Di-Chem (D) vacated the premises, and Mel Frank (P) sued for breach of the lease. The trial court awarded judgment to Mel Frank (P), and Di-Chem (D) appealed, contending that the trial court should have found that the city's actions constituted extraordinary circumstances rendering the performance of the lease impossible.

ISSUE: Is a tenant relieved from the obligation to pay rent due to a subsequent governmental regulation that prohibits the tenant from legally using the premises for its originally intended purpose if there is a serviceable use still available consistent with the use provision in the lease even if the use of the premises is less valuable or less profitable or even unprofitable?

HOLDING AND DECISION: (Lavorato, J.) No. A tenant is not relieved from the obligation to pay rent due to a subsequent governmental regulation that prohibits the tenant from legally using the premises for its originally intended purpose if there is a serviceable use still available consistent with the use provision in the lease even if the use of the premises is less valuable or less profitable or even unprofitable. The fact of unprofitability of the lease does not necessarily mean that the tenant's use has been substantially frustrated as to relieve rent payment. The facts of this case fall within the parameters of § 265 of the Restatement (Second) of Contracts, which provides that where, after a contract is made, a party's principal purpose is substantially frustrated without his or her fault by the occurrence of an event the nonoccurrence of which was a basic assumption on which the contract was made, his or her remaining duties to render performance are discharged unless the language or the circumstances indicate the contrary. The rule deals with the problem that arises when a change in circumstances makes one party's performance virtually worthless to the other, frustrating the purpose in making the contract. Here, not all Di-Chem Co.'s (Di-Chem) (D) inventory consisted of hazardous material. Di-Chem (D) did not establish that its principal purpose for leasing the facility—storing and distributing chemicals—was substantially frustrated by the city's actions. Nor did Di-Chem (D) present evidence as to the nature of its inventory and what percentage of the inventory consisted of hazardous chemicals. Thus, there was no evidence from which the trial court could have found that the city's actions substantially frustrated Di-Chem's (D) principal purpose of storing and distributing chemicals. Put another way, there was insufficient evidence that the city's action deprived Di-Chem (D) of the beneficial enjoyment of the property for other uses, i.e., storing and distributing nonhazardous chemicals. Di-Chem failed to establish its affirmative defense of what it termed impossibility. Affirmed.

ANALYSIS

The introduction to the Restatement (Second) of Contracts (Restatement) covers impossibility of performance, but with a different title: "Impracticability of

Continued on next page.

Performance and Frustration of Purpose." Restatement (Second) of Contracts Ch. 11 at 309 (1981). According to the Restatement, contract liability is strict liability. The obligor is therefore liable in damages for the breach of a contract even if he or she is without fault and even if circumstances have made the contract more burdensome or less desirable than anticipated. An obligor who does not wish to undertake so extensive an obligation may contract for a lesser one by using one of a variety of common clauses. For example, the obligor may reserve a right to cancel the contract. The extent of the obligation then depends on the application of the rules of interpretation. Furthermore, even though the obligor has not restricted his or her obligation by agreement, a court may still grant relief where an extraordinary circumstance may make performance so vitally different from what was reasonably to be expected as to alter the essential nature of that performance. In these circumstances, the court must determine whether justice requires a departure from the general rule that the obligor bear the risk that the contract may become more burdensome or less desirable. Whether extraordinary circumstances exist justifying discharge is a question of law for the court. In the *Mel Frank Tool* case, the court found that the tenant Di-Chem Co. (D) failed to present sufficient evidence to establish such extraordinary circumstances.

Quicknotes

AFFIRMATIVE DEFENSE A manner of defending oneself against a claim not by denying the truth of the charge but by the introduction of some evidence challenging the plaintiff's right to bring the claim.

BREACH OF CONTRACT Unlawful failure by a party to perform its obligations pursuant to contract.

LEASE An agreement or contract that creates a relationship between a landlord and tenant (real property) or lessor and lessee (real or personal property).

TENANT An individual who enjoys the use and occupation of the property of another for a specified period.

Alaska Packers' Association v. Domenico

Fishing company (D) v. Seaman (P)

117 F. 99 (9th Cir. 1902)

NATURE OF CASE: Appeal from judgment for plaintiffs in libel action for breach of contract.

FACT SUMMARY: Seamen (P), who had agreed to ship from San Francisco to Alaska at a fixed pay, refused to continue working once they reached Alaska, and demanded a new contract with more compensation.

RULE OF LAW

A promise to pay a person for doing that which he or she is already under contract to do is without consideration.

FACTS: A group of seamen (P) entered into a written contract with Alaska Packers' Association (Packers') (D) to go from San Francisco to Alaska on the Packers' (D) ships, and to work as sailors and fishermen. Compensation was fixed at $60 for the season, and two cents for each salmon caught. Once they had reached port in Alaska, the seamen (P) refused to continue work and demanded that compensation be increased to $100. A superintendent for Packers' (D), unable to hire a new crew, drew up a new contract, substituted in the sum of $100, and signed it although he expressed doubt at the time that he had the authority to do so. The seamen (P) resumed work, but upon the ship's return to San Francisco, Packers' (D) refused to honor the new contract. The seamen (P) filed a libel action for breach of contract.

ISSUE: Is a promise to pay a person for doing that which he or she is already under contract to do is without consideration?

HOLDING AND DECISION: (Ross, J.) No. A promise to pay a person for doing that which he or she is already under contract to do is without consideration. No astute reasoning can change the plain fact that the party who refuses to perform, and thereby coerces a promise from the other party to pay him or her an increased compensation for doing that which he or she is legally bound to do, takes an unjustifiable advantage of the necessities of the other party. The parties in the present case have not voluntarily rescinded or modified their contract. The Alaska Packers' Associations' (Packers') (D) second contract with the seamen (P) is unenforceable although the seamen (P) completed their performance in reliance on it. Reversed and remanded.

ANALYSIS

A few cases have held that the promise to pay additional compensation is enforceable. Consideration is found in the promisee's giving up of his or her power to breach the first contract. In other words, by refusing to continue work, the promisee has invoked the option to pay money damages rather than to invest his or her labor in further performance. This view has been questioned on the ground that a promisee may have the power to breach a contract, but certainly not the legal right, and in any event, he or she should not be encouraged to do so.

Quicknotes

CONSIDERATION Value given by one party in exchange for performance, or a promise to perform, by another party.

PREEXISTING DUTY A common-law doctrine that renders unenforceable a promise to perform a duty, that the promisor is already legally obligated to perform.

Kelsey-Hayes Co. v. Galtaco Redlaw Castings Corp.

Buyer (P) v. Seller (D)

749 F. Supp. 794 (E.D. Mich. 1990)

NATURE OF CASE: Pending motions for summary judgment for defendant and for plaintiff to amend the complaint alleging breach of contract.

FACT SUMMARY: When Galtaco Redlaw Castings Corp. (D) experienced financial losses and threatened to shut down operations, Kelsey-Hayes Co. (P), which had signed a three-year requirements contract, was forced to agree to pay higher prices to keep operations going.

RULE OF LAW

A subsequent contract or modification is invalid and therefore does not supersede an earlier contract when the subsequent contract was entered into under duress.

FACTS: Galtaco Redlaw Castings Corp. (Galtaco) (D) supplied Kelsey-Hayes Co. (P) with castings that were incorporated into brake assemblies sold to automobile manufacturers, including Chrysler and Ford. Facing financial losses, Galtaco (D) decided to cease its production of castings but offered its customers an agreement to keep its foundries operating for several months in exchange for a price increase of 30 percent. Since Kelsey-Hayes (P) could not find an alternate source of castings, it further agreed to another price hike of 30 percent when it signed a contract in 1989 for another year. Kelsey-Hayes (P) protested the breach of the original 1987 contract and later sued, alleging that the contract modifications were agreed to under duress because Galtaco (D) had threatened to breach its contract and go out of business, stopping production and delivery of castings, unless Kelsey-Hayes (P) agreed to significant price hikes. Galtaco (D) alleged that Kelsey-Hayes (P) could not sue for breach of the earlier contract because it had entered into a superseding contract and moved for summary judgment.

ISSUE: Is a subsequent contract or modification invalid and does it therefore not supersede an earlier contract when the subsequent contract was entered into under duress?

HOLDING AND DECISION: (Cohn, J.) Yes. A subsequent contract or modification is invalid and therefore does not supersede an earlier contract when the subsequent contract was entered into under duress. There is sufficient evidence for a reasonable finder of fact to determine that Kelsey-Hayes Co. (Kelsey-Hayes) (P) was under duress when it executed the 1989 agreements. A contract is voidable if a party's assent was induced through an improper threat by another party that leaves the victim no reasonable alternative. Economic duress can exist in the absence of an illegal threat. In addition, Kelsey-Hayes (P) presents a triable issue of fact since it lacked a reasonable alternative, other than acquiescence to Galtaco Redlaw Castings Corp.'s (Galtaco) (D) demands for a contract modification. Galtaco's (D) motion for summary judgment is denied. Kelsey-Hayes's (P) motion to amend is granted.

ANALYSIS

The court in this case reviewed the history in Michigan of the doctrine of economic duress. Early decisions held that in order to make a claim of duress, a person must be subjected to the threat of an unlawful act in nature of a tort or crime. The doctrine of duress has been greatly expanded since its common-law origin, however, to include any wrongful threat.

Quicknotes

DURESS Unlawful threats or other coercive behavior by one person that causes another to commit acts he or she would not otherwise do.

MODIFICATION A change to the terms of a contract without altering its general purpose.

Brookside Farms v. Mama Rizzo's, Inc.

Seller (P) v. Buyer (D)

873 F. Supp. 1029 (S.D. Texas 1995)

NATURE OF CASE: Pending motions for summary judgment.

FACT SUMMARY: Brookside Farms (P) alleged that Mama Rizzo's, Inc. (D) breached its contract to purchase fresh basil leaves.

RULE OF LAW

A contract that does not satisfy the statute of frauds, but is valid in other respects, is enforceable with respect to goods for which payment has been made and accepted or which have been received and accepted.

FACTS: Brookside Farms (Brookside) (P) and Mama Rizzo's, Inc. (MRI) (D) had entered into a written requirements agreement whereby MRI (D) agreed to buy a minimum of 91,000 pounds of fresh basil leaves for one year. MRI (D) later requested that additional parts of the stems of the basil leaves be removed, a task not specifically required under the original contract, and Brookside (P) agreed, in exchange for a $0.50 per pound price increase. Because the contract contained a clause forbidding oral modification, MRI (D) agreed to make a notation of the price change on its copy of the contract. MRI (D) later discontinued its order, but then resumed its orders under the contract. Two more shipments were made and paid for at a higher price. When a check issued for payment by MRI (D) was dishonored by MRI's (D) bank, Brookside (P) sued for damages and breach of contract. MRI (D) countersued, alleging Brookside (P) breached the contract by raising prices in violation of the express language of the contract. Both parties moved for summary judgment.

ISSUE: Is a contract that does not satisfy the statute of frauds, but is valid in other respects, enforceable with respect to goods for which payment has been made and accepted or which have been received and accepted?

HOLDING AND DECISION: (Kent, J.) Yes. A contract that does not satisfy the statute of frauds, but is valid in other respects, is enforceable with respect to goods for which payment has been made and accepted or which have been received and accepted. Valid oral modification of the contract occurred on both estoppel and statutory grounds. It is undisputed that the parties agreed to alter the purchase price of the basil leaves. The actual later conduct of the parties involved the order, shipment, and acceptance of 24,430 pounds of basil leaves, 3,041 pounds of which were paid for by a bad check on Mama Rizzo's, Inc (MRI) (D) part. Receipt and acceptance either of goods or of the price constitutes an unambiguous overt admission by both parties that a contract actually exists. Brookside Farms' (Brookside) (P) motion for partial summary judgment is granted on the claim that MRI (D) is liable to Brookside (P) for $20,526 in payment for the 3,041 pounds of basil leaves accepted but not paid for. Brookside (P) did not breach its contractual obligations, and MRI (D) is liable for a material breach of its obligation to buy a total of 91,000 pounds of basil. Plaintiff's motion for partial summary judgment is denied as to attorneys' fees and is granted as to claims that (1) MRI breached the executory portion of the parties' contract, (2) MRI is liable in the amount of $20,526.75 for the payment of the 3,041 pounds of basil accepted but not paid for, and (3) MRI is liable under the Perishable Agricultural and Commodities Act. Defendant's motion for summary judgment is denied on all counts for the same reasons including the counterclaim MRI is entitled to recover overpayments from Plaintiff for amounts it paid for basil. Defendant's counterclaim for overpayment is dismissed with prejudice. All relief not specifically granted herein is also denied. All parties must bear their own taxable costs incurred to date and may not file further pleadings in the matters set forth in this Order. For further relief to which the parties feel they are entitled, parties must turn to the Fifth Circuit. Plaintiff's motion for partial summary judgment granted and Defendant's petitions denied.

ANALYSIS

There was also a "no-oral-modifications" clause in the contract in this case. At common law, such clauses were held to be ineffective in restricting later modifications. Under the Uniform Commercial Code § 2-209(2), such a clause may be used to create a private statute of frauds between the parties.

Quicknotes

ESTOPPEL An equitable doctrine precluding a party from asserting a right to the detriment of another who justifiably relied on the conduct.

MODIFICATION A change to the terms of a contract without altering its general purpose.

Continued on next page.

STATUTE OF FRAUDS A statute that requires specified types of contracts to be in writing in order to be binding.

WAIVER CLAUSE A clause in a contract providing for the intentional or voluntary forfeiture of a recognized right.

CHAPTER 9

Consequences of Nonperformance: Express Conditions, Material Breach, and Anticipatory Repudiation

Quick Reference Rules of Law

Oppenheimer & Co. v. Oppenheim, Appel, Dixon & Co.

Commercial tenant (P) v. Proposed subtenant (D)

N.Y. Ct. App., 86 N.Y.2d 685, 636 N.Y.S.2d 734, 660 N.E.2d 415 (1995)

NATURE OF CASE: Appeal from reversal of judgment notwithstanding the verdict for defendant in action for breach of contract.

FACT SUMMARY: Oppenheimer & Co. (Oppenheimer) (P), a commercial tenant in a building, entered into a letter agreement with Oppenheim, Appel, Dixon & Co. (Oppenheim) (D), which was to be Oppenheimer's (P) subtenant, setting forth certain conditions precedent to the formation and existence of a sublease between them. One condition was that Oppenheimer (P) would deliver to Oppenheim (D), by a specified date, written consent from the landlord for certain work that Oppenheim (D) wanted done to the space it was to occupy. If this condition was not met, the sublease would become null and void. Although Oppenheimer (P) informed Oppenheim (D) that the landlord had given verbal approval for the work, it did not meet the deadline specified in the agreement for providing the landlord's written approval. Oppenheim (D) refused to go through with the transaction on the grounds that the condition in the agreement had not been met, and Oppenheimer (P) sued for breach of contract, contending that Oppenheim (D) waived or was equitably estopped from invoking the condition precedent regarding the landlord's written consent, and that, in any event, the doctrine of substantial performance applied and that Oppenheimer's (P) failure to provide the written consent was inconsequential. Oppenheim (D) countered that because there was no ambiguity as to the condition precedent in the letter agreement, the doctrine of substantial performance was inapplicable.

RULE OF LAW

The doctrine of substantial performance is not applicable to an unambiguous express condition in a contract.

FACTS: Oppenheimer & Co. (Oppenheimer) (P), a commercial tenant in a building known as One New York Plaza, had three years left on its lease. It was induced to move to a different building owned by Olympia & York Company (O & Y), which agreed to make the rental payments due under Oppenheimer's (P) rental agreement in the event it was unable to sublease its prior space in One New York Plaza. Oppenheimer (P) entered into a letter agreement for a sublease with Oppenheim, Appel, Dixon & Co. (Oppenheim) (D), an existing tenant in One New York Plaza that wanted to expand its tenancy to the floor that Oppenheimer (P) had occupied. The letter agreement set forth certain conditions precedent to the formation and existence of a sublease between them. One condition was that Oppenheimer (P) would deliver to Oppenheim (D), by January 30, 1987, a written consent from the landlord for certain work that Oppenheim (D) wanted done to the space it was to occupy. If this condition was not met, the sublease would become "null and void and of no further force and effect," and neither party was to have "any rights against nor obligations to the other." The parties extended the deadline to February 25, 1987, but although Oppenheimer (P) informed Oppenheim (D) that the landlord had given verbal approval for the work by that modified deadline, it did not meet the deadline for providing the landlord's written consent, which Oppenheimer (P) eventually provided on March 20, 1987. Oppenheim (D) refused to go through with the transaction on the grounds that the condition in the agreement had not been met, and Oppenheimer (P) sued for breach of contract, contending that Oppenheim (D) waived or was equitably estopped from invoking the condition precedent regarding the landlord's written consent, and that, in any event, the doctrine of substantial performance applied and that Oppenheimer's (P) failure to provide the written consent was inconsequential. Oppenheimer (P) alleged in its complaint that it had substantially performed the conditions set forth in the letter agreement. The trial court permitted the jury to consider whether Oppenheimer (P) had substantially performed the conditions in the letter agreement, and, concluding that Oppenheimer (P) had substantially performed, the jury awarded Oppenheimer (P) $1.2 million. Oppenheim (D) moved for judgment notwithstanding the verdict, which the trial court granted, ruling as a matter of law that the doctrine of substantial performance was inapplicable, given that the letter agreement was free of all ambiguity in setting the deadline that Oppenheimer (P) concededly did not honor. The state's intermediate appellate court reversed, concluding that the question of substantial compliance had been properly submitted to the jury and that Oppenheimer's (P) failure to deliver the landlord's written consent was inconsequential. Oppenheim (D) appealed, and the state's highest court granted review.

ISSUE: Is the doctrine of substantial performance applicable to an unambiguous express condition in a contract?

HOLDING AND DECISION: (Ciparick, J.). No. The doctrine of substantial performance is not applicable to an unambiguous express condition in a contract.

Continued on next page.

A condition precedent is an act or event, other than a lapse of time, that, unless the condition is excused, must occur before a duty to perform a promise in the agreement arises. Conditions can be express or implied. Express conditions are those agreed to and imposed by the parties themselves, whereas implied or constructive conditions are those imposed by a court to prevent injustice. Express conditions must be literally performed, whereas constructive conditions, which ordinarily arise from language of promise, are subject to the precept that substantial compliance is sufficient. Thus, courts will strictly enforce the terms of an express condition, unless such a condition violates public policy, but will shape the contours of an implied condition to avoid hardship or forfeiture by the obligee. Where the terms of an express condition are unambiguous, the court must honor those terms, regardless of whether doing so may result in hardship or forfeiture, since the terms clearly reflect the agreement reached by the parties. Applying these principles here, it is undisputed that the language in the letter agreement between the parties unambiguously sets forth an express condition precedent, and that, therefore, there is no leeway to interpret that language other than as written. Because the condition precedent agreed to by the parties is perfectly clear, and it is undisputed that Oppenheimer & Co. (Oppenheimer) (P) failed to fulfill that condition, there is no justifiable basis for applying the doctrine of substantial performance to the parties' agreement. Where, as here, parties have made an event a condition of their agreement, there is no mitigating standard of materiality or substantiality applicable to the nonoccurrence of that event, so that the doctrine of substantial performance cannot be applied to excuse the condition's nonoccurrence. Moreover, Oppenheimer (P) never asserted that it suffered a forfeiture, or conferred a benefit on Oppenheim, Appel, Dixon & Co. (Oppenheim) (D), so that there are no grounds for any kind of equitable intervention to prevent a forfeiture or unjust enrichment. Moreover, the general principle that substantial performance is ordinarily not applicable to excuse the nonoccurrence of an express condition precedent—rather than being universally applicable to all categories of breach of contract—is consistent with the state's precedents. In sum, freedom of contract prevails in an arm's length transaction between sophisticated parties such as the ones in this case, and, in the absence of countervailing public policy concerns, there is no reason to relieve them of the consequences of their bargain. If they are dissatisfied with the consequences of their agreement, "the time to say so [was] at the bargaining table." Lastly, it was not for the jury to decide the issue of substantial performance, which is an issue to be decided as a matter of law by the court. Reversed.

ANALYSIS

Although, as this case illustrates, an express condition ordinarily is strictly enforced, such a condition may nevertheless be excused by waiver, breach, or forfeiture. If an obligor waives the condition, the obligor must perform notwithstanding the nonoccurrence of the condition. Waiver can be affected either by words or conduct that convey the obligor's intent to perform despite the condition's nonoccurrence. Usually, a court will not find that the obligor has waived an express condition unless the obligor's intent to do so is patently clear, since a party must unambiguously intend to waive a contract right before it is relinquished. Here, although Oppenheimer & Co. (P) claimed in its complaint that Oppenheim, Appel, Dixon & Co. (D) waived the condition at issue, none of the facts of the case supported that claim.

Quicknotes

CONDITION PRECEDENT The happening of an uncertain occurrence that is necessary before a particular right or interest may be obtained or an action performed.

CONSTRUCTIVE CONDITION A condition that is not expressly stated in or implied by the terms of an agreement but is imposed by law.

ESTOP Prevent or bar.

EXPRESS CONDITION A condition that is expressly stated in the terms of a written instrument.

IMPLIED CONDITION A condition that is not expressly stated in the terms of an agreement but is inferred from the parties' conduct or the type of dealings involved.

JUDGMENT NOTWITHSTANDING THE VERDICT (JNOV) A judgment entered by the trial judge reversing a jury verdict if the jury's determination has no basis in law or fact.

MATERIALITY Importance; the degree of relevance or necessity to the particular matter.

SUBSTANTIAL PERFORMANCE Performance of all the essential obligations pursuant to an agreement.

UNJUST ENRICHMENT The principle of retaining a benefit given to one by another, without compensating the giver, in situations where compensation is reasonably expected.

J. N. A. Realty Corp. v. Cross Bay Chelsea, Inc.

Lessor (P) v. Lessee (D)

N.Y. Ct. App., 42 N.Y.2d 392, 366 N.E.2d 1313 (1977)

NATURE OF CASE: Appeal of reversal of an unsuccessful ejectment action.

FACT SUMMARY: Cross Bay Chelsea (D) negligently failed to give lessor J. N. A. Realty Corp. (P) notice of intent to exercise a lease renewal option.

RULE OF LAW

Equity will protect a tenant who negligently fails to exercise a renewal option if failure to do so will result in forfeiture.

FACTS: J. N. A. Realty Corp. (JNA) (P) executed a commercial lease to Cross Bay Chelsea's (Cross Bay) (D) predecessor. When the predecessor assigned the lease to Cross Bay (D), the lease terms were amended to provide for a 24-year renewal option on six-month notice by Cross Bay (D). When the six-month mark approached, JNA (P) did not remind Cross Bay (D), which did not send notice, although it had real or constructive knowledge of its duty to do so. JNA (P) began negotiating with a prospective new tenant and demanded that Cross Bay (D), which had spent some $15,000 in improvements, vacate. When Cross Bay (D) failed to do so, JNA (P) filed an ejectment action. The trial court found in favor of Cross Bay (D), and the appellate term affirmed. The appellate division reversed. Cross Bay (D) appealed.

ISSUE: Will equity protect a tenant who negligently fails to exercise a renewal option if failure to do so will result in forfeiture?

HOLDING AND DECISION: (Wachtler, J.) Yes. Equity will protect a tenant who negligently fails to exercise a renewal option if failure to do so will result in forfeiture. While a party has no legal interest in a renewal period until the required notice is given, courts have recognized an equitable interest against forfeiture where a tenant has made improvements, and the failure to give notice was not willful, and the landlord is not harmed by equity's intervention. Here, Cross Bay Chelsea, Inc. (D) invested not only the cost of purchasing the lease but put in $15,000 in improvements. Thus, a failure by equity to intervene will result in forfeiture. However, as J. N. A. Realty Corp. (JNA) (P) has been negotiating with a prospective tenant, JNA (P) may be harmed by intervention. This must be resolved at the trial level. Reversed and remanded.

DISSENT: (Breitel, C.J.) Tenant investment alone is not enough to justify intervention. This is an area that readily lends itself to manipulation and distortion, and a court should not be so ready to give relief. To do so injects great uncertainty into commercial transactions.

ANALYSIS

A vast majority of jurisdictions will grant equitable relief when a party fails to exercise an option. However, the sorts of situations where such relief will be given vary greatly. More courts will grant relief to a tenant than to one holding a real estate purchase or stock option right, for instance.

Quicknotes

EJECTMENT An action to oust someone in possession of real property unlawfully and to restore possession to the party lawfully entitled to it.

INTERVENTION The method by which a party, not an initial party to the action, is admitted to the action in order to assert an interest in the subject matter of a lawsuit.

Jacob & Youngs, Inc. v. Kent

Home builder (P) v. Homebuyer (D)

N.Y. Ct. App., 230 N.Y. 239, 129 N.E. 889 (1921)

NATURE OF CASE: Appeal from reversal of a directed verdict for defendant in action for damages for breach of a construction contract.

FACT SUMMARY: Jacobs & Youngs (P) was hired to build a $77,000 country home for Kent (D). When the dwelling was completed, it was discovered that through an oversight, pipe, not of Reading manufacture (though of comparable quality and price), which had been specified in the contract, was used. Kent (D) refused to make final payment of $3,483.46 upon learning of this.

RULE OF LAW

The measure of damages for breach of a construction contract where the breaching party has substantially performed with trivial deviation is the difference between the value of the construction as contracted for and the construction as built, rather than complete forfeiture by the breaching party.

FACTS: Jacobs & Youngs (Jacobs) (P) built a country home for $77,000 for Kent (D) and sued for $3,483.46 that remained unpaid. Almost a year after completion, Kent (D) discovered that not all pipe in the home was of Reading manufacture as specified in the contract. Kent (D) ordered the plumbing replaced, but as it was encased in the walls, except in those spots where it must necessarily remain exposed, Jacobs (P) refused to replace the pipe, stating that the pipe used was of comparable price and quality. It appears that the omission was neither fraudulent nor willful and was due to oversight. Kent (D) refused to pay the balance of the construction cost still due.

ISSUE: Is the measure of damages for breach of a construction contract where the breaching party has substantially performed with trivial deviation the difference between the value of the construction as contracted for and the construction as built, rather than complete forfeiture by the breaching party?

HOLDING AND DECISION: (Cardozo, J.) Yes. The measure of damages for breach of a construction contract where the breaching party has substantially performed with trivial deviation is the difference between the value of the construction as contracted for and the construction as built, rather than complete forfeiture by the breaching party. Where the significance of the default or omission is grievously out of proportion to the oppression of the forfeiture, the breach is considered trivial and innocent. A change will not be tolerated if it is so dominant and pervasive as to frustrate the purpose of the contract. The contractor cannot install anything he or she believes to be just as good. It is a matter of degree judged by the purpose to be served, the desire to be gratified, the excuse for deviation from the letter, and the cruelty of enforced adherence. Under the circumstances, the measure of damages should not be the cost of replacing the pipe, which would be great. Instead, the difference in value between the dwelling as specified and the dwelling as constructed should be the measure even though it may be nominal or nothing. Usually, the owner is entitled to the cost of completion, but not where it is grossly unfair and out of proportion to the good to be obtained. This simply is a rule to promote justice when there is substantial performance with trivial deviation. Affirmed.

DISSENT: (McLaughlin, J.) Jacobs & Youngs (P) failed to perform as specified. It makes no difference why Kent (D) wanted a particular kind of pipe. Failure to use the kind of pipe specified was either intentional or due to gross neglect which amounted to the same thing.

ANALYSIS

Substantial performance cannot occur where the breach is intentional as it is the antithesis of material breach. The part unperformed must not destroy the purpose or value of the contract. Because here there is a dissatisfied landowner who stands to retain the defective structure built on his land, there arises the problem of unjust enrichment. Usually, it would appear the owner would pocket the damages he or she collected rather than remedying the defect by tearing out the wrong pipe and replacing it with the specified pipe. The owner would have a home substantially in compliance and a sum of money greatly in excess of the harm suffered by him or her. Note that under the doctrine of *de minimus non curat lex*, the law is not concerned with trifles, trivial defects, and even if willful, will be ignored. The party who claims substantial performance has still breached the contract and is liable for damages, but in a lesser amount than for a willful breach.

Quicknotes

DE MINIMUS NON CURAT LEX Not of sufficient significance to invoke legal action.

SUBSTANTIAL PERFORMANCE Performance of all the essential obligations pursuant to an agreement.

Sackett v. Spindler

Shareholder (P) v. Publisher (D)

Cal. Ct. App., 248 Cal. App. 2d 220, 56 Cal. Rptr. 435 (1967)

NATURE OF CASE: Appeal from a trial court decision favoring a cross-complaint for breach of contract attached to a suit to recover money had and received.

FACT SUMMARY: Sackett's (P) continued delay in making the overdue final installment on the $85,000 purchase price for all 6,316 outstanding shares of S&S Newspaper was answered, after several extensions of time, by Spindler's (D) notice that there would be no sale. But a later offer by Spindler (D) to nonetheless accept a tender of the balance in cash or its equivalent (to which there was no reply) followed Sackett's (P) rejected request that he pay the balance over a period of time through a liquidating trust.

RULE OF LAW

A party can repudiate a contract where the other party thereto has committed a material—and therefore total—breach of the contract by continually failing to make required payments thereunder.

FACTS: Sackett (P) had a written contract with Spindler (D) to purchase from Spindler (D) all outstanding shares of S&S Newspapers for $85,000, to be paid in three installments. Sackett (P) made his initial installment of $6,000 on July 10, 1961 (when it was due); paid $19,800 on July 21 (to cover the $20,000 installment due on July 14); and gave a $59,200 check on August 10 (to cover the final $59,000 installment due on August 15). The agreement provided for 6 percent interest on any unpaid balance and delivery of the stock upon final payment under the contract. Therefore, when the $59,200 check bounced for insufficient funds on September 1, Spindler (D) reclaimed the shares of stock he had already put in escrow with Sackett's (P) attorneys. There followed a series of messages: Sackett (P) promised to pay a September 22 payment of $3,944.26 (to provide working capital); Sackett (P) sent an October 4 telegram saying his divorce proceedings would no longer block payment; Spindler's (D) attorney sent a letter dated October 5 to Sackett's (P) lawyer notifying that the sale would not take place because of the delay in final payment; Sackett's lawyer (P) on October 6 telephoned Spindler's (D) lawyer with a final offer to accept payment of the balance in cash or its equivalent (which was in response to Sackett's (P) unacceptable offer to pay the sum over a period of time through a liquidating trust). During this time, the company needed working capital so Spindler (D): (1) mortgaged $4,000 of his personal property, (2) sold half of his stock for $10,000 in November, (3) changed operations, and (4) bought back for $10,000 those shares he had sold in November and sold all outstanding shares—about a year after the original agreement had been entered into—for $22,000 (netting $20,680 after payment of brokerage commission). Thereafter, Sackett (P), sued Spindler (D) for money had and received, and Spindler (D) cross-complained for breach of contract. Spindler (D) was awarded $34,575.74 plus interest by the trial court. The state's intermediate appellate court granted review.

ISSUE: Can a party repudiate a contract where the other party thereto has committed a material—and therefore total—breach of the contract by continually failing to make required payments thereunder?

HOLDING AND DECISION: (Molinari, P.J.) Yes. A party can repudiate a contract where the other party thereto has committed a material—and therefore total—breach of the contract by continually failing to make required payments thereunder. Unlike a partial breach, a total breach (which is any material failure to perform as promised) renders proper a repudiation of the contract by the nonbreaching party. In this case, Spindler (D) was more than justified in terminating the contract on October 5. The following factors point to the material nature of the breach, which makes Spindler's (D) repudiation proper: (1) there was a high degree of uncertainty as to whether Sackett (P) intended to complete the contract and, if he did, when he would deign to do so; and (2) Sackett's (P) failure to perform could in no way be characterized as innocent, having been brought about by gross negligence or willful conduct. There was, therefore, no unlawful repudiation on which to base a release from the duties Sackett (P) had under the contract. Furthermore, Spindler's (D) repudiation, coming as it did before tender of final payment was made, and Spindler's (D) performance was to thereby become due, was anticipatory in nature. So, his later offer to accept cash tender nullified that repudiation, as did Sackett's (P) own offer to pay through a trust (inasmuch as it evidenced a disregard for any repudiation and a desire to treat the contract as still being in full force). Finally, since the general rule requiring damages to be measured by the difference between contract and market prices can be modified to use other measures, such as sale price, when market price is unreliable or unavailable, the decision is affirmed as modified.

Continued on next page.

ANALYSIS

Had Sackett's (P) actions not constituted a material breach but only a partial breach, Spindler's (D) October 5 letter might well have been interpreted to amount to a material breach on his part. That would have given Sackett (P) the option of suing for damages or canceling the contract, suing to recover his partial payment, and escaping any other duties to perform under the contract. Of course, with the price of the stock declining, as it was in this case, the first option would be of no use.

Quicknotes

MATERIAL BREACH Breach of a contract's terms by one party that is so substantial as to relieve the other party from its obligations pursuant thereto.

REPUDIATION The actions or statements of a party to a contract that evidence his or her intent not to perform, or to continue performance, of his or her duties or obligations thereunder.

Truman L. Flatt & Sons Co. v. Schupf

Vendee (P) v. Vendor (D)

Ill. App. Ct., 271 Ill. App. 3d 983, 649 N.E.2d 990 (1995)

NATURE OF CASE: Appeal from summary judgment for defendants in suit for specific performance of a real estate contract.

FACT SUMMARY: Flatt (P) backed out of a contract to purchase land from Schupf (D) when a condition that a rezoning request be granted was not satisfied, but later changed his mind and sued for specific performance of the contract.

RULE OF LAW

An anticipatory repudiation may be retracted by the repudiating party unless the other party has, before the withdrawal, manifested an election to rescind the contract or changed its position in reliance on the repudiation.

FACTS: Flatt (P) had contracted with Schupf (D) to purchase some land for $160,000, contingent upon rezoning of the property. When his request for rezoning was denied, Flatt (P) wrote Schupf (D) offering a lower price for the land. When Schupf (D) did not accept the lower offer, Flatt (P) decided to go ahead with the purchase as provided by the contract and wrote a letter on June 14 informing Schupf (D). Schupf (D) replied on July 8 that the failure to waive the rezoning requirements, as well as the new offer to buy the property at less than contract price, had effectively voided the contract. Flatt (P) then sued for specific performance and the court granted Schupf's (D) motion for summary judgment because Flatt (P) had allegedly repudiated the contract. Flatt (P) appealed, claiming that he had not repudiated the contract and, even if he had, he timely retracted that repudiation.

ISSUE: May an anticipatory repudiation be retracted by the repudiating party unless the other party has, before the withdrawal, manifested an election to rescind the contract or changed its position in reliance on the repudiation?

HOLDING AND DECISION: (Knecht, P.J.) Yes. An anticipatory repudiation may be retracted by the repudiating party unless the other party has, before the withdrawal, manifested an election to rescind the contract or changed its position in reliance on the repudiation. Here assuming Flatt's (P) request for a lower price constituted an anticipatory repudiation of the contract, he successfully retracted that repudiation in his letter of June 14, because Schupf (D) had not yet materially changed her position or indicated to Flatt (P) any intent to treat the contract as rescinded. Reversed and remanded.

ANALYSIS

The doctrine of anticipatory repudiation requires a clear manifestation of intent not to perform. Doubtful and indefinite statements that performance may or may not take place are not enough. The letter in this case created, at most, an ambiguous implication whether performance would occur.

Quicknotes

ANTICIPATORY REPUDIATION Breach of a contract subsequent to formation but prior to the time performance is due.

RELIANCE Dependence on a fact that causes a party to act or refrain from acting.

RESCISSION The canceling of an agreement and the return of the parties to their positions prior to the formation of the contract.

Hornell Brewing Co. v. Spry

Supplier (P) v. Distributor (D)

N.Y. Sup. Ct., 174 Misc. 2d 451, 664 N.Y.S.2d 698 (1997)

NATURE OF CASE: Action for declaratory judgment that defendant's rights have been terminated.

FACT SUMMARY: Hornell Brewing Co. (Hornell) (P) sought declaratory relief after Spry (D), who had an exclusive right to distribute Hornell's (P) beverages in Canada, failed to provide adequate assurance of due performance.

RULE OF LAW

One party's failure to respond to a request for adequate assurance of due performance constitutes a breach of the agreement, entitling the other party to suspend performance and terminate the agreement.

FACTS: Spry (D) was granted the exclusive right to purchase Hornell Brewing Co.'s (Hornell) (P) beverages, including the popular "Arizona" drink, for distribution in Canada. When Spry (D) failed to remit timely payment for shipments of beverages received from Hornell (P), Hornell (P) de facto terminated its relationship with Spry (D). When Hornell (P) requested a declaratory judgment that Spry (D) had no continuing rights with respect to distribution of Hornell's (P) beverages, Spry (D) alleged that adequate assurance had been provided and that Hornell (P) had no right to demand any further assurances.

ISSUE: Does one party's failure to respond to a request for adequate assurance of due performance constitute a breach of the agreement, entitling the other party to suspend performance and terminate the agreement?

HOLDING AND DECISION: (Gans, J.) Yes. One party's failure to respond to a request for adequate assurance of due performance constitutes a breach of the agreement, entitling the other party to suspend performance and terminate the agreement. An enforceable contract existed between the parties based on the uncontroverted facts of their conduct. Hornell Brewing Co (Hornell) (P) had reasonable grounds for insecurity after several missed payments and bad checks, and properly requested assurances from the buyer, Spry (D), that he would be able to make the payments on time. When Spry (D) failed to adequately reply, Hornell (P) was entitled to suspend his performance and terminate the agreement. Hornell's (P) request for a declaratory judgment is granted.

ANALYSIS

Under the Uniform Commercial Code § 2-609 a party that has reasonable grounds for insecurity may demand adequate assurance of due performance. Although this section applies only to the sale of goods, the Restatement (Second) of Contracts has a similar provision. Adequate assurance may take the form of a letter of credit or a bond.

Quicknotes

ADEQUATE ASSURANCES A situation in which one party is excused from performance of his or her obligations under a contract if the other party to the contract indicates that he or she does not intend to perform when the time for performance thereunder arrives; the nonbreaching party is excused from further performance unless he or she receives adequate assurances that performance will be rendered.

DECLARATORY JUDGMENT A judgment of the court establishing the rights and other legal relations of the parties in a controversy.

CHAPTER 10

Expectation Damages: Principles of Limitations

Quick Reference Rules of Law

CHAPTER 10

11. *Roth v. Speck.* An employee who wrongfully terminates his or her employment will be liable for any lost profits that can be established (where appropriate) and the difference in salary that the employer would be forced to pay someone of comparable skills. 162

Crabby's, Inc. v. Hamilton

Seller of real estate (P) v. Buyer of real estate (D)

Mo. Ct. App., 244 S.W.3d 209 (2008)

NATURE OF CASE: Appeal from judgment awarding damages to seller of land in action for breach of contract.

FACT SUMMARY: After Paragon Ventures, L.L.C. and Hamilton (collectively, Buyers) (D) refused to close on an agreement to purchase real estate from Crabby's, Inc. (Seller) (P), and after Seller (P) brought suit for breach of contract on which Seller (P) prevailed, Buyers (D) contended that they had not waived a financing contingency provision in the agreement, and that the trial court had erroneously calculated Seller's (P) damages.

RULE OF LAW

(1) A buyer under a real estate contract waives a condition in that contract through clear, unequivocal, and decisive acts showing the buyer's intentional relinquishment of the benefit of the condition.

(2) The sale price obtained in a sale of real property made by highly motivated sellers after a breach of contract for sale of the property constitutes substantial evidence of the property's fair market value where the subsequent sale is made just under a year after the breach.

FACTS: Crabby's, Inc. (Seller) (P) put up for sale a restaurant and the land it was on. Hamilton, along with Paragon Ventures, L.L.C. (collectively, Buyers) (D), agreed to purchase the property for $290,000. The contract contained a financing contingency provision that made it contingent on "Buyer's [sic] ability to obtain a conventional loan or loans in the amount of $232,000, payable over a period of not less than 15 years and bearing interest at a rate of not more than 5.5 percent per annum." The contract also provided Buyers (D) would use reasonable diligence in seeking to obtain such a loan or loans, and if Buyers (D) did not furnish Seller (P) with a copy of an effective written loan commitment within 30 days from the contract's effective date, the contract would automatically terminate. Buyers (D) applied for and were approved by a bank for a loan in the amount of $340,000.00. The bank agreed to loan them $225,000.00 amortized over 15 years on the real estate, $65,000.00 amortized over seven years on the equipment, and a $50,000.00 revolving line of credit all at the rate of interest of prime plus 1.5 percent. Buyers (D) did not apply for a loan with any other financial institution, and they did not furnish Seller (P) with a copy of an effective written loan commitment within 30 days of the effective date of the contract. The parties extended the contract's closing date by around two weeks to permit certain repairs. This extension did not otherwise modify the contract's terms. Following this extension, the parties discussed other additional repairs, which led to an agreement whereby Buyers (D) would receive a credit of $1,373.54 against the purchase price in lieu of additional repairs being made. This agreement also did not otherwise modify the contract's terms. By a second extension agreement, the closing date was again extended, by a little over two weeks, and the parties also entered into an agreement that allowed Buyers (D) to take possession of the property prior to closing so that they could start cleaning it. Buyers (D) obtained a key and took possession. Around this same time period, Buyers (D) made application for appropriate licenses to operate a restaurant on the property and had the utilities for the property transferred into Buyers' (D) name. Nothing in any of the subsequent agreements entered into between the parties altered any of the terms of the financing contingency contained in the original contract. Then, two days before the extended closing date, Buyers (D) informed Seller (P) of their intention not to close, notwithstanding that all matters required for closing had been addressed and all necessary paperwork was ready. Around a week later, Buyers (D) entered into an agreement to purchase a different restaurant and accompanying property for $170,000, and that sale closed. After Buyers (D) refused to close on Seller's (P) property, Seller's (P) realtor continuously tried to sell the property. About 11 months after Buyers (D) refused to close, the property sold for $235,000. Thereafter, Seller (P) brought a breach of contract action against Buyers (D), seeking damages equal to the difference between Buyers' (D) $290,000 contract price and the $235,000 price actually obtained when the property subsequently sold. Seller (P) also claimed real estate and personal property taxes, utilities, and mortgage interest accruing during that period as damages. The trial court determined Buyers (D) had breached the contract, and it awarded $95,547.30 to Seller (P). Buyers (D) appealed, arguing that the trial court had erred in finding they had breached the contract, arguing that by its terms the contract automatically terminated when they failed to provide Seller (P) with a copy of an effective written loan commitment as required by the financing contingency. They also argued that they had used reasonable diligence in finding a loan under the financing contingency, and, finally, they contended that the trial court's judgment was not supported by substantial evidence of

Continued on next page.

the fair market value of the property as of the date the contract was breached by Buyers (D). In response, Seller (P) argued that Buyers (D) had waived the financing contingency provisions, and that the trial court's damages calculation was not erroneous. The state's intermediate appellate court granted review.

ISSUE:

(1) Does a buyer under a real estate contract waive a condition in that contract through clear, unequivocal, and decisive acts showing the buyer's intentional relinquishment of the benefit of the condition?

(2) Does the sale price obtained in a sale of real property made by highly motivated sellers after a breach of contract for sale of the property constitute substantial evidence of the property's fair market value where the subsequent sale is made just under a year after the breach?

HOLDING AND DECISION: (Lynch, C.J.)

(1) Yes. A buyer under a real estate contract waives a condition in that contract through clear, unequivocal, and decisive acts showing the buyer's intentional relinquishment of the benefit of the condition. A provision in a real estate contract that makes the contract contingent upon the buyer's obtaining financing is a condition. Upon the nonoccurrence of the condition, the buyer is excused from performance. However, the buyer can elect to waive the contingency and proceed with the contract under the rule that a party may waive any condition of a contract in that party's favor. Parties to agreements may waive provisions of the contracts between them, and they may do so either by an express agreement or through their conduct. Here, Hamilton, along with Paragon Ventures, L.L.C. (collectively, Buyers) (D) waived the condition through their conduct, which manifested a clear, unequivocal, and decisive intentional relinquishment of the condition's benefits to them. Buyers (D) did not furnish Crabby's, Inc. (Seller) (P) with a copy of an effective written loan commitment within the time specified in the condition, so that the contract automatically terminated within 30 days of its being entered. However, after that date, Buyers (D) entered into several contract amendments extending the closing date, providing Buyers (D) with a credit on the purchase price for repairs, and granting them the right to take possession of the property—which they did. Buyers (D) also put the property's utilities in their names, and, as late as just a few days before the extended closing date, were working on obtaining the licenses necessary for operating a restaurant on the property. Nothing in the contract amendments or subsequent agreements modified the financing contingency, which the parties expressly agreed remained unchanged. Thus, the only reasonable explanation possible for and consistent with Buyers' (D) signatures on these documents is their waiver of this contract requirement and the resulting automatic termination of the contract. Moreover, Buyers' (D) failure to apply for financing on the exact terms set out in the financing contingency and their failure to seek a loan on such terms with more than one lender evidence Buyers' (D) failure to use reasonable diligence to obtain such financing as required by the contingency. Combined with their other conduct, these failures also evidence Buyers' (D) waiver of the entire financing contingency. All these actions by Buyers (D) are clear, unequivocal, and decisive acts showing Buyers' (D) intentional relinquishment of the benefit of the entire financing contingency, and they are so consistent with the intention to waive that contingency that no other reasonable explanation is possible. Affirmed as to this issue.

(2) Yes. The sale price obtained in a sale of real property made by highly motivated sellers after a breach of contract for sale of the property constitutes substantial evidence of the property's fair market value where the subsequent sale is made just under a year after the breach. Contrary to Buyers' (D) arguments, the subsequent sale was not too remote in time to constitute substantial evidence of fair market value and the sale was not a compelled sale. Therefore, the sale price obtained in the subsequent sale ($235,000) constituted substantial evidence of the property's fair market value. A seller's measure of damages for a buyer's breach of a contract for the sale of land with a structure on it is the difference between the purchase price and the fair market value of the property on the date of breach. If a seller sells the property within a reasonable time after breach, the sale price so obtained constitutes some evidence of market value. Here, Buyers (D) contend that 11 months after breach is not a "reasonable time." State precedent provides that this timeframe does constitute a reasonable time. Accordingly, as a matter of law, the subsequent sale by Seller (P) occurred within a reasonable time after the date of Buyers' (D) breach of the contract, such that it provided substantial evidence to support the trial court's determination of the fair market value of the property on the date of Buyer's (D) breach of the contract. Buyers (D) also contend that the subsequent sale was a compelled sale and, therefore, may not be used as evidence of fair market value, which is defined as a price obtained by a seller who is not under a compulsion to sell from a buyer who is not under a compulsion to buy. Here, although the evidence shows that Seller (P) was highly motivated to sell the property, there is no evidence that Seller (P) was under a compulsion to sell, or that the sale

Continued on next page.

was in any way a forced or distress sale. Therefore, the sale price Seller (P) obtained in the subsequent sale is substantial evidence of the fair market value of the property on the date of the breach. Affirmed as to this issue.

ANALYSIS

Real estate conditions are intended to protect the buyer. Therefore, they are a condition of the buyer's duty but not a condition of the seller's duty under the contract. Thus, here, Seller (P) had no affirmative duties under the financing contingency.

Quicknotes

BREACH OF CONTRACT Unlawful failure by a party to perform its obligations pursuant to contract.

DAMAGES Monetary compensation that may be awarded by the court to a party who has sustained injury or loss to his or her person, property, or rights due to another party's unlawful act, omission, or negligence.

FAIR MARKET VALUE Price of particular property or goods a buyer would offer and a seller would accept in the open market following full disclosure.

Handicapped Children's Education Board v. Lukaszewski

Employer (P) v. Speech therapist (D)

Wis. Sup. Ct., 112 Wis. 2d 197, 332 N.W.2d 774 (1983)

NATURE OF CASE: Appeal of award of damages for breach of contract.

FACT SUMMARY: Lukaszewski (D) reneged on a contract to provide speech therapy services on behalf of the Handicapped Children's Education Board (P).

RULE OF LAW

An employer who has to obtain an employee at a higher price upon breach of an employment contract may recover the difference.

FACTS: Lukaszewski (D) contracted with the Handicapped Children's Education Board (Board) (P) to provide speech therapy services. Subsequently, Lukaszewski (D) was offered a better position. She resigned, but the resignation was rejected by the Board (P). Lukaszewski (D) then obtained medical documentation that the stress of the job was resulting in hypertension, whereupon she ceased appearing for work. The Board (P) searched for a replacement. The only applicant was more qualified, so the Board (P) had to hire at a higher salary. The Board (P) sued for the difference. The trial court entered judgment for the Board (P). The appellate court reversed, holding that a breach had occurred, but since the Board (P) had obtained a more qualified employee, it had not been damaged. The Board appealed.

ISSUE: May an employer who has to obtain an employee at a higher price upon breach of an employment contract recover the difference?

HOLDING AND DECISION: (Callow, J.) Yes. An employer who has to obtain an employee at a higher price upon breach of an employment contract may recover the difference. The nonbreaching party is entitled to full compensation for the loss of its bargain. The court of appeals felt that the Handicapped Children's Education Board (Board) (P) had lost nothing, because the Board (P), although paying more, obtained a better "product." This is an incorrect analysis. The Board (P) did not contract for a better teacher at a higher price; it contracted for Lukaszewski (D) at a lower price. Since Lukaszewski's (D) breach forced the Board (P) to lose its bargained-for price, it is entitled to recover from Lukaszewski (D). Affirmed in part and reversed in part.

DISSENT: (Day, J.) Lukaszewski's (D) reason for leaving was legitimate, and therefore no breach occurred.

ANALYSIS

The dissent did not address the coverability of damages issue. It suggested that the contract had been legitimately terminated. The dissent did not state the precise legal basis therefor, but it would seem impossibility or impracticability of performance would be the grounds.

Quicknotes

BREACH OF CONTRACT Unlawful failure by a party to perform its obligations pursuant to contract.

IMPRACTICABILITY A doctrine relieving the parties to a contract from liability for nonperformance of their duties thereunder if the subject matter of the contract ceases to exist.

American Standard, Inc. v. Schectman

Landowner (P) v. Construction grader (D)

N.Y. App. Div., 80 A.D.2d 318, 439 N.Y.S.2d 529 (1981)

NATURE OF CASE: Appeal from award of damages for breach of contract.

FACT SUMMARY: Schectman (D) contended that the correct measure of damages for his failure to complete grading American Standard, Inc.'s (P) land was the diminution in value of the land, rather than the cost of completion.

RULE OF LAW

Only where the cost of completing the contract would entail unreasonable economic waste will the measure of damages for breach of a construction contract be diminution in value of the property in relation to what its value would have been if performance had been properly completed.

FACTS: Schectman (D) contracted to grade and to take down certain foundations to one foot below grade on American Standard, Inc.'s (American) (P) land. Schectman's (D) performance substantially deviated from the grading specifications in the contract. American (P) sued for breach and was awarded damages equal to the cost of completing the grading properly. Schectman (D) appealed, contending the trial court erred by refusing to admit evidence that American (P) sold the property for only $3,000 less than its full market value and therefore it suffered no appreciable loss due to the breach. As a result, Schectman (D) argued, the correct measure of damages was this $3,000 diminution in value of the property due to the breach, rather than the cost of completion.

ISSUE: Will the measure of damages for breach of a construction contract be diminution in the value of the property in relation to what its value would have been if performance had been properly completed only where the cost of completion would entail unreasonable economic waste?

HOLDING AND DECISION: (Hancock, J.) Yes. Only where the cost of completing the contract would entail unreasonable economic waste will the measure of damages for breach of a construction contract be diminution in value of the property in relation to what its value would have been if performance had been properly completed. Only where such cost of completion would entail unreasonable economic waste will the measure of damages be the diminution in the value of the property caused by the breach. Completing the job properly in this case would not require destruction of past work, only that performance be completed. The fact that the sale price of the property was not markedly affected by the breach is irrelevant to the measure of damages determination. No unreasonable economic waste would result from awarding cost of completion damages, therefore that measure was properly used. Affirmed.

ANALYSIS

Some commentators criticize the result in this case as bestowing upon American Standard, Inc. (P) a windfall recovery. Not only was it able to sell the property for virtually its fair market value, $183,000, but it also received a judgment against Schectman (D) for $90,000. Other commentators justify cost of completion awards as protecting the plaintiff's subjective value ascribed to the property.

Quicknotes

WASTE The mistreatment of another's property by someone in lawful possession.

WINDFALL Sudden gain.

Hadley v. Baxendale

Mill operator (P) v. Shipping company (D)

Ex. Ch., 156 Eng. Rep. 145 (1854)

NATURE OF CASE: Action for damages for breach of a carrier contract.

FACT SUMMARY: Hadley (P), a mill operator in Gloucester, arranged to have Baxendale's (D) company, a carrier, ship his broken mill shaft to the engineer in Greenwich for a copy to be made. Hadley (P) suffered a £300 loss when Baxendale (D) unreasonably delayed shipping the mill shaft, causing the mill to be shut down longer than anticipated.

RULE OF LAW

A party injured by the breach of a contract may recover as damages those damages that are the direct, natural and immediate consequence of the breach and that can reasonably be said to have been in the contemplation of the parties when the contract was made.

FACTS: Hadley (P), a mill operator in Gloucester, arranged to have Baxendale's (D) shipping company return his broken mill shaft to the engineer in Greenwich who was to make a duplicate. Hadley (P) delivered the broken shaft to Baxendale (D), who in consideration for Hadley's (P) fee promised to deliver the shaft to Greenwich in a reasonable time. Baxendale (D) did not know that the mill was shut down while awaiting the new shaft. Baxendale (D) was negligent in delivering the shaft within a reasonable time. Reopening of the mill was delayed five days, costing Hadley (P) lost profits and paid-out wages of £300. Hadley (P) had paid Baxendale (D) £24 to ship the mill shaft. Baxendale (D) paid into court £25 in satisfaction of Hadley's (P) claim. The jury awarded an additional £25 for a total £50 award.

ISSUE: May a party injured by the breach of a contract recover as damages those damages that are the direct, natural, and immediate consequence of the breach and that can reasonably be said to have been in the contemplation of the parties when the contract was made?

HOLDING AND DECISION: (Baron Edward Hall Alderson, J.) Yes. A party injured by the breach of a contract may recover as damages those damages that are the direct, natural and immediate consequence of the breach and that can reasonably be said to have been in the contemplation of the parties when the contract was made. The jury requires a rule for its guidance in awarding damages justly. When a party breaches its contract, the damages he or she pays ought to be those arising naturally from the breach itself and, in addition, those as may reasonably be supposed to have been in contemplation of the parties, at the time they made the contract, as the probable result of the breach of it. Therefore, if the special circumstances under which the contract was made were known to both parties, the resulting damages upon breach would be those reasonably contemplated as arising under those communicated and known circumstances. But if the special circumstances were unknown, then damages can be only those expected to arise generally from the breach. Hadley's (P) telling Baxendale (D) that he ran a mill and that the mill shaft that he wanted shipped was broken did not notify Baxendale (D) that the mill was shut down. Baxendale (D) could have believed reasonably that Hadley (P) had a spare shaft or that the shaft to be shipped was not the only defective machinery at the mill. Here, it does not follow that a loss of profits could fairly or reasonably have been contemplated by both parties in case of breach. Such a loss would not have flowed naturally from the breach without the special circumstances having been communicated to Baxendale (D). Reversed and remanded.

ANALYSIS

This case lays down two rules guiding damages. First, only those damages as may fairly and reasonably be considered arising from the breach itself may be awarded. Second, those damages that may reasonably be supposed to have been in contemplation of the parties at the time they made the contract as the probable result of a breach of it may be awarded. The second is distinguished from the first because with the latter, both parties are aware of the special circumstances under which the contract is made. Usually, those special circumstances are communicated by the plaintiff to the defendant before the making of the contract. But that is not an absolute condition. If the consequences of the breach are foreseeable, the party that breaches will be liable for the lost profits or expectation damages. Foreseeability and assumption of the risk are ways of describing the bargain. If there is an assumption of the risk, the seller or carrier must necessarily be aware of the consequences. A later English case held that there would be a lesser foreseeability for a common carrier than a seller, as a seller would tend to know the purpose and use of the item sold, while the common carrier probably would not know the use of all items it carried. If all loss went on to the seller, this would obviously be an incentive not to enter into contracts. Courts

Continued on next page.

balance what has become a "seller-beware" attitude by placing limitations on full recovery. The loss must be foreseeable when the contract is entered. It cannot be overly speculative. The seller's breach must be judged by willingness, negligence, bad faith, and availability of replacement items. Restatement (First) § 331(2) would allow recovery in the situation in this case under an alternative theory. If the breach were one preventing the use and operation of property from which profits would have been made, damages can be measured by the rental value of the property or by interest on the value of the property. Uniform Commercial Code § 2-715(2) allows the buyer consequential damages for any loss that results from general or particular needs of which the seller had reason to know.

Quicknotes

CONSEQUENTIAL DAMAGES Monetary compensation that may be recovered in order to compensate for injuries or losses sustained as a result of damages that are not the direct or foreseeable result of the act of a party, but that nevertheless are the consequence of such act and that must be specifically pled and demonstrated.

U.C.C. § 2-715(2) Provides that any damages that seller is aware of and cannot cover against are includable as consequential damages.

Florafax International, Inc. v. GTE Market Resources, Inc.

Customer (P) v. Telecommunications company (D)

Okla. Sup. Ct., 933 P.2d 282 (1997)

NATURE OF CASE: Appeal from an order for plaintiff for lost profits.

FACT SUMMARY: Florafax International, Inc. (Florafax) (P) sued GTE Market Resources, Inc. (GTE) (D) for breach of contract and claimed damages for lost profits it stood to make from a collateral contract Florafax (P) had with a third party, but allegedly lost because of GTE's (D) breach.

RULE OF LAW

For recovery of lost profits, sufficient certainty must be shown that reasonable minds might believe from a preponderance of the evidence that such damages were actually suffered.

FACTS: Florafax International, Inc. (Florafax) (P), a flowers-by-wire company, had an agreement with a leading marketer of floral products to handle direct consumer telephone and Internet orders. Florafax (P) then entered into an agreement with GTE Market Resources, Inc. (GTE) (D) for telecommunication and telemarketing services. GTE (D) failed to provide sufficient telemarketing sales representatives to handle the Mother's Day calls for orders and, as a result, Florafax (P) lost customers. GTE's (D) failure to perform also led to termination of an agreement Florafax (P) had with a third-party client and to additional costs Florafax (P) incurred when taking steps necessary to set up its own call answering center to perform the duties GTE (D) failed to provide. Florafax (P) sued GTE (D) for breach of contract and sought damages for its lost profits. The jury determined that GTE (D) breached its contract with Florafax (P) and awarded damages for all lost profits. GTE (D) appealed, claiming that lost profit damages cannot include profits from third-party collateral contracts, or, if they are recoverable, they must be limited to a sixty-day period, since profits beyond that time would be too remote, speculative, or uncertain.

ISSUE: For recovery of lost profits, must sufficient certainty be shown that reasonable minds might believe from a preponderance of the evidence that such damages were actually suffered?

HOLDING AND DECISION: (Lavender, J.) Yes. For recovery of lost profits, sufficient certainty must be shown that reasonable minds might believe from a preponderance of the evidence that such damages were actually suffered. Once it is clear loss of business profits has been suffered by virtue of the breach, it is proper to let the jury decide what the loss is from the admissible evidence. In this case, not only was the fact and causation of lost profit damages adequately shown to a reasonable certainty, but the amount of lost profit damages awarded was sufficiently shown through competent evidence contained in the record to take the matter out of the realm of mere speculation, conjecture, and surmise. Affirmed.

ANALYSIS

The court explained the holding of *Hadley v. Baxendale*, 156 Eng. Rep. 145 (1854). Loss of future or anticipated profits is recoverable in a breach of contract action if the loss is within the contemplation of the parties at the time the contract was made, or if the loss flows directly or proximately from the breach and the loss is capable of reasonably accurate measurement or estimate. This case fell under the second branch of the formulation.

Quicknotes

COLLATERAL CONTRACT A contract made prior to or contemporaneous with another contract.

SPECIAL DAMAGES Damages caused by a specific act that are not the usual consequence of that act and that must be specifically pled and proven.

Rockingham County v. Luten Bridge Co.

Customer (P) v. Telecommunications company (D)

35 F.2d 301 (4th Cir. 1929)

NATURE OF CASE: Appeal from directed verdict for plaintiff in action in damages for breach of contract.

FACT SUMMARY: Luten Bridge Co. (P) continued a construction contract after Rockingham County (D) had wrongfully notified it that the contract was being repudiated.

RULE OF LAW

After an absolute repudiation or a refusal to perform, the other party may not continue its performance in order to recover damages based on full performance.

FACTS: Rockingham County (D) contracted with Luten Bridge Co. (Luten) (P) to construct a bridge. The contract was approved by a 3 to 2 majority of the County Commission, but after the contract was approved, one of the majority members resigned and the other two failed to attend any more meetings. The minority, along with another commissioner, then acted as the Commission. After Luten (P) had begun minimal work, the newly constituted Commission (D), due to adverse public opinion, wrongfully repudiated the contract and informed Luten (P) that it would not perform. Luten (P), which had expended only a small amount of money on labor and materials at that point—perhaps gambling that the original majority on the Commission would reinstate the contract—proceeded to complete the bridge and brought suit in damages for breach of the entire contract. The trial court entered a directed verdict for Luten (P) on the full amount of its claim. The court of appeals granted review.

ISSUE: After an absolute repudiation or a refusal to perform, may the other party continue its performance in order to recover damages based on full performance?

HOLDING AND DECISION: (Parker, J.) No. After an absolute repudiation or a refusal to perform, the other party may not continue its performance in order to recover damages based on full performance. While Rockingham County (D) had no right to repudiate the contract, Luten Bridge Co. (Luten) (P) had a duty to cease its performance upon notification of an absolute, unqualified repudiation or a refusal to perform. Damages are then fixed at the moment of breach. The bridge could not be sold to anyone other than the County (D) and its completion therefore in no way mitigated damages. Luten's (P) only real interest was in lost profits, which it could have recovered after the breach. Luten (P) may not recover for construction and material costs after the repudiation. Reversed and remanded.

ANALYSIS

The rule of mitigation of damages basically states that one cannot sue for a loss he or she could have avoided. Uniform Commercial Code § 2-610(a) states that a new party must be employed to mitigate damages, e.g., breach of employment contracts. Only reasonable mitigation efforts are required. No penalty is assessed for failing to successfully mitigate so long as a reasonable attempt was made. Failure to make a reasonable attempt will cause damages to be correspondingly reduced.

Quicknotes

COLLATERAL CONTRACT A contract made prior to or contemporaneous with another contract.

REPUDIATION The actions or statements of a party to a contract that evidence his or her intent not to perform, or to continue performance, of his or her duties or obligations thereunder.

SPECIAL DAMAGES Damages caused by a specific act that are not the usual consequence of that act and that must be specifically pled and proven.

Maness v. Collins

Former employee (P) v. Former employer (D)

Tenn. Ct. App., 2010 WL 4629614 (2010)

NATURE OF CASE: Appeal from judgment for plaintiff in action for breach of employment agreement, and cross-appeal from judgment for defendants on damages.

FACT SUMMARY: Maness (P) sold his business to SKM, LLC (D) and its owners (D). Maness (P) contended that SKM (D) and the owners (D) breached the agreement for employment he had with them when they terminated him before the three-year employment term was up. SKM (D) and the owners (D) contended that they did not breach the agreement because they had just cause to terminate Maness (P), and that he was not entitled to damages because he had failed to mitigate his damages by looking for comparable work after his termination, notwithstanding that a noncompetition agreement prohibited him from doing so.

RULE OF LAW

(1) The termination of an employee who is employed under an employment agreement for a specific term is not affected for just cause where the employer actively hinders the employee from performing his or her duties.

(2) An employer who has breached an employment agreement by terminating an employee covered under the agreement may not rely on the defense of mitigation of damages absent evidence that suitable alternative employment was available to the terminated employee.

FACTS: Maness (P), via an asset purchase agreement, sold his business to SKM, LLC (D), owned by three co-equal partners, Collins (D), Mike Smith (D), and Mike's son, Josh Smith (D). Josh Smith (D) was responsible for day-to-day management of the company. The agreement provided Maness (P) would be an employee of SKM (D) for three years as a production manager and would be paid an annual salary. Maness (P) also entered a noncompetition agreement that prohibited him from competing directly or indirectly with SKM (D) throughout the United States for five years. As part of the noncompetition agreement, he averred that his skills were such that he could easily find alternative, commensurate employment or work that would not violate the provisions of the agreement. The relationship between Maness (P) and the company's owners deteriorated, as they clashed over his management style and restricted his authority to discipline and fire employees. In fact, they rehired an employee he had fired. Josh Smith (D) held a meeting with the SKM (D) employees in which he told them that Maness (P) no longer had any authority to correct employees or tell them what to do, but Maness (P) was not informed of this meeting, nor were the other owners. When he complained, Maness (P) claimed, Mike Smith (D) told him to just stay in his office at his desk and draw his money. Maness (P), perceiving his authority to have been undercut and finding employees increasingly disrespectful and belligerent toward him, became dissatisfied and idle. At some point, he reported to ownership that he had observed Josh Smith (D) in a drug transaction. Shortly thereafter, around five months after Maness (P) started working for SKM (D) as an employee, his employment was terminated on the grounds that he failed to fulfill his job duties and that his actions and attitude were detrimental to the company's success. Maness (P) did not actively seek other work after his employment with SKM (D) was terminated. Maness (P) filed suit against SKM (D) and its owners, alleging breach of Maness's (P) employment agreement and asserting that the noncompetition agreement was unenforceable. At trial, Maness's (P) testimony about Josh Smith (D) was corroborated by SKM (D) employees, who attested to Josh Smith's (D) workplace drug use and dealing, and who attested to the meeting at which Josh Smith (D) informed employees that Maness (P) had no authority to discipline or terminate employees. The owners testified that Maness (P) was not interested in acquiring new customers, which they wanted him to do, and that he became idle and unproductive after they removed his authority to discipline and terminate employees. They believed there was just cause to fire him. Josh Smith (D) also testified that although he had a drug problem and used drugs in the workplace, such use did not affect his performance, and he also testified that he never engaged in drug transactions at work. The trial court found that Josh Smith (D) had a severe drug addiction problem, and that Maness's (P) performance had been satisfactory until his authority had been undercut and removed. The court also found that although Maness (P) acted unprofessionally by becoming idle, he was dealing daily with "a drug-addicted business owner," namely, Josh Smith (D). Accordingly, the trial court found that the company and owners did not meet their burden of proof to show just cause for terminating Maness's (P) employment under the employment agreement. As to damages, the court found Maness (P) had a duty to mitigate his damages but took no action to do so by looking for other work. Maness (P) argued that looking for comparable work would have been pointless, as he was prohibited from doing so by the

Continued on next page.

noncompetition agreement. The trial court determined that, in light of Maness's (P) failure to make any effort to find work, he failed to mitigate his damages and that such failure to mitigate precluded any award for damages. The parties cross-appealed and the state's intermediate appellate court granted review.

ISSUE:

(1) Is the termination of an employee who is employed under an employment agreement for a specific term effected for just cause where the employer actively hinders the employee from performing his or her duties?

(2) May an employer who has breached an employment agreement by terminating an employee covered under the agreement rely on the defense of mitigation of damages absent evidence that suitable alternative employment was available to the terminated employee?

HOLDING AND DECISION: (Kirby, J.)

(1) No. The termination of an employee who is employed under an employment agreement for a specific term is not effected for just cause where the employer actively hinders the employee from performing his or her duties. The asset purchase agreement did not expressly specify that Maness (P) could be terminated for cause, just or otherwise. Therefore, under the plain language of the employment agreement, SKM (D) had an essentially unqualified obligation to employ Maness (P) for a period of three years at the annual salary specified. However, state precedent provides that even where an employment agreement is for a definite term, the employer may nevertheless discharge the employee for just cause. Thus, SKM (D) and the owners (D) could terminate Maness's (P) employment for just cause without breaching the agreement. Whether Maness's (P) termination was for just cause is a question of fact, determined in light of all the circumstances. Here, viewed in isolation, Maness's (P) conduct would have provided just cause for his termination. However, the trial court, correctly viewing his conduct in the context of all the circumstances, determined, as a matter of fact, that Maness (P) was actively prevented from fulfilling his job responsibilities by Josh Smith (D) and SKM (D). Each party to a contract is under an implied obligation to restrain from doing any act that would delay or prevent the other party's performance of the contract, and each party has the right to proceed, free of hindrance by the other party. Therefore, SKM (D) and the owners (D) did not have just cause to terminate Maness (P), and, therefore, they breached the asset purchase agreement, under which Maness (P) is entitled to recover. Affirmed as to this issue.

(2) No. An employer who has breached an employment agreement by terminating an employee covered under the agreement may not rely on the defense of mitigation of damages absent evidence that suitable alternative employment was available to the terminated employee. A party who has been wronged by a breach of contract [here, Maness (P)] may not unreasonably sit idly by and allow damages to accumulate. This is known as the doctrine of avoidable consequences, often referred to as the plaintiff's obligation to mitigate his damages. Here, SKM (D) and the owners (D) failed to present evidence that comparable, suitable employment was available to Maness (P). Under state case law, the failure to mitigate damages is an affirmative defense, and where there has been a breach of an employment agreement by an employer, "the employer must prove both availability of suitable and comparable substitute employment and a lack of reasonable diligence on the part of the employee." Such evidence is necessary to quantify an employee's damages, since the measure of those damages is the compensation that the employee who has been wrongfully discharged would have received if the contract had been carried out according to its terms, provided that the employee has been unable to find comparable employment. Without such evidence, the computation of the employee's damages becomes problematic, since the employee may be entitled to some recovery despite a failure to mitigate, given that only the amount that the plaintiff would have earned in the exercise of reasonable diligence is applied to reduce his or her contractual damages. It is only where an employee through such diligence finds work that pays as much as, or more, than what the employee earned under the original employment agreement that the employee will be entitled to no recovery. If no proof of comparable, suitable substitute employment is presented to the trial court, then the trial court has no basis on which to determine the amount by which the plaintiff's damages should be reduced. Even where, as here, an employee avers that he could find alternative, commensurate employment or work, such a contractual acknowledgment does not relieve the breaching employer from presenting evidence of suitable, comparable employment to prove the plaintiff's failure to mitigate damages. Such an acknowledgement is not equivalent to a stipulation that the employee would have earned compensation that equaled or exceeded the compensation he would have received pursuant to the employment agreement. Thus, a trial court could not determine how much the employee would have been able to earn from alternative, commensurate work, and, therefore, the court would not be able to determine the amount by which the employee's

Continued on next page.

damages should be reduced. Hence, in the absence of evidence that suitable alternative employment was available to Maness (P), SKM (D) and the owners (D) cannot rely on the affirmative defense of mitigation of damages. Reversed as to this issue. Affirmed in part, reversed in part, and remanded.

ANALYSIS

This decision illustrates the general rule that a breaching employer has the burden of proving the availability of substantially equivalent employment as part of its mitigation of damages defense. Some courts have carved out an exception to this general rule, holding that an employer is released from its burden of proving the availability of such equivalent employment if the employer proves that an employee has not made any reasonable efforts to obtain such work. Here, the court expressly rejected SKM's (D) and the owners' (D) invitation to adopt such an exception, reasoning that adopting the exception would create problems in calculating damages. In light of SKM's (D) and the owners' (D) failure to provide evidence of the availability of substantially equivalent employment, the trial court clearly erred in holding that Maness's (P) alleged failure to mitigate precluded him from any award of damages at all, as it had no evidence of how much to reduce his recovery by.

Quicknotes

BURDEN OF PROOF The duty of a party to introduce evidence to support a fact that is in dispute in an action.

DAMAGES Monetary compensation that may be awarded by the court to a party who has sustained injury or loss to his or her person, property, or rights due to another party's unlawful act, omission, or negligence.

Jetz Service Co. v. Salina Properties

Lessee (P) v. Lessor (D)

Kan. Ct. App., 19 Kan. App. 2d 144, 865 P.2d 1051 (1993)

NATURE OF CASE: Appeal from damages award for plaintiff in action for breach of a lease agreement.

FACT SUMMARY: Jetz Service Co. (P), which installs and maintains coin-operated laundry equipment, was awarded damages to cover its lost profits when Salina Properties (D) breached its lease.

RULE OF LAW

If the injured party could and would have entered into the subsequent contract, even if the contract had not been broken, and could have had the benefit of both, the party can be said to have "lost volume" and the subsequent transaction is not a substitute for the broken contract.

FACTS: Salina Properties' (D) predecessor in title leased 175 square feet of an apartment complex to Jetz Service Co. (P) for use as a coin-operated laundry facility. Jetz Service (P) was entitled to the first $300 per month or 50 percent, whichever was greater, of the gross receipts from the machines it installed there. Salina Properties (D) disconnected all Jetz Service's (P) machines sixteen months before the end of its lease agreement and replaced them with its own equipment. Jetz Service (P) retrieved its property and stored it in one of its warehouses. Four sets of the laundry equipment were subsequently leased in the Kansas City area, although other suitable laundry equipment was available to complete this transaction. When Jetz Service (P) sued for damages, the trial court determined Jetz Service (P) was a "lost volume" lessee and awarded judgment for loss of profits and damages in the amount requested. Salina Properties (D) appealed, claiming that Jetz Service (P) failed to mitigate its damages and failed to prove the requisite elements to recover lost profits.

ISSUE: If the injured party could and would have entered into the subsequent contract, even if the contract had not been broken, and could have had the benefit of both, can the party be said to have "lost volume" and is the subsequent transaction not a substitute for the broken contract?

HOLDING AND DECISION: (Larson, J.) Yes. If the injured party could and would have entered into the subsequent contract, even if the contract had not been broken, and could have had the benefit of both, the party can be said to have "lost volume" and the subsequent transaction is not a substitute for the broken contract. Adequate authority exists to apply the lost volume rule to volume providers of services. The evidence here showed that Jetz Service (P) had several warehouses in which it had available for lease about 1,500 washers and dryers, thus it would have been able to fulfill the Kansas City lease without using the machines from Salina Properties (D), and it would have been able to enter into both transactions irrespective of the breach by Salina Properties (D). The trial court properly applied the status of "lost volume" lessee to Jetz Service (P) under the facts of this case. There was substantial competent evidence to justify the trial court's findings and judgment. Affirmed.

ANALYSIS

The calculation of lost future profits was based upon historical past profits generated during the seven-month period preceding the breach by Salina Properties (D). Lost profits are presumed to have been contemplated by the parties. Fixed expenses or overhead are not deducted when computing lost profits.

Quicknotes

LOST-VOLUME SELLER A seller who can accommodate more than one buyer and for whom a buyer's breach does not release the goods for sale to another customer; in such a case, the appropriate measure of damages is the net profit the seller would have earned pursuant to the sale.

Zapata Hermanos Sucesores, S.A. v. Hearthside Baking Company, Inc.

Supplier (P) v. Debtor (D)

313 F.3d 385 (7th Cir. 2002), (2003)

NATURE OF CASE: Appeal from award of attorneys' fees in action for breach of contract brought under international treaty.

FACT SUMMARY: Lenell (D), a U.S. corporation that had been found to have breached its supply contract with Zapata Hermanos Sucesores, S.A. (Zapata), a Mexican corporation, contended that neither the Convention on Contracts for the International Sale of Goods nor the inherent authority of the trial court entitled Zapata to an award of all the attorneys' fees Zapata incurred in prosecuting its breach of contract action.

RULE OF LAW

(1) The term "loss" in Article 74 of the Convention on Contracts for the International Sale of Goods does not include attorneys' fees incurred in the litigation of a suit for breach of contract.

(2) A trial court does not have inherent authority to punish a litigant's bad faith, but nontortious, breach of contract through an award of attorneys' fees.

FACTS: Zapata Hermanos Sucesores, S.A. (Zapata) (P), a Mexican corporation that supplied Lenell (D), a U.S. corporation, sued Lenell (D) in U.S. District Court for breach of contract and won. Based both on a provision of the Convention on Contracts for the International Sale of Goods (the Convention), and on the inherent authority of the courts to punish the conduct of litigation in bad faith, the district judge ordered Lenell (D) to pay Zapata (P) $550,000 in attorneys' fees. The Convention, of which both the United States and Mexico are signatories, provides remedies for breach of international contracts for the sale of goods. Zapata (P) brought suit under the Convention for money due for 110 invoices, amounting to around $900,000, and also sought prejudgment interest plus attorneys' fees, which it contended are "losses" within the meaning of the Convention and are therefore an automatic entitlement of a plaintiff who prevails in a suit under the Convention. Article 74 of the Convention provides that "damages for breach of contract by one party consist of a sum equal to the loss, including loss of profit, suffered by the other party as a consequence of the breach," provided the consequence was foreseeable at the time the contract was made. Article 7(2) provides that "questions concerning matters governed by this Convention which are not expressly settled in it are to be settled in conformity with the general principles on which it is based or, in the absence of such principles, in conformity with the law applicable by virtue of the rules of private international law [i.e., conflicts of law rules]." The court of appeals granted review.

ISSUE:

(1) Does the term "loss" in Article 74 of the Convention on Contracts for the International Sale of Goods include attorneys' fees incurred in the litigation of a suit for breach of contract?

(2) Does a trial court have inherent authority to punish a litigant's bad faith, but nontortious, breach of contract through an award of attorneys' fees?

HOLDING AND DECISION: (Posner, J.)

(1) No. The term "loss" in Article 74 of the Convention on Contracts for the International Sale of Goods does not include attorneys' fees incurred in the litigation of a suit for breach of contract. Neither the Convention on Contracts for the International Sale of Goods' (the Convention) background nor the cases under it indicate that "loss" is intended to include attorneys' fees. Although there is no suggestion to the contrary, it is clear that "loss" does not include attorneys' fees incurred in the litigation of a suit for breach of contract, though certain pre-litigation legal expenditures, for example expenditures designed to mitigate the plaintiff's damages, would probably be covered as "incidental" damages. The Convention is about contracts, not about procedure. The principles for determining when a losing party must reimburse the winner for the latter's expense of litigation are usually not a part of substantive contract law but are a part of procedural law. Although the Convention could have addressed the question of attorneys' fees, it did not, and there are no "principles" that can be drawn out of the provisions of the Convention for determining whether "loss" includes attorneys' fees. Therefore, the issue must be resolved by choice of law principles and under the substantive contract law of the nation, the laws of which must be applied. Under Zapata Hermanos Sucesores, S.A.'s (Zapata) (P) reading, the Convention would get his attorneys' fees reimbursed more-or-less automatically. But this raises numerous problems. For example, if the defendant won, he could, under Zapata's interpretation, invoke the domestic law, if, as is likely other than in the United States, that domestic law entitled either side that wins to reimbursement of his fees by the loser. Also, a winning plaintiff might be

Continued on next page.

able to waive his right to attorneys' fees under the Convention in favor of domestic law, which might be more-or-less generous than Article 74, since Article 74 requires that any loss must, to be recoverable, be foreseeable, which beyond some level attorneys' fees, though reasonable ex post, might not be. Finally, it is unlikely that the United States would have signed the Convention had it thought that in doing so it was abandoning the hallowed American rule. A vast majority of the signatories of the Convention are nations in which the loser pays attorneys' fees and costs, so the question whether "loss" includes attorneys' fees would have held little interest for these nations. For all these reasons, "loss" in Article 74 does not include attorneys' fees. Reversed as to this issue.

(2) No. A trial court does not have inherent authority to punish a litigant's bad faith, but nontortious, breach of contract through an award of attorneys' fees. The trial judge based his award of attorneys' fees in part on his desire to punish Lenell (D) for having failed to pay money it conceded it owed to Zapata (P). However, under U.S. common law (the law deciding any issues not expressly governed by the Convention), a breach of contract is not wrongful because it is neither tortious nor criminal on its own. Ordinarily, a breaching party will have to pay damages, and sometimes a breach can increase economic efficiency, which explains why the law does not view breaches, without more, as wrongful conduct. While common-law courts will sometimes award punitive damages for breach of contract in bad faith, to prevail, a plaintiff must show that the breach of contract involved tortious misconduct, such as duress or fraud or abuse of fiduciary duty. Zapata (P) did not assert such misconduct here. In fact, Zapata (P) did not even request punitive damages, and the trial judge had no authority to award attorneys' fees in lieu of such damages. The issue of punitive damages as a sanction for breach of contract is a matter of substantive law, and, under the Erie doctrine, the federal court must follow state law on this issue and the trial judge cannot circumvent this doctrine by renaming punitive damages "attorneys' fees." "The inherent authority of federal courts to punish misconduct before them is not a grant of authority to do good, rectify shortcomings of the common law (as by using an award of attorneys' fees to make up for an absence that the judge may deem regrettable of punitive damages for certain breaches of contract), or undermine the American rule on the award of attorneys' fees to the prevailing party in the absence of statute." Instead, the trial court's authority to punish is a residual one, limited to punishing misconduct occurring in the litigation itself, not in the events giving rise to the litigation or not adequately dealt with by other rules, such as Rules 11 and 37 of the Federal Rules of Civil Procedure, which Lenell (D) has not been accused of violating. Thus, the judge could have punished Lenell (D) only for misconduct in the litigation itself, and if the judge was punishing Lenell (D) for failing to pay Zapata (P) what it conceded it owed Zapata (D), this fault is largely attributable to the judge himself for failing to grant partial summary judgment early in the proceedings based on his erroneous belief that he could not do so unless the grant would give rise to an appealable judgment. Reversed as to this issue.

ANALYSIS

As noted by the court, the so-called American Rule governing the award of attorneys' fees in litigation in the federal courts is that attorneys' fees are not ordinarily recoverable in the absence of a statute or enforceable contract providing therefor. The United States is in the minority of commercial jurisdictions that do not make prevailing parties truly whole by saddling their adversaries with the winners' legal expenses, an omission that does not (as does the vast majority of other jurisdictions' fee-shifting approach) put the winners in contract disputes into the same economic position as if the breaching parties had performed their required obligations under the contracts. There are exceptions to the American rule, however, that justify the awarding of attorneys' fees to the prevailing party, including the possibilities that the parties may have a valid contract term allowing for attorneys' fees, there may be an applicable statute granting such fees, or there may be an established court rule that allows for recovery.

Quicknotes

BREACH OF CONTRACT Unlawful failure by a party to perform its obligations pursuant to contract.

Erlich v. Menezes

Homeowners (P) v. Contractor (D)

Cal. Sup. Ct., 21 Cal. 4th 543, 981 P.2d 978 (1999)

NATURE OF CASE: Appeal by contractor from adverse ruling in suit by homeowners.

FACT SUMMARY: Barry and Sandra Erlich (P) contracted with John Menezes (D) to build their "dream house." They moved in in December 1990. In February 1991, heavy rains came, and the house leaked from every conceivable location. The Erlichs (P) not only sued Menezes (D) for negligent breach of contract in the construction of their home but also sought damages for emotional distress.

RULE OF LAW

Damages for mental suffering and emotional distress are generally not recoverable in an action for the breach of an ordinary commercial contract.

FACTS: Barry and Sandra Erlich (P) contracted with John Menezes (D), a licensed general contractor, to build a "dream house" on their ocean-view lot. The house was built and the Erlichs (P) moved in in December 1990. In February 1991, the rains came, and the house leaked from every conceivable location. Despite extensive repair efforts, which included using sledgehammers and jackhammers to cut holes in the exterior walls and ceilings, application of new waterproofing materials on portions of the roof and exterior walls, and more caulk, the house leaked from the windows and the roofs, and water seeped between the floors. Independent inspections revealed serious errors in the construction of the home's structural components. The Erlichs (P) sued Menezes (D) for breach of contract, fraud, negligent misrepresentation, and negligent construction. At trial, the Erlichs (P) testified that they suffered emotional distress as a result of the defective condition of the house and by Menezes's (D) invasive and unsuccessful repair attempts. The jury found that Menezes (D) had breached his construction contract by negligently constructing the house but was not guilty of fraud or negligent misrepresentation. The jury awarded $406,700 as the cost of repairs, as well as $100,000 damages for emotional distress caused by the negligent construction, and Barry Erlich (P) received an additional $50,000 for physical pain and $15,000 for lost earnings. The court of appeals affirmed, and Menezes (D) appealed.

ISSUE: Are damages for mental suffering and emotional distress generally recoverable in an action for the breach of an ordinary commercial contract?

HOLDING AND DECISION: (Brown, J.) No. Damages for mental suffering and emotional distress are generally not recoverable in an action for the breach of an ordinary commercial contract. A preexisting contractual relationship, without more, will not support a recovery for mental suffering where the defendant's tortious conduct has resulted only in economic injury to the plaintiff. Unless the defendant has assumed a duty to plaintiff in which the emotional condition of the plaintiff is an object, recovery is available only if the emotional distress arises out of the defendant's breach of some other legal duty and the emotional distress is proximately caused by breach of the independent duty; even then, with rare exceptions, a breach of the duty must threaten physical injury, not simply damage to property or financial interests. Here, although the jury found that the contractor Menezes (D) had breached his construction contract by negligently constructing the house, the Erlichs (P) were not entitled to recover damages for mental distress since the claim for negligent breach of a contract is not sufficient to support tort damages for violation of an independent tort duty. Even assuming Menezes's (D) negligence constituted a breach of a sufficient independent duty to the Erlichs (P), such a finding would not entitle them to emotional distress damages on the facts alleged. The breach (the negligent construction of the house) did not cause physical injury. The only physical injury alleged was for Barry Erlich's (P) heart disease, which flowed from the emotional distress and not directly from the negligent construction. No California case has ever allowed recovery for emotional distress arising solely out of property damage. Cases permitting recovery for emotional distress typically involve mental anguish stemming from more personal undertakings, the traumatic results of which were unavoidable, such as, for example, an infant injured during childbirth, misdiagnosed venereal disease and subsequent failure of a marriage, a fatal waterskiing accident, or the failure to adequately preserve a corpse. Reversed and remanded.

ANALYSIS

In *Erlich,* the court explained that recovery for emotional disturbance will be excluded unless the breach also caused bodily harm or the contract or the breach is of such a kind that serious emotional disturbance was a particularly likely result, since to permit emotional distress damages in cases of negligent construction of a personal residence when the negligent construction causes gross interference with the normal use and

Continued on next page.

habitability of the residence would make the financial risks of construction agreements difficult to predict. Contract damages must be clearly ascertainable in both nature and origin, and a rule focusing not on the risks that the contracting parties voluntarily assume, but on one party's possible future reaction to inadequate performance, cannot provide any reasonable limit on liability. As noted in *Erlich*, however, tort damages have been permitted in contract cases where a breach of duty directly causes physical injury; for breach of the covenant of good faith and fair dealing in insurance contracts; for wrongful discharge in violation of fundamental public policy; or where the contract was fraudulently induced. In each of these cases, the duty that gives rise to tort liability is either completely independent of the contract or arises from conduct that is both intentional and intended to harm.

Quicknotes

BREACH OF CONTRACT Unlawful failure by a party to perform its obligations pursuant to contract.

EMOTIONAL DISTRESS Extreme personal suffering that results in another's conduct and for which damages may be sought.

Roth v. Speck

Beauty shop owner (P) v. Employee (D)

D.C. Mun. Ct. App., 126 A.2d 153 (1956)

NATURE OF CASE: Action for breach of employment contract.

FACT SUMMARY: Roth (P) hired Speck (D) to work in his beauty shop for one year, but Speck (D) quit after six and one-half months.

RULE OF LAW

An employee who wrongfully terminates his or her employment will be liable for any lost profits that can be established (where appropriate) and the difference in salary that the employer would be forced to pay someone of comparable skills.

FACTS: Roth (P) hired Speck (D) for one year to be a beautician in his beauty shop. Speck (D) wrongfully quit after six and one-half months. Roth (P) brought suit for damages. At trial, the court found lost profits could not be estimated because of the seasonal nature of the business and other factors. It found that Speck (D) had another job with a $25 per week salary increase and that no satisfactory replacement could be found for the salary Roth (P) had paid Speck (D). The court awarded Roth (P) $1.00 in damages since he had been unable to satisfactorily establish the amount of his injury.

ISSUE: Is an employee who wrongfully terminates his or her employment, liable for any lost profits that can be established (where appropriate) and the difference in salary that the employer would be forced to pay someone of comparable skills?

HOLDING AND DECISION: (Quinn, J.) Yes. An employee who wrongfully terminates his or her employment will be liable for any lost profits that can be established (where appropriate) and the difference in salary that the employer would be forced to pay someone of comparable skills. One of the measures of damages when an employee wrongfully terminates his or her employment is, in effect, "replacement" cost, i.e., the cost of hiring another employee of comparable ability if one could not be found at the same salary. The evidence adduced herein was that no satisfactory replacement could be found. Speck's (D) new employer offered him $25 per week more to work for him. This is a proper measure of damages since it appears that Roth (P) would have to offer $25 per week more to find comparable help. Since lost profits could not be estimated due to too many intangible factors, Roth (P) cannot recover these damages. Reversed granting a limited new trial.

ANALYSIS

Damages for lost profits will be awarded only where, at the time the contract was entered, the employee knew or should have known that if he or she wrongfully terminated the employment, the employer would lose profits. The burden is on the employee to establish that his or her commissions would have been greater than his or her guaranteed salary to mitigate his or her damages. Mere difficulty in proof will not excuse the defendant of this burden.

Quicknotes

MITIGATION OF DAMAGES A plaintiff's implied obligation to take reasonable steps to avoid further damages after injury has occurred.

CHAPTER 11

Alternatives to Expectation Damages: Reliance and Restitutionary Damages, Specific Performance, and Agreed Remedies

Quick Reference Rules of Law

Wartzman v. Hightower Productions, Ltd.

Law firm (D) v. Corporation (P)

Md. Ct. Spec. App., 53 Md. App. 656, 456 A.2d 82 (1983)

NATURE OF CASE: Appeal from award of damages for breach of contract.

FACT SUMMARY: Hightower Productions, Ltd. (Hightower) (P) hired Wartzman (D), a law firm, to incorporate it, and when Wartzman (D) forgot a vital part of the process, Hightower (P), forced to cancel its project, sued Wartzman (D) for damages.

RULE OF LAW

Where a breach has prevented an anticipated gain and proof of loss is difficult to ascertain, a party can recover damages based upon his or her reliance interest on the contract, less any loss that can be proven that the injured party would have suffered if the contract were performed.

FACTS: Three men conceived of Hightower Productions, Ltd. (Hightower) (P) as a corporate promotional venture in which an entertainer would live in a mobile perch to establish the world record for flagpole sitting. They hired Wartzman (D), a law firm, to incorporate it so they could sell stock to raise money for the venture. Wartzman (D) filed the articles of incorporation, and Hightower (P) hired an entertainer, a company to build the perch, and public relations specialists, and it sold stock. Hightower (P) still needed to sell more stock when Wartzman (D) announced that Hightower (P) had been structured incorrectly and that a securities attorney would need to be hired for approximately $15,000. Hightower (P) asked Wartzman (D) to pay the costs of restructuring, but they refused. The stockholders decided to discontinue the project because of the added costs that accrued because of this mistake. Hightower (P) sued Wartzman (D) for failure to create a corporation authorized to issue stock. The jury returned a verdict in favor of Hightower (P), and Wartzman (D) appealed.

ISSUE: Where a breach has prevented an anticipated gain and proof of loss is difficult to ascertain, can a party recover damages based on his or her reliance interest on the contract, less any loss that can be proven that the injured party would have suffered if the contract were performed?

HOLDING AND DECISION: (Getty, J.) Yes. Where a breach has prevented an anticipated gain and proof of loss is difficult to ascertain, a party can recover damages based upon his or her reliance interest on the contract, less any loss that can be proven that the injured party would have suffered if the contract were performed. If anticipated profits are too speculative to be determined, moneys spent in part performance or in preparation for performing the contract are recoverable. These damages are limited if it can be shown that full performance would have resulted in a loss. It is the responsibility of the breaching party to show that performance of the contract would have resulted in a net loss. Ordinarily, profits lost due to a breach of contract are recoverable. Wartzman (D) contended that its failure to incorporate Hightower Productions, Ltd. (Hightower) (P) correctly was only a collateral issue as to why the project failed. However, the project could have worked only if stock had been sold to raise money. Without this, there were no funds to continue. Additionally, it would be impossible to prove that the project would have ultimately failed. Therefore, reliance damages were an appropriate remedy. The jury instructions were correct in that the ultimate success of the venture need not be proven, nor could Wartzman (D) have claimed that Hightower (P) did not mitigate its damages by hiring a securities attorney for $15,000. It was not required to spend huge amounts of money to mitigate. Affirmed.

ANALYSIS

One of the main factors affecting determination of how much a party receives in reliance damages is whether that party tried to mitigate its damages. Here, the court held that Hightower Productions, Ltd. (P) had no duty to mitigate; rather Wartzman (D) bore the responsibility of mitigating damages by paying for the securities expert itself. Some courts use this "equal opportunity" exception, but it is not accepted by all courts.

Quicknotes

BREACH OF CONTRACT Unlawful failure by a party to perform its obligations pursuant to contract.

MITIGATION Reduction in penalty.

Walser v. Toyota Motor Sales, U.S.A., Inc.

Dealer (P) v. Auto manufacturer (D)

43 F.3d 396 (8th Cir. 1994)

NATURE OF CASE: Appeal from damages award for plaintiffs in a promissory estoppel claim.

FACT SUMMARY: Walser (P) alleged that the district court erred in instructing the jury that damages were limited to the out-of-pocket expenditures made in reliance on Toyota Motor Sales, U.S.A, Inc.'s (D) promise of a dealership.

RULE OF LAW

In determining damages on a promissory estoppel claim for breach, whether to charge full contract damages or something less is a matter of discretion delegated to district courts.

FACTS: Walser (P) was negotiating with Toyota Motor Sales, U.S.A., Inc. (D) for a Lexus dealership and was told that a letter of intent had been formally approved by Lexus management. In reliance on that statement, Walser's (P) father had agreed to purchase property for the proposed Lexus dealership. When informed that Lexus would not be issuing the letter of intent to him, Walser (P) sued for breach of contract, promissory estoppel, fraud, joint venture, statutory breach, intentional interference with contractual relations, and interference with a prospective business advantage. The district court dismissed all charges except for the promissory estoppel, breach of contract, and fraud claims. The jury returned a verdict in favor of Walser (P) only on the promissory estoppel claim and awarded damages in accordance with the district court's instructions to limit damages to out-of-pocket expenses. Walser (P) appealed, claiming the district court had erred in its instructions.

ISSUE: In determining damages on a promissory estoppel claim for breach, is whether to charge full contract damages or something less a matter of discretion delegated to district courts?

HOLDING AND DECISION: (Hansen, J.) Yes. In determining damages on a promissory estoppel claim for breach, whether to charge full contract damages or something less is a matter of discretion delegated to district courts. A district court's discretionary decision will not be disturbed on review if that decision remains within the range of choices available to the district court, accounts for all relevant factors, and does not constitute a clear error of judgment. The district court did not abuse its discretion in limiting the award of damages on the promissory estoppel claim to out-of-pocket expenses. Affirmed.

ANALYSIS

Some courts have held that recovery for promissory estoppel cases should be limited only to the amount of actual reliance. Other courts have granted expectation damages and lost profits. Certainty and foreseeability are other factors considered by courts in making damages awards.

Quicknotes

BREACH OF CONTRACT Unlawful failure by a party to perform its obligations pursuant to contract.

FRAUD A false representation of facts with the intent that another will rely on the misrepresentation to his or her detriment.

INTERFERENCE WITH CONTRACTUAL RELATIONS An intentional tort whereby a defendant intentionally elicits the breach of a valid contract resulting in damages.

JOINT VENTURE Venture undertaken based on an express or implied agreement among the members, with a common purpose and interest, and an equal power of control.

PROMISEE The party to whom a promise is made.

PROMISOR The party who promises to render an obligation to another in the future.

PROMISSORY ESTOPPEL A promise that is enforceable if the promisor should reasonably expect that it will induce action or forbearance on the part of the promisee, does in fact cause such action or forbearance, and is the only means of avoiding injustice.

RELIANCE Dependence on a fact that causes a party to act or refrain from acting.

United States ex rel. Coastal Steel Erectors, Inc. v. Algernon Blair, Inc.

Federal government (P) v. General contractor (D)

479 F.2d 638 (4th Cir. 1973)

NATURE OF CASE: Appeal by subcontractor in action to recover in quantum meruit for labor and equipment furnished.

FACT SUMMARY: Algernon Blair, Inc. (Blair) (D), as general contractor, was sued by its subcontractor in the name of the United States (P) to recover for the labor and equipment that had been supplied before the subcontractor ceased work on the project due to a breach of contract by Blair (D).

RULE OF LAW

A subcontractor who justifiably ceases work under a contract because of the prime contractor's breach may recover in quantum meruit the value of labor and equipment already furnished pursuant to the contract irrespective of whether he or she would have been entitled to recover in a suit on the contract.

FACTS: Algernon Blair, Inc. (Blair) (D) was acting as general contractor in constructing a naval base and had subcontracted certain work to Coastal Steel Erectors, Inc. (Coastal). Coastal stopped performance when 28 percent of its work was done because of a material breach of the subcontract by Blair (D). Another subcontractor was hired to complete the job. Coastal then brought an action, in the name of the United States (P), to recover for labor and equipment furnished. The district court found $37,000 was still due Coastal under the contract but held that it would have lost more than that if it had to complete the contract. Therefore, there could be no recovery on the contract.

ISSUE: May a subcontractor who justifiably ceases work under a contract because of the prime contractor's breach recover in quantum meruit the value of labor and equipment already furnished pursuant to the contract irrespective of whether he or she would have been entitled to recover in a suit on the contract?

HOLDING AND DECISION: (Craven, J.) Yes. A subcontractor who justifiably ceases work under a contract because of the prime contractor's breach may recover in quantum meruit the value of labor and equipment already furnished pursuant to the contract irrespective of whether he or she would have been entitled to recover in a suit on the contract. Whether or not the subcontractor would be entitled to recover in a suit on the contract, a subcontractor who justifiably ceases work under a contract because of the prime contractor's breach, as in this case, may recover in quantum meruit the value of the labor and equipment already supplied. The impact of quantum meruit is to allow a promisee, such as Coastal Steel Erectors, Inc. (Coastal), to recover the value of services it gave to the defendant irrespective of whether it would have lost money on the contract and been unable to recover in a suit on the contract. The standard for measuring the reasonable value of services rendered is the amount for which such services could have been purchased from one in the plaintiff's position at the time and place the services were rendered. The case must be remanded for a finding as to the reasonable value of the labor and equipment Coastal furnished. Reversed and remanded.

ANALYSIS

According to Professor George E. Palmer, the courts regularly deny restitution of the value of the plaintiff's performance where he or she has fully performed and the defendant's obligation is to pay money. He notes this is incongruous, since restitution of an amount in excess of the contract price for full performance has been permitted in many decisions where the plaintiff has only partially performed. 1 George E. Palmer, *The Law of Restitution* 378–379 (1978).

Quicknotes

MATERIAL BREACH Breach of a contract's terms by one party that is so substantial as to relieve the other party from its obligations pursuant thereto.

QUANTUM MERUIT Equitable doctrine allowing recovery for labor and materials provided by one party, even though no contract was entered, in order to avoid unjust enrichment by the benefited party.

RESTITUTION The return or restoration of some thing to its rightful owner to prevent unjust enrichment.

Lancellotti v. Thomas

Purchaser of business (P) v. Business owner (D)

Pa. Super. Ct., 341 Pa. Super. 1, 491 A.2d 117 (1985)

NATURE OF CASE: Appeal of award of damages for breach of contract.

FACT SUMMARY: Lancellotti (P) backed out of an agreement to purchase a business from Thomas (D) who had been paid $25,000.

RULE OF LAW

A party breaching a contract may be entitled to restitution to prevent forfeiture.

FACTS: Lancellotti (P) contracted to buy Thomas's (D) business. Pursuant to this, Lancellotti (P) paid $25,000. A dispute subsequently arose regarding certain improvements called for in the contract, and Lancellotti (P) eventually abandoned the business. Lancellotti (P) sued for a return of the $25,000. Thomas (D) counterclaimed for $6,665 in rent, which had been deferred under the contract. The trial court instructed the jury that a breaching party was not entitled to restitution. The jury awarded Thomas (D) $6,665. Lancellotti (P) appealed.

ISSUE: May a party breaching a contract be entitled to restitution to prevent forfeiture?

HOLDING AND DECISION: (Spaeth, P.J.) Yes. A party breaching a contract may be entitled to restitution to prevent forfeiture. The common-law rule held that a breaching party was not so entitled, on the premise that a wrongdoer should not profit from his or her wrongdoing. However, the common-law rule has been slowly eroded. Recognizing that the purpose of contract law is not to punish, courts have increasingly permitted breaching parties to recover if forfeiture would otherwise occur and prejudice to the nonbreaching party will not occur. This is the position of the Uniform Commercial Code and Restatement (Second) of Contracts § 374. Here, the trial court instructed the jury that a breaching party could not recover, so once the jury found that Lancellotti (P) had breached, his recourse was foreclosed. The matter must be remanded for a determination of whether restitution would be granted to the appellant.

DISSENT: (Tamilia, J.) The Uniform Commercial Code, cited by the majority, is inapplicable here, as the contract did not involve goods. This being so, any departure from the common-law rule must come from the Pennsylvania Supreme Court, which as yet has not seen fit to change the common-law rule in this jurisdiction and has not adopted the Restatement (Second) position. Most important, however, for determining the outcome of the case—and ignored by the majority—is the trial court's determination that the agreement clearly captures the parties' agreement. The record shows that Lancellotti (P) engaged in bad faith "sharp practice"; to provide him with restitution is to reward him for his bad faith conduct—a result inconsistent with equity.

ANALYSIS

The acceptance of the rule stated here has been slow in coming. While the law of contracts is not criminal law, the breaching party does appear to have "done wrong." For this reason, the law has been reluctant to help the breaching party. The rule has evolved as contract law has come to focus more on economics and less on morality.

Quicknotes

EQUITY Fairness; justice; the determination of a matter consistent with principles of fairness and not in strict compliance with rules of law.

FORFEITURE The loss of a right or interest as a penalty for failing to fulfill an obligation.

RESTITUTION The return or restoration of some thing to its rightful owner to prevent unjust enrichment.

Shaffer v. George Washington University

Student (P) v. Private university (D)

27 F.4th 754 (D.C. Cir. 2022)

NATURE OF CASE: Appeals from dismissals for failure to state a claim of two putative class actions asserting, inter alia, breach of contract and unjust enrichment.

FACT SUMMARY: In two separate putative class actions, students (P) and parents (P) (collectively, the Plaintiffs) (P) of American University (American) (D) and George Washington University (GWU) (D) (collectively, the Universities) (D), contended that by responding to the COVID-19 pandemic by transitioning to online education from in-person learning and by refusing to refund prorated tuition payments or fees, the Universities (D), inter alia, breached their express and implied contractual obligations to the students, or, alternatively, were unjustly enriched. The Universities (D) asserted that the Plaintiffs (P) failed to state any claims.

RULE OF LAW

(1) A breach of contract claim premised on the breach of an express promise will not survive a motion to dismiss for failure to state a claim where the plaintiff fails to plausibly allege the existence of an express contract between the plaintiff and defendant.

(2) A breach of contract claim premised on the breach of an implied promise will survive a motion to dismiss for failure to state a claim where the plaintiff plausibly alleges the existence of an implied-in-fact contract between the plaintiff and defendant.

(3) An unjust enrichment claim will survive a motion to dismiss for failure to state a claim where the claim is raised in the alternative to a breach of contract claim and it is plausible that the contract at issue is invalid, subject to avoidance, or otherwise ineffective to regulate the parties' obligations and the claim otherwise states a plausible claim for unjust enrichment.

FACTS: In response to the global COVID-19 pandemic, and government shutdown orders that resulted, American University (American) (D) and George Washington University (GWU) (D) (collectively, the Universities) (D), like numerous other institutions of higher learning, transitioned to online learning programs and largely shut down campus activities. Before the pandemic, the Universities (D) charged higher rates for on-campus programs than for the programs' online counterparts, sometimes charging more than half for on-campus instruction. When the pandemic became full-blown, in March 2020, the Universities (D) shifted all on-campus classes to online learning in mid-March 2020 and held classes virtually for the rest of the semester. The Universities (D) also suspended events and activities. However, neither American (D) nor GWU (D) offered prorated refunds of spring 2020 tuition or fees. Both Universities' (D) pre-pandemic communications contained numerous references to the benefits of their on-campus instruction, and the Universities (D) had a history of providing on-campus instruction to students who paid the tuition associated with such instruction (as opposed to online instruction). The Universities (D) also had "reservation of rights" provisions in their communications, stating that the Universities (D) reserved the right to amend their policies and information contained in their catalogs, with or without notice, specifically reserving the right to change courses, programs, fees, and the academic calendar, or to make other changes deemed necessary or desirable, giving advance notice of change when possible. However, the reservation or rights did not specifically address emergencies or other force majeure events or allocate the risk of such events between the schools and students. In two separate putative class actions brought in federal district courts, parents (P) and students (P) (collectively, the Plaintiffs) (P) of the Universities (D) alleged that the Universities (D), inter alia, breached their express and implied contractual obligations to the students, or, alternatively, were unjustly enriched. Specifically, the Plaintiffs (P) alleged that the Universities (D) expressly or impliedly promised to provide on-campus instruction to the students (P) in exchange for the on-campus tuition (versus online tuition) the students (P) paid. The Plaintiffs (P) also alleged that the Universities (D) breached their promises to provide certain activities and benefits in exchange for the fees the students (P) paid (e.g., sports center fees, technology fees, and the like). In the alternative, the Plaintiffs (P) alleged that the Universities (D) were unjustly enriched by shifting to online instruction and not refunding any portion of the tuition and fees paid for on-campus instruction and activities. The Plaintiffs (P) also brought claims for conversion and violation of consumer protection laws. The Universities (D) moved to dismiss the actions for failure to state a claim, and the respective district courts granted the Universities' (D) motions. One of the district courts concluded that the schools' written materials did not give rise to an enforceable contractual promise for in-person instruction, and also that the Plaintiffs' (P) unjust enrichment claim was inappropriate because it required the

Continued on next page.

court to displace the terms of the alleged contract. The other district court concluded that, at most, the school had impliedly promised to make a good-faith effort to provide on-campus education, while retaining the right to deviate from the traditional model if it reasonably deemed it necessary to do so. That court also determined that the Plaintiffs (P) failed to plausibly allege that the school violated promises to provide services in exchange for the fees at issue, and it held that the Plaintiffs' (P) contract claims precluded their unjust enrichment claims and that, alternatively, the students failed to plausibly allege it was unjust under the circumstances for the school to retain their entire tuition and fee payments. The Plaintiffs (P) appealed, and the Court of Appeals for the District of Columbia granted review.

ISSUE:

(1) Will a breach of contract claim premised on the breach of an express promise survive a motion to dismiss for failure to state a claim where the plaintiff fails to plausibly allege the existence of an express contract between the plaintiff and defendant?
(2) Will a breach of contract claim premised on the breach of an implied promise survive a motion to dismiss for failure to state a claim where the plaintiff plausibly alleges the existence of an implied-in-fact contract between the plaintiff and defendant?
(3) Will an unjust enrichment claim survive a motion to dismiss for failure to state a claim where the claim is raised in the alternative to a breach of contract claim and it is plausible that the contract at issue is invalid, subject to avoidance, or otherwise ineffective to regulate the parties' obligations and the claim otherwise states a plausible claim for unjust enrichment?

HOLDING AND DECISION: (Edwards, J.)

(1) No. A breach of contract claim premised on the breach of an express promise will not survive a motion to dismiss for failure to state a claim where the plaintiff fails to plausibly allege the existence of an express contract between the plaintiff and defendant. To prevail on a claim of breach of contract, a party must establish: (1) a valid contract between the parties; (2) an obligation or duty arising out of the contract; (3) a breach of that duty; and (4) damages caused by breach. The relationship between a university and its students is contractual in nature. In this regard, the terms of a contract between a university and its students set down in a university's bulletin become a part of that contract, but merely because the bulletin contains language on a topic is not enough to support a finding that the language amounts to a contractual obligation. Whether a given section of a university bulletin becomes part of the contractual obligations between the students and the university depends on general principles of contract construction, and other university publications and communications may constitute part of the contract. Although contracts should be construed by reference to the norms of conduct and expectations founded on them, so that usual practices surrounding a contractual relationship can themselves be raised to the level of a contractual obligation, words that merely express an expectancy regarding future conduct do not suffice to create a contractual obligation susceptible of enforcement. Here, one of the students' (P) and parents' (P) (collectively, the Plaintiffs) (P) claims is that a material term of their contracts with the Universities (D), whether express or implied, was that American University (D) and George Washington University (D) (collectively, the Universities) (D) would provide on-campus education and experiences in exchange for their tuition and fees. However, the Plaintiffs (P) have failed to plausibly allege the parties had express contracts with such a term, as they point to no language indicating that the provision of in-person education and on-campus services was an explicit term of the parties' agreements. Accordingly, the Plaintiffs' (P) claim for breach of an express contract was correctly dismissed for failing to state a claim.
(2) Yes. A breach of contract claim premised on the breach of an implied promise will survive a motion to dismiss for failure to state a claim where the plaintiff plausibly alleges the existence of an implied-in-fact contract between the plaintiff and defendant. Accepting the complaints' factual allegations as true and drawing all reasonable inferences from those allegations in the Plaintiffs' (P) favor, the Plaintiffs (P) have adequately alleged that the Universities (D) breached an implied-in-fact contract to provide in-person education in exchange for tuition, as well as an implied-in-fact contract to provide some benefits in exchange for fees. To survive a motion to dismiss at this early stage, the Plaintiffs (P) need allege only sufficient factual matter, accepted as true, to state a claim to relief that is plausible on its face. Here, it is plausible that the Universities (D) implicitly agreed to provide on-campus instruction based on the Universities' (D) communications, which emphasized the benefits of such instruction and highlighted the different ways that the Universities (D) provided such on-campus instruction. It can also be inferred from the higher rates the Universities (D) charged for on-campus instruction, as opposed to online instruction, that the Universities (D) promised in-person education in exchange for the Plaintiffs' (P) tuition payments. Such a promise may also be inferred from the Universities' (D) historic practice of providing on-campus instruction to students who paid the tuition associated with traditional

Continued on next page.

on-campus—rather than online—education. For these reasons, the Plaintiffs (P) have stated a claim that the Universities (D) breached an implied agreement to provide in-person instruction, and that the Plaintiffs (P) suffered harm from such breach. Although the Universities (D) assert that the reservation of rights language in their communications is a defense to such a breach, such language does not say anything about allocation of risk, and, therefore, the reservation of rights language would not necessarily as a matter of law be viewed by a reasonable person as allocating the entire financial consequences of the pandemic change to online classes to the students. In fact, there is nothing that the Universities (D) cite that would suggest that they have retained unfettered rights to shut down on-campus educational activities and use online learning in their place after students have paid tuition for traditional on-campus courses, especially given that the Universities (D) have never done so in the past. The Universities (D) also argue that even if the Plaintiffs (P) have plausibly alleged that the Universities (D) made enforceable promises to provide in-person education, the contract claims nonetheless fail because the Plaintiffs (P) fail to allege cognizable damages. The argument is based on the premise that courts are prohibited from reviewing claims that test the quality or value of the education students receive. This argument, however, is rejected because determining whether the Universities (D) breached implied promises to provide on-campus instruction would not require a court to subjectively value the quality of the Plaintiffs' (P) education, and, in any event, the Universities' (D) argument to the contrary overlooks the fact that the Universities (D) themselves charge different rates for online and in-person instruction. Because the Universities (D) fail to raise adequate defenses at this point to the Plaintiffs' (P) plausible breach-of-contract claims, the district courts must resolve in the first instance whether the parties contracted for in-person education as alleged. If the district courts conclude that the Universities (D) made such promises, and that providing in-person instruction was a basic assumption on which the contracts were made, the Universities (D) may still have strong arguments that the pandemic and resulting government-issued shutdown orders discharged their duties to perform. Accordingly, at this early stage of the proceedings, the district courts' dismissals of the Plaintiffs' (P) claims relating to the breach of implied-in-fact contracts for the provision of on-campus instruction in exchange for tuition, and implied-in-fact contracts for the provision of certain benefits and services in exchange for fees, are reversed.

(3) Yes. An unjust enrichment claim will survive a motion to dismiss for failure to state a claim where the claim is raised in the alternative to a breach of contract claim and it is plausible that the contract at issue is invalid, subject to avoidance, or otherwise ineffective to regulate the parties' obligations and the claim otherwise states a plausible claim for unjust enrichment. Unjust enrichment occurs when: (1) the plaintiff conferred a benefit on the defendant; (2) the defendant retains the benefit; and (3) under the circumstances, the defendant's retention of the benefit is unjust. In such a case, the recipient of the benefit has a duty to make restitution to the other party. However, an unjust enrichment claim will not lie when the parties have a contract governing an aspect of their relation, because a court will not displace the terms of that contract and impose some other duties not chosen by the parties. If such a contract is determined to be invalid, subject to avoidance, or otherwise ineffective to regulate the parties' obligations, the unjust enrichment claim is not precluded. Thus, the viability of the Plaintiffs' (P) unjust enrichment claim will depend on the district courts' determination on remand, after the issues are fully briefed, of whether the implied-in-fact contract for on-campus instruction was legitimate and enforceable. However, at this point in the proceedings, where the nature and enforceability of any promises the Universities (D) made remain unresolved, the Plaintiffs' (P) alternative claims for unjust enrichment may proceed past the pleadings stage, given that the Federal Rules of Civil Procedure (Fed. R. Civ. P.) expressly allow parties to advance inconsistent and alternative theories of recovery at the pleadings stage (Fed. R. Civ. P. 8(a)(3)). Although the Universities (D) point out that the Plaintiffs (P) are not claiming it was inequitable for the Universities (D) to retain the students' (P) entire tuition and fee payments, whether there was a net benefit to the Universities (D) is not a question that can be resolved at the motion-to-dismiss stage. For these reasons, the district courts' dismissals of the Plaintiffs' (P) unjust enrichments are reversed.

Affirmed in part, reversed in part, and remanded.

ANALYSIS

As the Restatement (Third) of Restitution and Unjust Enrichment § 2, cmt. c, observes, claims for restitution, which are made as part of unjust enrichment claims, can arise in a contractual context when a valuable performance has been rendered under a contract that is invalid, or subject to avoidance, or otherwise ineffective to regulate the parties' obligations. Here, because the contracts between the students (P) and parents (P) (collectively, the Plaintiffs) (P) and American University (D) and George Washington University

Continued on next page.

(D) (collectively, the Universities) (D) are not express written contracts, and, at most, are implied contracts, it is possible that the district courts on remand will determine that any contracts between the parties were illusory or did not cover the issues in dispute. The courts also conceivably could determine that even though the Universities (D) promised to provide in-person education and services, the need to comply with government shutdown orders discharged their duty to perform, or that the pandemic constituted a supervening change of circumstances that excused their performance. In such event, the Plaintiffs' (P) unjust enrichment claims would be triggered, providing the Plaintiffs (P) with the possibility of restitution if the district courts determine that by transitioning to online courses, the Universities (D) gained a net benefit that it would be inequitable for the Universities (D) to keep and that would require the Universities (D) to refund to the Plaintiffs (P) a portion of the funds they paid to the Universities (D).

Quicknotes

BREACH OF CONTRACT Unlawful failure by a party to perform its obligations pursuant to contract.

CLASS ACTION A suit commenced by a representative on behalf of an ascertainable group that is too large to appear in court, shares a commonality of interests, and will benefit from a successful result.

CONVERSION The act of depriving an owner of his or her property without permission or justification.

EXPRESS CONTRACT A contract the terms of which are specifically stated; may be oral or written.

EXPRESS PROMISE The expression of an intention to act, or to forbear from acting, granting a right to the promisee to expect and enforce its performance.

FORCE MAJEURE Superior force; an event or effect that cannot be anticipated or controlled

IMPLIED-IN-FACT CONTRACT Conditions that arise by physical or moral inference: (a) prerequisites or circumstances that a reasonable person would assume necessary to render or receive performance; and (b) the good-faith cooperation of the promisee in receiving the performance of the promisor.

MATERIAL TERM OF CONTRACT A fact without the existence of which a contract would not have been entered.

UNJUST ENRICHMENT The principle of retaining a benefit given to one by another, without compensating the giver, in situations where compensation is reasonably expected.

City Stores Co. v. Ammerman

Department stores (P) v. Promoters (D)

266 F. Supp. 766 (D.D.C. 1967), *aff'd*, 394 F.2d 950 (D.C. Cir. 1968)

NATURE OF CASE: Action for specific performance of a contract.

FACT SUMMARY: Promoters (D) of a proposed shopping center, in return for Lansburgh's Department Store's (P) expression of preference for their site over that of a competitor's, agreed, in the event they were issued a permit, to offer Lansburgh (P) a tenancy on rental and terms equal to that of the other stores in the center and then reneged on the offer.

RULE OF LAW

(1) A binding option contract is formed, despite the existence of express and implied conditions precedent and material terms remaining to be decided, where the substance of the agreement is clear.

(2) An option contract involving further negotiations on details and construction of a building may be specifically enforced where damages would be inadequate or impracticable, and the importance of specific performance to the plaintiff outweighs the difficulties of supervision by the court.

FACTS: Ammerman (D), the promoter of a proposed suburban shopping center, was having considerable difficulty in persuading the Board of County Supervisors to rezone the land for that use. In order to impress the Board, Ammerman (D) secured from Lansburgh's Department Store (Lansburgh's) (P), which was owned by City Stores Co. (P), a letter expressing its preference for the project over that of Ammerman's (D) major competitor. In return, Ammerman (D) agreed, in the event he was successful in receiving a building permit, to accept Lansburgh's (P) as a tenant on the rental and terms at least equal to that of the other stores in the center. Ammerman (D), who had promised another tenant to keep the stores in the center down to three, refused to accept Lansburgh's (P) when Sears offered it better terms. Lansburgh's (P) sued for specific performance, and Ammerman (D) defended on the grounds that the option with Lansburgh's (P) was lacking in material terms, and therefore void, that specific performance was not an appropriate remedy, and that it would result in hardship to them.

ISSUE:

(1) Is a binding option contract formed, despite the existence of express and implied conditions precedent and material terms remaining to be decided, where the substance of the agreement is clear?

(2) May an option contract involving further negotiations on details and construction of a building be specifically enforced where damages would be inadequate or impracticable, and the importance of specific performance to the plaintiff outweighs the difficulties of supervision by the court?

HOLDING AND DECISION: (Gasch, J.)

(1) Yes. A binding option contract is formed, despite the existence of express and implied conditions precedent and material terms remaining to be decided, where the substance of the agreement is clear. The rule that where material terms remain to be decided, there is no contract at all, applies only where the parties fail to reach an enforceable agreement. An option contract, though in the form of an offer, is a true contract that is binding on the offeror and subject to the offeree's acceptance or rejection. The option here, although lacking in material terms, is nonetheless a binding contract.

(2) Yes. An option contract involving further negotiations on details and construction of a building may be specifically enforced where damages would be inadequate or impracticable, and the importance of specific performance to the plaintiff outweighs the difficulties of supervision by the court. Here, while the crucial elements of rate of rental and the amount of space can readily be determined from other leases entered by Ammerman (D), some details of design, construction, and price of the building to be occupied were left open for further negotiations. However, it would be unfair to allow Ammerman (D), who has already reaped the benefits of his bargain with Lansburgh's Department Store's (Lansburgh's) (P), to object merely on the ground of the incompleteness or uncertainty of the agreement. Even were it possible to arrive at a precise measure of damages for breach of this contract—which it is not—money damages would not compensate Lansburgh's (P) for its loss of the right to participate in the shopping center. Finally, the difficulties of supervision are here diminished since the court can look to the other leases the promoters have made for guidance. As for any hardship the promoters may suffer as a result of not being able to accept Sears, they have not suggested that this would ruin them financially, but only that they would make less money. This is not

Continued on next page.

a sufficient basis to deny specific performance. The option will be specifically enforced.

ANALYSIS

More courts are today willing to depart from the established rule that equity will not order specific performance of a building or repair contract by emphasizing the inadequacy of the damages factor. These courts have variously held that damages are inadequate where the contract calls for construction on the contractor's own land, where the plaintiff is financially unable to complete the work and not await an award of damages before he can live in the house, or where a business tenant seeks repairs on a short-term lease. Even where damages are arguably inadequate, many courts, reluctant to oversee the enforcement of their decrees and the attendant supervision required, will still refuse to order specific performance.

Quicknotes

OPTION CONTRACT A contract pursuant to which a seller agrees that property will be available for the buyer to purchase at a specified price and within a certain time period.

SPECIFIC PERFORMANCE An equitable remedy whereby the court requires the parties to perform their obligations pursuant to a contract.

Reier Broadcasting Company, Inc. v. Kramer

Broadcasting company/employer (P) v. Athletic coach/employee (D)

Mont. Sup. Ct., 316 Mont. 301, 72 P.3d 944 (2003)

NATURE OF CASE: Appeal from order denying motion for relief from judgment in suit seeking an injunction to prevent a breach of an employment agreement.

FACT SUMMARY: Reier Broadcasting Company, Inc. (Reier) (P) contended that a personal services employment agreement it had with Kramer (D) was not subject to a state statute that prohibited the use of an injunction to prevent of a breach of a contract that could not be specifically enforced.

RULE OF LAW

A statute that provides that an injunction may not be granted to prevent the breach of a contract, the performance of which would not be specifically enforced, applies to a negative covenant in a personal services employment agreement so that an injunction may not prevent the personal services from being performed elsewhere during the life of the contract.

FACTS: Reier Broadcasting Company, Inc. (Reier) (P), a broadcasting company that had exclusive rights to broadcast certain university athletic events until 2002, entered into an employment contract with Kramer (D), the university's head football coach, for exclusive rights with him. The contract remained in force until 2004 and specified that Kramer (D) could not provide similar services to any other broadcaster. When Reier's (P) contract with the university expired in 2002, the university sought bids from other broadcasters. Reier (P) noticed that the university's Request for Proposal required the successful offeror to broadcast interviews and conduct a commentary program with Kramer (D) in violation of the Reier-Kramer employment agreement. The university declined to change its Request for Proposal, and awarded broadcast rights to another broadcaster, Clear Channel Communication (Clear Channel). The university also notified Kramer (D) that he was expected to provide interviews to Clear Channel despite the exclusivity clause in his contract with Reier (P). Reier (P) brought suit for a temporary restraining order (TRO) and injunction to prevent Kramer (D) from providing services to Clear Channel. The TRO was granted, but the court declined to convert it into an injunction based on a state statute that prohibited the issuance of an injunction to prevent the breach of a contract the performance of which would not be specifically enforced. Reier (P) moved to alter or amend the court's judgment, and this motion was denied. The state's highest court granted review.

ISSUE: Does a statute that provides that an injunction may not be granted to prevent the breach of a contract, the performance of which would not be specifically enforced, apply to a negative covenant in a personal services employment agreement so that an injunction may not prevent the personal services from being performed elsewhere during the life of the contract?

HOLDING AND DECISION: (Leaphart, J.) Yes. A statute that provides that an injunction may not be granted to prevent the breach of a contract, the performance of which would not be specifically enforced, applies to a negative covenant in a personal services employment agreement so that an injunction may not prevent the personal services from being performed elsewhere during the life of the contract. The trial court correctly relied on a state statute that provides that "an obligation to render personal service" cannot be specifically enforced. The court also correctly reasoned that since the contract between Reier Broadcasting Company, Inc. (Reier) (P) and Kramer (D) was one for personal services, that contract could not be specifically enforced, so that it could not be enforced by injunction. Reier (P) argues that the statute prohibiting an injunction applies only to affirmative covenants, not to negative covenants that prohibit the performance of services that are special or unique. According to Reier (P), contracts based on special or unique personal services, or in which a person holds a unique position, may be indirectly enforced by restraining the person from providing services to another. This is an issue of first impression in this state. Other states that have ruled on this issue have interpreted statutes similar to the one here to prevent the enforcement of negative covenants in personal services contracts. Those courts have reasoned that an injunction of a negative covenant would amount to the enforcement of the affirmative part of the contract, and thus be in violation of the statute. Thus, here, if an injunction were granted, Kramer (D) could perform only for Reier (P), if at all—it's not just that he could not perform for Clear Channel—and this would result in the indirect specific enforcement of the contract. The reasoning of those courts is sound. Affirmed.

DISSENT: (Cotter, J.) Enforcement of the negative covenant in the contract between Reier Broadcasting Company, Inc. (Reier) (P) and Kramer (D) would not run afoul of the statute involved here, and it would not serve as an indirect enforcement of the affirmative part of the

Continued on next page.

contract. Reier (P) is simply seeking to prevent Kramer (D) from violating the noncompetition provisions of the contract—provisions that were specifically bargained for by Kramer (D) at the encouragement and behest of the university. The university, which helped negotiate the contract, is acting in bad faith, and its position is offensive. Additionally, a party that has accepted and used the benefits that it has contractually secured for itself is estopped from denying the validity of binding force of the contract. Therefore, not only should the negative covenant here be enforced by injunction, but, in addition, the university and Kramer (D) should be estopped from challenging the contract's enforceability.

ANALYSIS

The Restatement (Second) of Contracts position on this issue, in § 367(2), is that an injunction will not be issued if the probable result would be to compel an "undesirable" continuance of personal relations or "to leave the employee without other reasonable means of making a living." Also, the court in this case relied on California precedent, *Anderson v. Neal Institutes Co.*, 37 Cal. App. 174, 173 P. 779 (Cal. Ct. App. 1918), in reaching its conclusion. However, as the court points out, the California legislature responded immediately to that decision by amending the statute at issue to allow for the use of injunctive relief to enforce a negative covenant where the promised service is of a unique character the loss of which cannot be adequately compensated in damages. In its current form, the statute states, "[a]n injunction may not be granted . . . to prevent the breach of a contract the performance of which would not be specifically enforced . . . other than a contract in writing for the rendition of personal services . . . where the promised service is of a special, unique, [or] unusual . . . character, which gives it peculiar value. . . ." The court in this case could have suggested that if the state's legislature wanted to similarly amend the statute, it could have done so, and that its failure to so amend the statute is an indication that it did not intend to follow the California legislature's policy decision.

Quicknotes

BREACH The violation of an obligation imposed pursuant to contract or law, by acting or failing to act.

INJUNCTION A court order requiring a person to do, or prohibiting that person from doing, a specific act.

Barrie School v. Patch

Private school (P) v. Parent of student (D)

Md. Ct. App., 401 Md. 497, 933 A.2d 382 (2007)

NATURE OF CASE: Appeal from affirmance of judgment for defendants in action for breach of contract to enforce a liquidated damages provision.

FACT SUMMARY: The Barrie School (P) contended that it was not required to mitigate damages where the liquidated damages provisions of its enrollment contract were valid and did not constitute a penalty, so that the Patches (D), who had breached the enrollment contract, were required to pay the liquidated damages.

RULE OF LAW

A nonbreaching party has no duty to mitigate damages where the parties agree to a valid liquidated sum in the event of a breach.

FACTS: The Patches (D) enrolled their daughter in The Barrie School (P), a private school. They entered a re-enrollment agreement (the Agreement) with the school for the following academic year. The Agreement provided for a $1,000.00 nonrefundable deposit and payment of the remaining tuition balance of $13,490.00 in two installments. The Agreement contained an escape clause that allowed for unilateral cancellation, provided that the head of the school received written notice by certified letter before May 31, 2004. Under § 3 of the Agreement, the Patches (D) were obligated to pay the full tuition if they failed to meet the withdrawal deadline. The Patches (D) did not cancel the Agreement on or before May 31, 2004. Instead, 44 days later, they attempted to cancel by faxing a notice to the school, in which they demanded return of their deposit. The school demanded payment of the balance of the full amount of tuition, as required by the contract, but the Patches (D) refused to pay it. The school filed suit against the Patches (D) for breach of contract plus 12 percent interest, and attorney's fees. The Patches (D) countered by asserting that the Agreement had been procured by fraud, that it was a contract of adhesion, that the damages constituted a penalty, that The Barrie School (P) had a duty to mitigate any damages, and that the Agreement was unenforceable because it violated public policy and the state's anti-competition laws. The Patches (D) also counterclaimed for a return of their deposit, interest, and attorney's fees. Although no evidence of mitigation was presented at trial, it turned out the number of students enrolled for the academic year at issue exceeded the school's original budget projections. The trial court ruled that the contract was valid and had been breached by the Patches (D). It also ruled that there was no fraud in the inducement to enter into the Agreement, and that the Agreement was not a contract of adhesion. As to the liquidated damages provision, the court held that it was valid but also held that The Barrie School's (P) failure to mitigate its damages was fatal to its claim. Accordingly, the court entered judgment for the Patches (D). The state's intermediate appellate court affirmed, and the state's highest court granted review.

ISSUE: Does a nonbreaching party have a duty to mitigate damages where the parties agree to a valid liquidated sum in the event of a breach?

HOLDING AND DECISION: (Raker, J.) No. A nonbreaching party has no duty to mitigate damages where the parties agree to a valid liquidated sum in the event of a breach. The party seeking to set aside a liquidated damages provision has the burden of proving that the provision should not be enforced. This gives the nonbreaching party the advantage inherent in stipulated damages clauses, that of eliminating the need to prove damages. It also upholds the general principle that assumes that bargains are enforceable and that the party asking the court to invalidate a bargain should demonstrate the justice of his or her view. Valid liquidated damages clauses are enforceable, and the validity of such clauses is determined by looking to the stipulated loss at the time of the contract's formation, not actual losses resulting from breach. Here, the lower courts correctly determined that the liquidated damages clause at issue was not a penalty, because the specified damages amount was a reasonable forecast of just compensation for potential harm caused by a breach of the re-enrollment agreement (the Agreement), and because that amount was neither grossly excessive nor out of all proportion to an amount that might have been expected at the time of contracting. In addition, the actual damages resulting from breach would have been very difficult to estimate at the time of contracting, as it would be almost impossible to assign an exact amount as to the impact of losing one child for the school year. Despite the validity of the liquidated damages provision, the Patches (D) argue that, in keeping with general contract law principles, there exists a duty to mitigate damages even in the face of a valid liquidated damages clause. The mitigation of damages doctrine helps to determine the proper amount of damages for a breach of contract. Liquidated damages differ fundamentally from mitigation of damages. While mitigation is part of a court's assessment of actual damages that have resulted from a breach of contract, liquidated damages clauses are the remedy the parties to a contract have

Continued on next page.

determined to be proper in the event of breach. Where the parties to a contract have included a reasonable liquidated damages sum that stipulates damages in the event of breach, that sum replaces any determination of actual loss. From this, it logically follows that once a court has determined that a liquidate damages provision is valid, it need not inquire as to the amount of actual damages, and the need for mitigation of damages is precluded. To hold otherwise would blunt the Agreement's purpose. Here, the Agreement's liquidated damages clause specified a comprehensive sum that eliminated the need to calculate actual losses, including any mitigation of damages that might have occurred. Accordingly, The Barrie School (P) had no duty to mitigate damages. The same rationale applies to the Patches' (D) argument that the school suffered no actual harm, because it filled the spot that was to be taken by their daughter. The no-actual-harm defense negates the benefit of an agreed-upon or stipulated damages clause and deviates from the accepted principle that the time of contract formation is the appropriate point from which to judge the reasonableness of a stipulated amount of damages. Moreover, such a defense, if given effect, would potentially generate uncertainty in the calculation of damages, because courts could then give greater damages than contemplated when the damages actually exceeded the stipulated amount. Finally, as to the Patches' (D) arguments that the contract was one of adhesion and unconscionable, the lower courts did not err in concluding that the Agreement was neither. First, the Patches (D) were under no compulsion to send their daughter to The Barrie School (P), and, second, the Agreement was not extremely unfair. To the contrary, it gave the Patches (D) a meaningful opportunity to cancel the entire Agreement upon timely notification and receive a full refund. In sum, the Agreement was an arm's-length business transaction. Reversed and remanded.

DISSENT: (Bell, C.J.) The majority is wrong in concluding that where a liquidated damages clause is valid there is no need for the nonbreaching party to mitigate its damages. It is a long-held and well-settled, general principle of contract law that contract remedies are to be compensatory, not punitive. The majority maintains that the time of the contract formation is the appropriate point from which to judge the reasonableness of a liquidated damages provision. However, this prospective viewpoint is not the best vantage point for determining the reasonableness of the liquidated damages clause. Instead, because the validity of a liquidated damages clause does not become an issue until one of the parties breaches the contract, the review of a liquidated damages clause to determine whether it is a penalty should include the effect of the breach, at the least, whether actual damage have been incurred. Ordinarily, unless actual damages are extremely difficult to determine, the validity of a liquidated damages clause should be determined from all the circumstances—those existing at the making of the contract as well as those existing at the time of the breach, including consideration of the actual damages sustained. Here, it is clear the Patches (D) breached the re-enrollment agreement. However, the evidence shows that the school did not suffer harm commensurate to the sum fixed as liquidated damages. Awarding The Barrie School (P) a full year's tuition is grossly disproportionate to, and in excess of, the harm it actually suffered—which was none, since its enrollment projections were exceeded. Contrary to the majority's view, a no-actual-harm defense is consistent with liquidated damages provisions. If the actual loss is less than the stipulated amount, the liquidated damages will not be deemed a penalty unless they are excessive. However, if the actual loss is greater, then the stipulated amount will be the limit of recovery. Where, as here, if the stipulated amount will lead to an excessive recovery, the liquidated damages clause will be deemed a penalty, and the nonbreaching party will have to prove its actual damages—just as in any other breach of contract action.

ANALYSIS

It would seem under a "freedom of contract" approach, the penalty limitation on liquidated damage clauses should be abolished and such clauses should be enforced unless they are the product of some defect in the bargaining process, such as fraud or coercion. Some commentators advocate such a position. Others would create a presumption that a liquidated damages clause is valid absent a showing that the clause is unconscionable. Still, others would apply the penalty limitation to situations where there may be an opportunity and incentive to induce a breach, but otherwise would not impose the penalty limitation.

Quicknotes

BREACH OF CONTRACT Unlawful failure by a party to perform its obligations pursuant to contract.

COUNTERCLAIM An independent cause of action brought by a defendant to a lawsuit in order to oppose or deduct from the plaintiff's claim.

FRAUD A false representation of facts with the intent that another will rely on the misrepresentation to his or her detriment.

JUST COMPENSATION The right guaranteed by the Fifth Amendment to the United States Constitution that when property is taken for public use by the state, a person is to receive adequate compensation in order to restore

Continued on next page.

him or her to the position he or she enjoyed prior to the appropriation.

LIQUIDATED DAMAGES An amount of money specified in a contract representing the damages owed in the event of breach.

MITIGATION OF DAMAGES A plaintiff's implied obligation to take reasonable steps to avoid further damages after injury has occurred.

CHAPTER 12

Rights and Duties of Third Parties

Quick Reference Rules of Law

Vogan v. Hayes Appraisal Associates, Inc.

Borrowers (P) v. Appraiser (D)

Iowa Sup. Ct., 588 N.W.2d 420 (1999)

NATURE OF CASE: Appeal from adverse judgment by third-party contract beneficiaries.

FACT SUMMARY: Susan and Rollin Vogan (P) secured a mortgage from MidAmerica Savings Bank (MidAmerica) for $170,000 to build a house. The Vogans (P) hired builder Gary Markley of Char Enterprises, Inc. and MidAmerica contracted with Hayes Appraisal Associates, Inc. (Hayes Appraisal) (D) to do the initial appraisal and make periodic appraisals of the progress of the construction. MidAmerica was to release payments to the builder based upon the progress reports made by Hayes Appraisal (D). There were cost overruns and a second mortgage was necessary, including the addition of further funds. The Vogans (P) eventually brought suit against Hayes Appraisal (D) on a third-party beneficiary theory.

RULE OF LAW

Unless otherwise agreed between the promisor and promisee, a beneficiary of a promise is an intended beneficiary if recognition of a right to performance in the beneficiary is appropriate to effectuate the intention of the parties, and either the performance of the promise will satisfy an obligation of the promisee to pay money to the beneficiary, or the circumstances indicate that the promisee intends to give the beneficiary the benefit of the promised performance.

FACTS: Hayes Appraisal Associates, Inc. (Hayes Appraisal) (D) was hired by MidAmerica Savings Bank (MidAmerica) to monitor the progress of new home construction for the Vogans (P) who had obtained a construction loan from MidAmerica for $170,000. The contractor defaulted after all the original construction loan proceeds and a subsequent portion of a second mortgage loan had been paid out by the bank. The Vogans (P) sued and recovered a judgment against Hayes Appraisal (D) on a third-party beneficiary theory based on its failure to properly monitor the progress of the construction, thus allowing funds to be improperly released by the lender to the defaulting contractor. The court of appeals reversed the judgment on the basis that erroneous progress reports by Hayes Appraisal (D) were not the cause of any loss to the Vogans (P). The Vogans (P) appealed.

ISSUE: Unless otherwise agreed between the promisor and promisee, is a beneficiary of a promise an intended beneficiary if recognition of a right to performance in the beneficiary is appropriate to effectuate the intention of the parties, and either the performance of the promise will satisfy an obligation of the promisee to pay money to the beneficiary, or the circumstances indicate that the promisee intends to give the beneficiary the benefit of the promised performance?

HOLDING AND DECISION: (Carter, J.) Yes. Unless otherwise agreed between the promisor and promisee, a beneficiary of a promise is an intended beneficiary if recognition of a right to performance in the beneficiary is appropriate to effectuate the intention of the parties, and either the performance of the promise will satisfy an obligation of the promisee to pay money to the beneficiary, or the circumstances indicate that the promisee intends to give the beneficiary the benefit of the promised performance. The primary question in a third-party beneficiary case is whether the contract manifests intent to benefit a third party. The intent need not be to benefit a third party directly. Here, the Vogans (P), who were the borrowers, were third-party beneficiaries of the contract between the construction lender and Hayes Appraisal Associates, Inc. (Hayes Appraisal) (D), under which Hayes Appraisal (D) agreed to issue reports monitoring the general contractor's progress in the construction of the Vogans' (P) home where the appraiser's performance was to have been of pecuniary benefit to the Vogans (P), and the inspection reports issued by Hayes Appraisal (D) naming the Vogans (P) as home purchasers gave Hayes Appraisal (D) reason to know that the lender's purpose in contracting for periodic inspection reports was to provide protection for the money that the Vogans (P) had invested in the project. Accordingly, the jury could properly find that the faulty progress reports issued by Hayes Appraisal (D) to the construction lender, in which the appraiser overstated the extent of the contractor's progress, caused injury to the Vogans (P) where, when the initial construction loan funds were exhausted due to cost overruns, the Vogans (P) deposited their own funds into the construction account, and much of those funds was paid to the contractor based on Hayes Appraisal's (D) faulty reports, before the contractor defaulted. Court of appeals judgment vacated, and district court decision affirmed.

ANALYSIS

As noted by the *Vogan* court, recovery by the Vogans (P) from Hayes Appraisal Associates, Inc. (Hayes

Continued on next page.

Appraisal) (D) of sums advanced to the contractor by the construction lender based upon Hayes Appraisal's (D) faulty progress reports, in which the appraiser overstated the extent of the contractor's progress, was not beyond the appraiser's contemplation at the time it entered into the contract to provide the Vogans (P) with such progress reports. Thus, recovery did not violate the rule of *Hadley v. Baxendale*, 156 Eng. Rep. 145 (1854), even though, due to cost overruns, substantially more funds were advanced to the contractor than the amount of the original construction loan.

Quicknotes

INTENDED BENEFICIARY A third party who is the recipient of the benefit of a transaction undertaken by another.

PROMISEE The party to whom a promise is made.

THIRD-PARTY BENEFICIARY A party who benefits from a promise made pursuant to a contract although he or she is not a party to the agreement.

Chen v. Chen

Mother (P) v. Father (D)

Pa. Sup. Ct., 893 A.2d 87 (2006)

NATURE OF CASE: Appeal from affirmance of ruling permitting intervention in a parent's support action asserting breach of contract, and from judgment for plaintiff in that action.

FACT SUMMARY: Richard Chen (Father) (D) contended that his daughter, Theresa (Daughter), should not be permitted to intervene in a support action brought by his former wife and the daughter's mother, Wheamei Chen (Mother) (P), because, he contended, Daughter was only an incidental beneficiary, not an intended beneficiary, of the property settlement agreement (the Agreement) at issue.

RULE OF LAW

A child may not bring suit or intervene in an action to enforce support provisions of his or her parents' property settlement agreement where support payments are to be made to the custodial parent.

FACTS: When Richard Chen (Father) (D) and Wheamei Chen (Mother) (P) divorced, they entered into a property settlement agreement (the Agreement). At the time, they had a son and a daughter, Theresa (Daughter). Mother (P) received custody over Daughter, who was one year old, and, as part of the Agreement, Father (D) was to pay $25.00 per week child support for Daughter. Father (D) further agreed that upon obtaining regular employment or upon any increase in salary the $25.00 support award would be increased in accordance with the county's domestic relations guidelines. The Agreement was incorporated by reference but not merged into the divorce decree. Pursuant to the Agreement, Father (D) paid $25.00 per week to Mother (P) until Daughter's eighteenth birthday. However, he did not increase the payments as required for employment and salary increases. When Daughter turned 18, the county informed Mother (P) that support payments would cease. In response, Mother (P) filed a petition requesting enforcement of the property settlement agreement and a finding of contempt of court. Mother (P) sought to enforce the Agreement's provision for increases in child support and to collect total support/arrearages based upon Father's (D) salary increases over the almost 18 years the Agreement had been in effect. Shortly after turning 18, Daughter filed a petition to intervene as a party to Mother's (P) action, asserting that intervention was appropriate because she had a legally enforceable interest as a third-party intended beneficiary under the Agreement. The trial court, applying case law that relied on Restatement (Second) of Contracts, § 302, concluded that Daughter should be permitted to intervene. The court found that § 302's liberal standard of permitting intervention by a third party had been satisfied. Section 302 provides that a beneficiary is an intended beneficiary if recognition of a right to performance in the beneficiary will effectuate the intentions of the parties and the circumstances indicate that the promisee intended to give the beneficiary the benefit of the promised performance. Specifically, the court determined the parties to the Agreement clearly intended that the child support provision of the Agreement was to benefit Daughter throughout her minority. Daughter was permitted to intervene, whereupon Mother (P) withdrew as a party, leaving Daughter and Father (D) as party-opponents. Interpreting the Agreement as an independent contract, the trial court concluded that Father (D) had breached the contract and ordered him to pay around $59,000 in arrearages due under the Agreement. On appeal, the state's intermediate appellate court affirmed, finding that the trial court correctly permitted Daughter to intervene and correctly determined that Father (D) had breached the support provisions of the Agreement. In doing so, the court rejected Father's (D) argument that Daughter had no direct right to the payments, but only to her parents' support. The state's highest court granted review.

ISSUE: May a child may bring suit or intervene in an action to enforce support provisions of his or her parents' property settlement agreement where support payments are to be made to the custodial parent?

HOLDING AND DECISION: (Baer, J.) No. A child may not bring suit or intervene in an action to enforce support provisions of his or her parents' property settlement agreement where support payments are to be made to the custodial parent. The issue is one of first impression in this jurisdiction and is one purely of law. Richard Chen (Father) (D) contends that Theresa (Daughter) is not an intended beneficiary, but an incidental beneficiary. He argues that neither parent intended Daughter to receive the payments dollar for dollar, and that permitting children to intervene in their parents' support agreements will open the door to a child suing one or both of her parents by equating the right to be supported with the right to support payments. Under the state's procedural rules, a party has the right to intervene where the determination of the action "may affect any legally enforceable interest of such person whether or not such person may be bound by a judgment in the action."

Continued on next page.

Daughter asserts that she has a "legally enforceable interest" as an intended beneficiary to her parents' separation agreement. To determine whether Daughter has a legally enforceable interest, the property settlement agreement (the Agreement) is interpreted pursuant to contract principles because property settlement agreements incorporated but not merged into divorce decrees are considered independent contracts, interpreted according to the law of contracts. Under contract law principles, the intent of the parties is paramount. If the contract is unambiguous, the intent is determined from the contract itself. Here, the Agreement did not expressly name Daughter as an intended beneficiary. However, Daughter may still be considered an intended beneficiary if she satisfies the Restatement (Second) of Contract's two-part test. The first part of that test is a standing test, and the question here, under that first part, is whether recognition of a right in Daughter to seek performance of the provision to increase Father's (D) weekly payments upon employment or increases in salary in accordance with the support guidelines is "appropriate to effectuate the intentions of the parties." It is clear the second part of the test is satisfied, since circumstances indicate that Wheamei Chen (Mother) (P) intended to give Daughter the benefit of the promised performance. The question raised by the first part of the test raises competing policy considerations. On the one hand, support of minor children is favored, and parents are obligated to render such support in the best interests of minor children. Courts may abandon contract principles to uphold the best interests of minor children. The best interests of a minor child are not implicated here, however, because Daughter is grown, so that contract principles must be adhered to. Also at issue is a fundamental right of parents to direct the care, custody, and control of their children. Support agreements or orders do not provide for direct payment of support payments to minor children, and parents are given discretion as to how to direct support funds. Parents have the final say regarding the family's budget. Accordingly, many courts are reluctant, absent unusual circumstances such as the death of a parent, to allow children to enforce their parents' agreements where the custodial parent was a signatory to the agreement and the designated recipient of the payments. This reluctance is often rooted in a desire to promote familial harmony and foster the parent-child relationship, neither of which is served when a child litigates support obligations against a parent. Such an approach is correct. Strong public policy favors denying a child standing to seek the specific dollars one parent owes the other for the child's generalized support pursuant to a separation agreement, absent special circumstances such as a direct designation that a benefit be paid to the child or the custodial parent's inability to enforce the agreement due to death or disability. Here, Mother (P) and Father (D) clearly intended to provide support for Daughter, but they did not intend for her to receive payments directly. Instead, the Agreement left Mother (P) to exercise her prerogative as a parent to direct the care, custody, and control of Daughter, and to determine how to best use the support funds provided by Father (D). Accordingly, Daughter is not an intended beneficiary under § 302 and because recognition of Daughter's right to performance is not "appropriate to effectuate the intention of the parties." Reversed.

CONCURRENCE: (Cappy, C.J.) Insofar as the majority rests the case on contract law principles, its decision is correct. However, the majority should not have gone beyond the contract law issues presented, e.g., it should not have broadened the scope of the issue to include discussion of policy issues and other matters.

CONCURRENCE: (Castille, J.) The case should have been resolved on contract principle alone and could easily have been resolved by limiting the inquiry to whether § 302's two-part test was met. The majority correctly determined Theresa (Daughter) met part two of the test, and the key issue was whether she satisfied part one. To resolve this issue, the majority needlessly addressed extraneous policy issues. The issue could have been resolved by merely looking at the property settlement agreement's unambiguous language, which provided Richard Chen (Father) (D) would make support payments to Wheamei Chen (Mother) (P) for Daughter's benefit, not for Daughter to be the direct recipient of the payments. Accordingly, Daughter was not an intended beneficiary under § 302.

CONCURRENCE: (Saylor, J.) As the property settlement agreement was one for support, Therese (Daughter) was an intended beneficiary during her minority. The resolution of the question of whether she should be permitted to intervene is a policy question that can be answered without resort to contract principles or the overlay of the two-part test of § 302. As a policy matter, minor children should not be accorded standing to initiate such legal actions absent express statutory authority.

ANALYSIS

As this case intimates, courts generally permit children to enforce provisions of their parents' separation agreements that provide for benefits to flow directly to the children. In such cases, it is clear pursuant to the agreements' express provisions that the children are intended, rather than incidental, beneficiaries, and resolution of such cases can be accomplished through

Continued on next page.

contract principles alone, without resorting to policy considerations as the majority did in this case.

Quicknotes

BREACH OF CONTRACT Unlawful failure by a party to perform its obligations pursuant to contract.

CONTEMPT OF COURT Conduct that is intended to obstruct the court's effective administration of justice or to otherwise disrespect its authority.

DIVORCE DECREE A decree terminating a marriage.

INCIDENTAL BENEFICIARY A person for whom a trust is not specifically created and who has no right to assert an interest in the trust, yet derives incidental benefits therefrom.

INTENDED BENEFICIARY A third party who is the recipient of the benefit of a transaction undertaken by another.

INTERVENTION The method by which a party, not an initial party to the action, is admitted to the action in order to assert an interest in the subject matter of a lawsuit.

PROPERTY SETTLEMENT AGREEMENT An agreement entered into by spouses upon dissolution of the marriage that is either agreed to by the spouses and sanctioned by the court or based on the court's division of the marital estate following the divorce proceeding.

Herzog v. Irace

Assignee (P) v. Attorneys (D)

Me. Sup. Jud. Ct., 594 A.2d 1106 (1991)

NATURE OF CASE: Appeal of an award of damages for breach of assignment.

FACT SUMMARY: Although notified of Jones's assignment of a personal injury claim to Herzog (P), Jones's attorneys, Irace and Lowry (D), failed to pay the settlement to Herzog (P).

RULE OF LAW

An assignment is binding upon the obligor where there is an intent to relinquish the right to the assignee and the obligor is notified.

FACTS: Jones, who had been injured in a motorcycle accident, hired attorneys Irace and Lowry (collectively, the Attorneys) (D) to represent him in a personal injury action. Jones required surgery for his injuries, which was performed by Herzog (P), a physician. Since Jones was unable to pay for this treatment, he signed a letter stating that he "request[ed] that payment be made directly . . . to John Herzog" of money received in settlement for his claim. Herzog (P) notified the Attorneys (D) of the assignment in 1988. The following year Jones received a $20,000 settlement for his claim. Jones instructed the Attorneys (D) to pay the money to him rather than to Herzog (P). The Attorneys (D) followed this instruction; Jones failed to pay Herzog (P) for the medical treatment. Herzog (P) brought a breach of assignment action against the Attorneys y (D), and the trial court ruled in favor of Herzog (P). The superior court affirmed, and the Attorneys (D) appealed.

ISSUE: Is an assignment binding upon the obligor where there is an intent to relinquish the right and the obligor is notified?

HOLDING AND DECISION: (Brody, J.) Yes. An assignment is binding upon an obligor where there is an intent to relinquish the right to the assignee and the obligor is notified. The letter directing payment to be made directly to Herzog (P) clearly and unequivocally demonstrated Jones's intent to relinquish his control over any money received for his personal injury claim. Irace and Lowry (collectively, the Attorneys) (D) were duly notified of this assignment and therefore the settlement money should have been paid to Herzog (P). Although the assignment did interfere with the ethical obligations the Attorneys (D) owed to Jones, the professional conduct rules do not prohibit the client's right to assign the proceeds of a lawsuit to a third party. The client's right prevails over any limitations on his lawyers. Affirmed.

ANALYSIS

Although assignment of contract rights is generally valid, some limitations on the right exist. Nearly every jurisdiction has a statute that restricts the assignment of wages. Furthermore, public policy considerations may protect assignors who attempt to assign future rights. Restatement (Second) of Contracts § 317(2) does not allow assignment where the duty to the obligor would be materially changed.

Quicknotes

ASSIGNMENT A transaction in which a party conveys his or her entire interest in property to another.

OBLIGOR Promisor; party who has promised or is obligated to perform.

Sally Beauty Co. v. Nexxus Products Co.

Competitor (P) v. Beauty products company (D)

801 F.2d 1001 (7th Cir. 1986)

NATURE OF CASE: Appeal from summary judgment dismissing action for damages for breach of contract.

FACT SUMMARY: Nexxus Products Co. (Nexxus) (D) abrogated an exclusive distribution agreement when the distributor was purchased by Sally Beauty Co. (P), a direct competitor of Nexxus (D).

RULE OF LAW

A distribution agreement may be abrogated by the manufacturer if the distributor is purchased by a direct competitor of the manufacturer.

FACTS: Nexxus Products Co. (Nexxus) (D), a manufacturer of hair care products, contracted with Best Barber & Beauty Supply Co. (Best) for the latter to serve as exclusive distribution agent for Nexxus (D) products in most of the Texas market. Subsequent to this, Best was purchased by Sally Beauty Co. (Sally) (P), a wholly owned subsidiary of Alberto-Culver Co., a major manufacturer of hair care products and a direct competitor of Nexxus (D). Nexxus (D) soon thereafter abrogated the distribution agreement. Sally (P) sued for breach of contract. The district court entered summary judgment for Nexxus (D), dismissing the action on the grounds that the contact had been one for personal services and was therefore not assignable without Nexxus's (D) consent. The court of appeals granted review.

ISSUE: May a distribution agreement be abrogated by the manufacturer if the distributor is purchased by a direct competitor of the manufacturer?

HOLDING AND DECISION: (Cudahy, J.) Yes. A distribution agreement may be abrogated by the manufacturer if the distributor is purchased by a direct competitor of the manufacturer. [The court first held that because triable issues of fact existed, the district court erred in granting summary judgment on the basis of a personal service contract, although it did not find this to be reversible error. It then discussed the impact of the Uniform Commercial Code (U.C.C.).] An agreement for distribution of goods is not per se a contract for the sale of goods, but courts have generally held such agreements to be sufficiently similar that the U.C.C., which by its terms deals with "transactions in goods," should be applied. U.C.C. § 2-210(1) provides that a contractual right may be assigned except where the obligee has a substantial interest in having his or her original promisor perform or control the acts pertaining to the contract. Essentially, an obligee should not have to accept, via delegation, a bargain to which he or she did not agree. An exclusive distribution agreement, by its very nature, involves an implicit or explicit promise by the distributor to use its best efforts in executing the contract. Assignment of the contract to a competitor of the manufacturer of necessity raises the question of whether the distributor will use such efforts. This is sufficient under § 2-210(1) to allow a manufacturer to veto an assignment of an exclusive distribution contract, as Nexxus (D) did in this case. Affirmed.

DISSENT: (Posner, J.) It is improper for the court to conclude, as a matter of law, that Sally Beauty Co. (Sally) (P) will not use its best efforts in completing the contract. The court has decided the matter with no better foundation than judicial intuition about what businessppeople might consider reasonable. Merely because Sally (P) is a subsidiary of a company that manufactures hair products—most of which are cheaper than Nexxus Products Co.'s (Nexxus) (D) products and aimed at a different market—does not mean, without further factual findings, that it will not use its best efforts to market Nexxus products. Precedent requires a factual inquiry into whether a change in business form is likely to impair performance of the contract, not a per se rule. This is especially true here, where the facts tend to indicate that Sally's (P) acquisition of Best Barber & Beauty Supply Co. would not especially hurt Nexxus (D), since Alberto-Culver Co. does not have a monopoly on the market and Sally (P) carries brands that compete with those manufactured by Alberto-Culver. Instead of creating a per se rule, the majority should have a remanded for a factual inquiry "on whether the merger so altered the conditions of performance that Nexxus (D) is entitled to declare the contract broken."

ANALYSIS

The laws of most jurisdictions treat contracts for goods and services differently. Contracts for services are usually per se nonassignable without consent. Contracts for goods, subject to the Uniform Commercial Code (U.C.C.), are held to the standard quoted in the main opinion. As the present case illustrates, some contracts have elements of both goods and services, and the two can be sufficiently analogous to warrant application of U.C.C. principles in the services situation.

Continued on next page.

Quicknotes

ABROGATE Annul; cancel; void.

ASSIGNMENT A transaction in which a party conveys his or her entire interest in property to another.

U.C.C. § 2-210 A party may perform his duty through a delegate unless agreed otherwise or unless the other party has a substantial interest in having his or her original promisor perform or control the acts required by the contract.

Glossary

Common Latin Words and Phrases Encountered in the Law

A FORTIORI: Because one fact exists or has been proven, therefore a second fact that is related to the first fact must also exist.

A PRIORI: From the cause to the effect. A term of logic used to denote that when one generally accepted truth is shown to be a cause, another particular effect must necessarily follow.

AB INITIO: From the beginning; a condition that has existed throughout, as in a marriage that was void ab initio.

ACTUS REUS: The wrongful act; in criminal law, such action as is sufficient to trigger criminal liability.

AD VALOREM: According to value; an ad valorem tax is imposed upon an item located within the taxing jurisdiction calculated by the value of such item.

AMICUS CURIAE: Friend of the court. Its most common usage takes the form of an amicus curiae brief, filed by a person who is not a party to an action but is nonetheless allowed to offer an argument supporting his or her legal interests.

ARGUENDO: In arguing. A statement, possibly hypothetical, made for the purpose of argument.

BILL QUIA TIMET: A bill to quiet title (establish ownership) to real property.

BONA FIDE: True, honest, or genuine. May refer to a person's legal position based on good faith or lacking notice of fraud (such as a bona fide purchaser for value) or to the authenticity of a particular document (such as a bona fide last will and testament).

CAUSA MORTIS: With approaching death in mind. A gift causa mortis is a gift given by a party who feels certain that death is imminent.

CAVEAT EMPTOR: Let the buyer beware. This maxim is reflected in the rule of law that a buyer purchases at his or her own risk because it is the buyer's responsibility to examine, judge, test, and otherwise inspect what he or she is buying.

CERTIORARI: A writ of review. Petitions for review of a case by the United States Supreme Court are most often done by means of a writ of certiorari.

CONTRA: On the other hand. Opposite. Contrary to.

CORAM NOBIS: Before us; a writ of error directed to the court that originally rendered the judgment.

CORAM VOBIS: Before you; a writ of error directed by an appellate court to a lower court to correct a factual error.

CORPUS DELICTI: The body of the crime; the requisite elements of a crime amounting to objective proof that a crime has been committed.

CUM TESTAMENTO ANNEXO, ADMINISTRATOR (ADMINISTRATOR C.T.A.): With will annexed; an administrator c.t.a. settles an estate pursuant to a will in which he or she is not appointed.

DE BONIS NON, ADMINISTRATOR (ADMINISTRATOR D.B.N.): Of goods not administered; an administrator d.b.n. settles a partially settled estate.

DE FACTO: In fact; in reality; actually. Existing in fact but not officially approved or engendered.

DE JURE: By right; lawful. Describes a condition that is legitimate "as a matter of law," in contrast to the term "de facto," which connotes something existing in fact but not legally sanctioned or authorized. For example, de facto segregation refers to segregation brought about by housing patterns, etc., whereas de jure segregation refers to segregation created by law.

DE MINIMUS: Of minimal importance; insignificant; a trifle; not worth bothering about.

DE NOVO: Anew; a second time; afresh. A trial de novo is a new trial held at the appellate level as if the case originated there and the trial at a lower level had not taken place.

DICTA: Generally used as an abbreviated form of obiter dicta, a term describing those portions of a judicial opinion incidental or not necessary to resolution of the specific question before the court. Such nonessential statements and remarks are not considered to be binding precedent.

DUCES TECUM: Refers to a particular type of writ or subpoena requesting a party or organization to produce certain documents in their possession.

EN BANC: Full bench. Where a court sits with all justices present rather than the usual quorum.

EX PARTE: For one side or one party only. An ex parte proceeding is one undertaken for the benefit of only one party, without notice to, or an appearance by, an adverse party.

EX POST FACTO: After the fact. An ex post facto law is a law that retroactively changes the consequences of a prior act.

EX REL.: Abbreviated form of the term "ex relatione," meaning upon relation or information. When the state brings an action in which it has no interest against an individual at the instigation of one who has a private interest in the matter.

FORUM NON CONVENIENS: Inconvenient forum. Although a court may have jurisdiction over the case, the action should be tried in a more conveniently located court, one to which parties and witnesses may more easily travel, for example.

GUARDIAN AD LITEM: A guardian appointed by the court to represent a minor or incompetent person in a legal action.

HABEAS CORPUS: You have the body. The modern writ of habeas corpus is a writ directing that a person (body) being detained (such as a prisoner) be brought before the court so that the legality of his or her detention can be judicially ascertained.

IN CAMERA: In private, in chambers. When a hearing is held before a judge in his or her chambers or when all spectators are excluded from the courtroom.

IN FORMA PAUPERIS: In the manner of a pauper. A party who proceeds in forma pauperis because of his or her poverty is one who is allowed to bring suit without liability for costs.

INFRA: Below, under. A word referring the reader to a later part of a book. (The opposite of supra.)

IN LOCO PARENTIS: In the place of a parent.

IN PARI DELICTO: Equally wrong; a court of equity will not grant requested relief to an applicant who is in pari delicto, or as much at fault in the transactions giving rise to the controversy as is the opponent of the applicant.

IN PARI MATERIA: On like subject matter or upon the same matter. Statutes relating to the same person or things are said to be in pari materia. It is a general rule of statutory construction that such statutes should be construed together, i.e., looked at as if they together constituted one law.

IN PERSONAM: Against the person. Jurisdiction over the person of an individual.

IN RE: In the matter of. Used to designate a proceeding involving an estate or other property.

IN REM: Signifies an action against the res, or thing. An action in rem is basically one that is taken directly against property, as distinguished from an action in personam, i.e., against the person.

INTER ALIA: Among other things. Used to show that the whole of a statement, pleading, list, statute, etc., has not been set forth in its entirety.

INTER PARTES: Between the parties. May refer to contracts, conveyances, or other transactions having legal significance.

INTER VIVOS: Between the living. An inter vivos gift is a gift made by a living grantor, as distinguished from bequests contained in a will, which pass upon the death of the testator.

IPSO FACTO: By the mere fact itself.

JUS: Law or the entire body of law.

LEX LOCI: The law of the place; the notion that the rights of parties to a legal proceeding are governed by the law of the place where those rights arose.

MALUM IN SE: Evil or wrong in and of itself; inherently wrong. Describes an act that is wrong by its very nature, as opposed to one which would not be wrong but for the fact that there is a specific legal prohibition against it (malum prohibitum).

MALUM PROHIBITUM: Wrong because prohibited, but not inherently evil. Describes something that is wrong because it is expressly forbidden by law but that is not in and of itself evil, e.g., speeding.

MANDAMUS: We command. A writ directing an official to take a certain action.

MENS REA: A guilty mind; a criminal intent. A term used to signify the mental state that accompanies a crime or other prohibited act. Some crimes require only a general mens rea (general intent to do the prohibited act), but others, like assault with intent to murder, require the existence of a specific mens rea.

MODUS OPERANDI: Method of operating; generally refers to the manner or style of a criminal in committing crimes, admissible in appropriate cases as evidence of the identity of a defendant.

NEXUS: A connection to.

NISI PRIUS: A court of first impression. A nisi prius court is one where issues of fact are tried before a judge or jury.

N.O.V. (NON OBSTANTE VEREDICTO): Notwithstanding the verdict. A judgment n.o.v. is a judgment given in favor of one party despite the fact that a verdict was returned in favor of the other party, the justification being that the verdict either had no reasonable support in fact or was contrary to law.

NUNC PRO TUNC: Now for then. This phrase refers to actions that may be taken and will then have full retroactive effect.

PENDENTE LITE: Pending the suit; pending litigation underway.

PER CAPITA: By head; beneficiaries of an estate, if they take in equal shares, take per capita.

PER CURIAM: By the court; signifies an opinion ostensibly written "by the whole court" and with no identified author.

PER SE: By itself, in itself; inherently.

PER STIRPES: By representation. Used primarily in the law of wills to describe the method of distribution where a person, generally because of death, is unable to take that which is left to him or her by the will of another, and therefore his or her heirs divide such property between them rather than take under the will individually.

PRIMA FACIE: On its face, at first sight. A prima facie case is one that is sufficient on its face, meaning that the evidence supporting it is adequate to establish the case until contradicted or overcome by other evidence.

PRO TANTO: For so much; as far as it goes. Often used in eminent domain cases when a property owner receives partial payment for his or her land without prejudice to his or her right to bring suit for the full amount he or she claims the land to be worth.

QUANTUM MERUIT: As much as the party deserves. Refers to recovery based on the doctrine of unjust enrichment in those cases in which a party has rendered valuable services or furnished materials that were accepted and enjoyed by another under circumstances that would reasonably notify the recipient that the rendering party expected to be paid. In essence, the law implies a contract to pay the reasonable value of the services or materials furnished.

QUASI: Almost like; as if; nearly. Essentially used to signify that one subject or thing is almost analogous to another but that material differences between them do exist. For example, a quasi-criminal proceeding is one that is not strictly criminal but shares enough of the same characteristics to require some of the same safeguards (e.g., procedural due process must be followed in a parole hearing).

QUID PRO QUO: Something for something. In contract law, the consideration, something of value, passed between the parties to render the contract binding.

RES GESTAE: Things done. In evidence law, this principle justifies the admission of a statement that would otherwise be hearsay when it is made so closely to the event in question as to be said to be a part of it, or with such spontaneity as not to have the possibility of falsehood.

RES IPSA LOQUITUR: The thing speaks for itself. This doctrine gives rise to a rebuttable presumption of negligence when the instrumentality causing the injury was within the exclusive control of the defendant, and the injury was one that does not normally occur unless a person has been negligent.

RES JUDICATA: A matter adjudged. Doctrine that provides that once a court of competent jurisdiction has rendered a final judgment or decree on the merits, that judgment or decree is conclusive upon the parties to the case and prevents them from engaging in any other litigation on the points and issues determined therein.

RESPONDEAT SUPERIOR: Let the master reply. This doctrine holds the master liable for the wrongful acts of his or her servant (or the principal for his or her agent) in those cases in which the servant (or agent) was acting within the scope of his or her authority at the time of the injury.

STARE DECISIS: To stand by or adhere to that which has been decided. The common-law doctrine of stare decisis attempts to give security and certainty to the law by following the policy that once a principle of law as applicable to a certain set of facts has been set forth in a decision, it forms a precedent that will subsequently be followed, even though a different decision might be made were it the first time the question had arisen. Of course, stare decisis is not an inviolable principle and is departed from in instances where there is good cause (e.g., considerations of public policy led the Supreme Court to disregard prior decisions sanctioning segregation).

SUPRA: Above. A word referring a reader to an earlier part of a book. (The opposite of infra.)

ULTRA VIRES: Beyond the power. This phrase is most commonly used to refer to actions taken by a corporation that are beyond the power or legal authority of the corporation.

Addendum of French Derivatives

CHATTEL: Tangible personal property.

CY PRES: Doctrine permitting courts to apply trust funds to purposes not expressed in the trust but necessary to carry out the settlor's intent.

IN PAIS: Not pursuant to legal proceedings.

PER AUTRE VIE: For another's life; during another's life. In property law, an estate may be granted that will terminate upon the death of someone other than the grantee.

PROFIT A PRENDRE: A license to remove minerals or other produce from land.

VOIR DIRE: Process of questioning jurors as to their predispositions about the case or parties to a proceeding in order to identify those jurors displaying bias or prejudice.